D0166428

*Social History of Africa*

# BURYING SM

*Social History of Africa*
Series Editors
Allen Isaacman and Luise White

BURYING SM
*The Politics of Knowledge and the
Sociology of Power in Africa*
David William Cohen and E. S. Atieno Odhiambo

COLONIAL CONSCRIPTS
*The Tirailleurs Senegalais in French West Africa,
1857–1960*
Myron Echenberg

LAW IN COLONIAL AFRICA
Kristin Mann and Richard Roberts
(editors)

PEASANTS, TRADERS, AND WIVES
*Shona Women in the History of Zimbabwe, 1870–1939*
Elizabeth Schmidt
*(forthcoming)*

WOMEN OF PHOKENG
*Consciousness, Life Strategy, and Migrancy
in South Africa, 1900–1983*
Belinda Bezzoli
(with the assistance of Mmantho Nkotsoe)

# BURYING SM

## The Politics of Knowledge and the Sociology of Power in Africa

David William Cohen
Northwestern University

E. S. Atieno Odhiambo
Rice University

HEINEMANN
Portsmouth, NH

JAMES CURREY
London

Heinemann
A division of Reed Elsevier Inc.
361 Hanover Street   Portsmouth, NH 03801-3912

**James Currey Ltd.**
54b Thornhill Square, Islington
London N1 B1E

ISBN 0−435−08061−X (Heinemann cloth)
ISBN 0−435−08063−6 (Heinemann paper)
ISBN 0−85255−656−X (James Currey cloth)
ISBN 0−85255−606−3 (James Currey paper)

Copyright © 1992 by David William Cohen and E. S. Atieno Odhiambo. All rights reserved. No part of this book may be reproduced in any form or by electronic or mechanical means, including information storage and retrieval systems, without permission in writing from the publisher, except by a reviewer, who may quote brief passages in a review.

**Library of Congress Cataloging-in-Publication Data**

Cohen, David William.
   Burying SM: the politics of knowledge and the sociology of power
in Africa/David William Cohen, E. S. Atieno Odhiambo.
      p.   cm. − (Social history of Africa)
   Includes bibliographical references and index.
   ISBN 0−435−08061−X (cloth). − ISBN 0−435−08063−6 (pbk.)
      1. Otieno, Virginia Edith Wambui − Trials, litigation, etc.
2. Ochieng' Ougo, Joash − Trials, litigation, etc. 3. Otieno,
Silvanus Melea, d. 1985 − Death and burial. 4. Customary law − Kenya-
-Nairobi. 5. Burial laws (Luo law) I. Atieno Odhiambo, E. S.,
1946−      . II. Title. III. Series: Social history of Africa series.
   LAW
   344.6762'045 − dc20                                                          91−28283
   [346.7620445]                                                                      CIP

**British Library Cataloguing in Publication Data**

Cohen, David William, 1943−
   Burying SM: the politics of knowledge and the
   sociology of power in Africa.
   I. Title II. Odhiambo, E. S. Atieno, 1946−
   322.44092

   ISBN 0−85255−656−X
   ISBN 0−85255−606−3 pbk

Cover photo: Burying SM at Nyalgunga 23 May 1987. Courtesy of Nation Newspapers, Nairobi.
Cover design by Jenny Jensen Greenleaf
Text design by G&H Soho Ltd.
Printed in the United States of America

00 99       DA     5 6 7

The authors wish to dedicate this book to Virginia Wambui Otieno, *Simba Nyiri*, the Lion among Women; and to the memory of "a man more sinned against than sinning," Silvano Melea Otieno

| Ja Kager | Kager man |
| Man Umira | From Umira |
| Jou Chon | The wizards |
| Nene Yiro Jo* | From Long Ago |

May deep affection, and memory, and a love of knowledge, continue to replenish the productions of History.

With concern and respect.

And in memory of the late
Justice J. O. Nyarangi
who has well presided.

---

* Song of Ogola Opot, Luo harpist, 1957.

# KA MIBETIE KICHIEMO
# (An Anthem of Luo in Urban Centers)

Composed and recorded in 1965 by four Luo kids born in Kaloleni, Nairobi: "Ka Mibetie Kichiemo," by Paddy Gwada, Rocky Gwada, Jabanga, and Ogaye. Ashantis Band. Translated by E. S. Atieno Odhiambo.

| | |
|---|---|
| Ka mibetie | Wherever you sit |
| Kichiemo | Eating |
| Onego iparie | Think of the people |
| Jo-Dala | At *Dala* |
| | |
| Ka mibetie | Wherever you sit |
| Kimetho | Drinking |
| Onego iparie | Think of the people |
| Jo-Pacho | At *Pacho* |
| | |
| Ka mibetie | Wherever you sit |
| Kiloso | Talking |
| Onego iparie | You should think of |
| Meru | Your Mother |
| | |
| Ka mibetie | Wherever you sit |
| Kichiemo | Eating |
| Onego iparie | Think of the people |
| Jo-Pacho | At *Pacho* |

| | |
|---|---|
| Meru tuo | Your mother is sick |
| E dala | At home |
| Dogi | Return |
| Ikonyie meru | Help your mother |
| Aa, Juma | Oh, Juma |
| Wuoda! | My son! |

| | |
|---|---|
| Duogi | Return |
| E dala | Back home |
| Mondo Ikonyi | To provide for |
| Meru | Your mother |
| Aa, Juma | Oh, Juma |
| Wuoda! | My son! |
| | |
| Meru tuo | Your mother is sick |
| E dala | At home |
| Paro ga | Think of |
| Kibathi! | The others! |
| Aa, Juma | Oh, Juma |
| Wuoda! | My son! |

# CONTENTS

S. M. Otieno's genealogy xi

List of Photographs xii

Acknowledgments xiii

Introduction 1

1 One Body, Two Funerals 11

2 Orations of the Dead 21

3 Silences of the Living 30

4 Living Bodies and Their Knowledge 43

5 The Productions of Culture 59

6 The Constitution of an African State 75

7 Owino Misiani's Lamentation, 1987 88

Conclusion 92

Afterpiece 100

Notes 120

Texts Cited in Court 141

Bibliography 143

Index 154

# The "Genealogy" of Silvano Melea Otieno

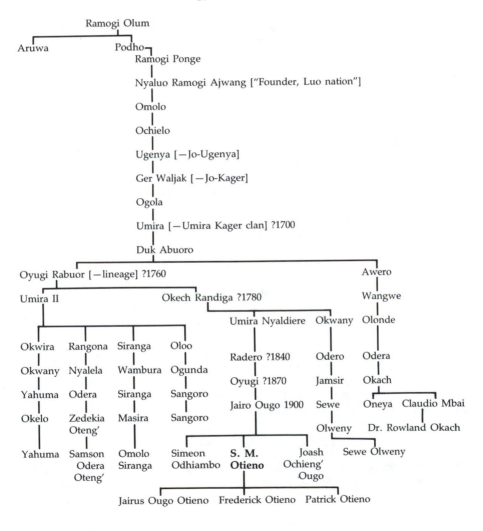

Ramogi Olum
Aruwa    Podho
Ramogi Ponge
Nyaluo Ramogi Ajwang ["Founder, Luo nation"]
Omolo
Ochielo
Ugenya [—Jo-Ugenya]
Ger Waljak [—Jo-Kager]
Ogola
Umira [—Umira Kager clan] ?1700
Duk Abuoro

Oyugi Rabuor [—lineage] ?1760          Awero
Umira II          Okech Randiga ?1780          Wangwe
Umira Nyaldiere   Okwany   Olonde

Okwira  Rangona  Siranga  Oloo
Okwany  Nyalela  Wambura  Ogunda   Radero ?1840   Odero   Odera
Yahuma  Odera    Siranga  Sangoro  Oyugi ?1870    Jamsir  Okach
Okelo   Zedekia  Masira   Sangoro  Jairo Ougo 1900  Sewe   Oneya  Claudio Mbai
        Oteng'                                       Olweny  Dr. Rowland Okach

Yahuma  Samson   Omolo    Simeon    S. M.      Joash      Sewe Olweny
        Odera    Siranga  Odhiambo  **Otieno**  Ochieng'
        Oteng'                                  Ougo

Jairus Ougo Otieno   Frederick Otieno   Patrick Otieno

# LIST OF PHOTOGRAPHS

|  | Page |
|---|---|
| Silvano Melea Otieno (1931–1986) | 3 |
| Wambui Otieno at a press conference at her Langata residence, showing a court order that permits her to bury her husband | 8 |
| Joash Ochieng' Ougo (l) and Richard Kwach (r) leaving the Law Courts | 15 |
| Joash Ochieng' Ougo with Omolo Siranga | 25 |
| Rev. John Gatu (l), Rev. Timothy Njoya, and Wambui Otieno outside Saint Andrew's Church, Nairobi | 31 |
| Crowd control outside the Law Courts | 44 |
| Albert Ong'ang'o, a mason, giving testimony before the High Court at Westlands Cottage Hospital | 48 |
| Wambui Otieno leaving the court with her sons Munyua Otieno (l) and Patrick Otieno (r) | 65 |
| Joash Ochieng' Ougo and a cousin displaying the clothing in which SM will be buried | 70 |
| Wambui Otieno leaving the Law Courts with daughters and friends | 71 |
| John Khaminwa at Haverford College | 81 |
| Joash Ochieng' Ougo, Omolo Siranga, and others celebrating the Court of Appeal decision at One Ojijo Road | 94 |
| Mourning SM at Nyalgunga | 98 |

*Photographs have been kindly provided by* Nation Newspapers, *Nairobi, except for the photograph of John Khaminwa, which was provided courtesy of Haverford College.*

# ACKNOWLEDGMENTS

There are many people to whom the authors owe their separate and combined gratitude. We are especially grateful to James Currey who encouraged, or even commanded, us to write an "afterword" on the S. M. Otieno case to append to the complete manuscript in press of our *Siaya: The Historical Anthropology of an African Landscape*; to Elijah Oduor Ogutu, whose several words in correspondence in February 1987, brought home at an early stage the remarkable power and importance of this case to those close to the Otienos; to Luise White, who, in the most challenging of circumstances and with extraordinary courage, gained special insight into the meaning of the case for Kenyans in their everyday lives; to William Ochieng' and Ivan Karp, who from an early stage suggested clues to comprehending and representing the case; and to Lynn Thomas, whose own broader research and constant interest in the circumstances of women before the law in Africa provided us with material, interpretations, perspectives, and criticism beyond what one would expect of a young scholar deeply engaged in her own research.

E. S. Atieno Odhiambo specifically acknowledges Allen Matusow, the Dean of Humanities, Rice University, for providing generous support for summer research in London and South Africa, which in turn permitted presentations of the work in progress to the African Seminar, Saint Anthony's College, Oxford, in 1989 and to the University of Witwatersrand in 1990. Gratitude is expressed to the Johns Hopkins University in Baltimore, Northwestern University in Evanston, and Rice University for providing various kinds of support that made the completion of the manuscript possible. Shula Marks provided office facilities at the Institute for Commonwealth Studies, London. Tim Couzens and the Center for African Studies, University of Witwatersrand, provided a fellowship that made possible an extended period of writing and discussion in Johannesburg. Jane Audi Odhiambo and Bill Ochieng' provided a constant access to newspaper clippings in the aftermath of the case. Thanks are extended to the members of seminars and audiences at the International Studies Program, the University of Tennessee, the History Seminar at Rice University, the Red Lion Seminar in Chicago, and the German Historical Institute in London's conference in Berlin on "Hegemony" for most stimulating and productive discussions of portions of the work in progress. John Otumba Okayo kindly assisted with the discography on

SM. Terence O. Ranger in Oxford and David William Cohen in Evanston and Kingsport, Tennessee, provided unusual hospitality and settings for writing. And gratitude of a special kind is due to Caroline and Michael Odhiambo for explaining and textualizing "Tero Buru".

David William Cohen expresses his gratitude to the Department of History, The Johns Hopkins University, and Northwestern University for providing support and opportunities to complete this work. In Göttingen, Germany, Hans Medick and Alf Lüdtke provided a marvelous environment and stimulus within which some early writing on the case unfolded. Linda Gerstein and the administration of Haverford College provided information on John Khaminwa's visit to Haverford. Shula Marks assembled a most valuable collection of close and expert, yet not quite implicated, scholars of eastern and southern Africa who provided at a very early stage a remarkable and powerful discussion and critique of the work in its earliest draft. Peter Amuka, Patricia Stamp, Judith Butterman, Wangari Maathai, Gibson Kamau Kuria, Joanna Gwinn, and Duncan Okoth-Okombo generously shared their own work and thinking on the case at different stages in the project. Gabrielle Spiegel and Carroll Smith-Rosenberg provided challenging commentary in the University of Pennsylvania Seminar on Language, Text, and the Body. Useful suggestions and criticism were drawn from seminars, conferences, and lecture audiences at The Johns Hopkins University, Northwestern University, University of Minnesota, Rice University, the Sixth Roundtable in Anthropology and History at Bellagio, Italy, the American Ethnological Society meetings in Atlanta on "The Body," and the African Studies Association Annual Meeting in Baltimore. In these more formal academic settings and elsewhere, numerous individuals offered valuable readings of the case from their own knowledge or by reference to comparable situations elsewhere. Gretchen Elsner-Sommer has pressed one to examine and recenter the so-called margin. Friends in Anthropology and History at Johns Hopkins and Northwestern have been wonderful colleagues throughout the development of the book, sharing advice and ideas unstintingly. And students at Johns Hopkins and Northwestern have provided constant stimulation and challenging criticism as the manuscript progressed. Staff of the Program of African Studies, Northwestern—most particularly John B. Godfrey and Akbar Virmani—have shown remarkable patience and allowed considerable freedom to pursue the project, and staff have also assisted with the physical preparation of the text. Jennifer and Ben Cohen have provided a foundation of affection and support, and Jennifer assisted the research in a number of ways, while Ben and Wallace M. Cohen have offered provocative readings along the way.

Both authors recognize the special and most generous contributions of those who have accepted the challenge of entering commentaries and critiques within the book, as well as those in Kenya and elsewhere who "attended" the case and raised voices among diverse audiences and thereby began the processes of interpretation and representation through which meaning grows and knowledge is elaborated. These discussions will continue to envelop and surpass this present treatment of the case.

# INTRODUCTION

I had a farm in Africa, at the foot of the Ngong Hills. The Equator runs across these highlands, a hundred miles to the North, and the farm lay at an altitude of over six thousand feet. In the day-time you felt that you had got high up, near to the sun. . . .

The geographical position, and the height of the land combined to create a landscape that had not its like in all the world. . . . [I]t was Africa distilled up through six thousand feet, like the strong and refined essence of a continent. The colours were dry and burnt, like the colours in pottery. . . . The views were immensely wide. Everything that you saw made for greatness and freedom, and unequalled nobility. . . .

. . . Up in this high air you breathed easily, drawing in a vital assurance and lightness of heart. In the highlands you woke up in the morning and thought: Here I am, where I ought to be.[1]

The mist cleared away and the calves were led out and the milking of cows began, and the time was about nine o'clock in the morning. Then Olonana said, "Take [the visitors] . . . to Kikuya." On the small plain called Kabati [modern Karen near Karen von Blixen's old house] there is a white building [Mr. Rodney Chilton's present house] on the edge of the plain and that is the real place of Kikuya, and when you stand there you can see red buildings on the plain at the place we used to call Rora. That area belonged to the Ilkaputiei section. . . . [Olonana] died at Enomatasiani [about three or four miles east of modern Ngong township], and he died of illness. It seems as if he was bewitched, and he became sick and started roaming all over the country. Sometimes he climbed trees and he became somewhat insane until he died, at Enomatasiani.[2]

Mr. Otieno walked in . . . and said: ". . . I've bought a piece of land in Kiserian [Ngong]." . . . I remarked: "This is very unusual for a Luo to buy land right at the heart of Maasai and Kikuyu." . . . He replied to my remark: "We must change our outlook. One acre in Ngong is worth 10 in Siaya. It is common sense to buy land at Ngong! . . . I shall be buried at Kiserian [Ngong] and I have made this plainly clear to all parties that might be interested in my funeral. I shall be buried at Kiserian."[3]

We used to meet at the Bomas of Kenya Bar and he [Mr. Otieno] called me neighbour. . . . He and his wife used to sit at a place the bar's waiters called "SM corner" at the end of the counter. Most of the time they were together. ... [A]s a neighbour and a good friend, he used to consult me on land values. He had told me he was buying a plot at Ngong where he wanted to concentrate on farming. ... Mr. Otieno was very widely read and we would hold normal discussions while drinking. But particularly, he was fond of quoting Shakespeare and together we would joke a lot.[4]

It was a sunny, warm, brilliant Saturday in Nairobi, 20 December 1986. The southwestern suburb of Karen-Langata, immortalized by Isak Dinesen (Karen Blixen) in print and Meryl Streep on screen, looked "dry and burnt," dusty, and ever ethereal. The notables—Kenyans and Africans, not European settlers this Christmas week—moved about their neighborhood, among them doctors, lawyers, senior military officers. They were completing various pre-Christmas responsibilities. And some were readying their cars for the long drive up-country to the lands of their birth in the former Native Reserves, to their extensive farms in the Rift Valley, or to their oceanic properties along the Kenya coast.[5]

For the few others who would not be leaving town, this was a time to do some straightening up of their town and suburban investments: bars and butcheries in Athi River and Ongata Rongai, the small gardening plots in Limuru and Upper Matasia, and the kiosk in Buru Buru estate, Nairobi. It was a good time to visit, to chat, to be with friends and family. It was a time of heightened sociability. Indeed, it was a good day to consult uncles and elder brothers about the not-yet-completed dowry payment, and about the protocol of mourning a mother-in-law in the city as Khama Nyamogo[6] was doing that very afternoon, consulting with one of the authors of this work as well as with his paternal uncle, Dr. Zachariah Ogutu Nyamodi, at the latter's residence in Karen.

Silvano Melea Otieno was one such occupied, busy person that Saturday the 20th. Born a Luo in Nyamila village, Nyalgunga, Alego, in Siaya District in western Kenya, Otieno—popularly referred to as "SM"—was the doyen of Kenya's criminal lawyers. That morning, SM spoke with his wife Virginia Edith Wambui about the need to stock alcohol in the house for an anticipated afternoon visit by a *mzee* (an elder), an acquaintance of SM, and to set in place some hospitality for Christmas carousals. SM then headed to his law offices downtown where Wambui joined him later in the morning, and there they bantered more about Christmas doings. Around midday, SM left his offices with two nephews, Odhiambo Modi and Umira Odhiambo, and they headed for his compound in Karen. There he played host to the two of them, showing them around his lands, with two of his sons, Patrick Oyugi Otieno and Frederick Otieno, in tow.

Later in the afternoon, SM left his Langata patrimony in the company of his nephews and headed for the six-acre garden he owned at Upper Matasia on the outskirts of Ngong. He carried a parcel containing a dress for a daughter of Wambui who was also staying at the farm. When he reached his Upper Matasia lands he chatted with Tiras Waiyaki, a son to his wife Wambui Otieno by a former liaison.

A weekend yeoman, SM took his relatives around the *shamba* (farm) to view the cattle—six bulls in all—and some goats. SM expressed pride in his *shamba*, and many friends and relatives knew that the development of his Upper Matasia farm was becoming an important element of SM's life. On returning to the farm

Silvano Melea Otieno (1931–1986)

cottage from the walk, SM intimated that he was feeling unwell. He lay back onto a sofa. Tiras Waiyaki noticed that SM was having difficulty breathing and began massaging him, but to no avail. Waiyaki and the nephews moved SM to his Mercedes Benz and placed him on the rear seat. Waiyaki sat next to him, while one of the nephews drove in a rush to Nairobi Hospital. Silvano Melea Otieno was pronounced dead on arrival. It was 6:00 p.m. under a very azure afternoon sky.

At 7:40 that evening, Joash Ochieng' Ougo, SM's brother, 51 years old, senior foreman at the Kenya Railways Corporation, was visited at his residence, One Ojijo Road, in Parklands, Nairobi, by one of SM's stepdaughters, Elizabeth, and

Joshua Buliro, a former high-ranking Kenya diplomat. They carried to Ochieng' the news of SM's death. Elizabeth and Joshua then gave Ochieng' a lift to the City Mortuary. At the morgue, Ochieng' viewed the body in the company of one John Obonyo and a niece, Mrs. Jane Obuong' Abonyo, who was daughter to Otieno's sister Helen.

From the City Mortuary, Ochieng'—accompanied by his wife Rispa and his sister Idalia Awino—proceeded to SM's Langata residence. Ochieng' stayed at Langata for about ten minutes, and then took leave to inform other relatives of his brother's death. Ochieng' returned to Langata at about midnight. Virginia Edith Wambui, widow of SM, invited Ochieng' to sit down to discuss burial arrangements, making clear to Ochieng' that Otieno should be buried in Nairobi "according to his wishes."

Joash Ochieng' declined to discuss the matter there and then, pleading that it was too early to do so because "members of my clan who could talk about it had not come." Reportedly, the new widow Wambui was thoroughly annoyed with this response and she asked Ochieng' to leave her property.

The following day, 21 December, was an extraordinary one for Joash Ochieng'. He returned to Langata, and again Wambui was annoyed, so much so that the police were called three times to evict him from her house—called in by Wambui, according to Ochieng', or by a Mrs. Kimani, according to Wambui's legal counsel, John Mugalasinga Khaminwa.

Ochieng' returned to his house at One Ojijo Road, where he found Omolo Siranga, a member of their clan, the Umira Kager. Evidently, a decision was made at that point that funeral meetings would be held at Ochieng's house. Siranga and companions went out to inform various people to this effect, and word spread quickly across Nairobi. That evening some four hundred people turned up for the meeting at One Ojijo Road. Twenty or so people gave speeches reflecting various concerns about the death of SM and raising points in respect to the plans for an appropriate funeral. It was decided to form a committee to arrange all aspects of SM's burial. Omolo Siranga was drafted to chair this committee. The assembled "parliament" of the Umira Kager decided that evening that SM would be buried at his birthplace at Nyalgunga in Siaya. As later recounted, the process of decision making was an implicit one: " . . . the burial place was not an issue. It was already understood where he would be buried."[7]

Armed with these understandings and plans, and authorized by the meeting, Omolo Siranga went to Langata the next day, 22 December, to ask Wambui to allow the funeral throngs of the Umira Kager, and others, to assemble and mourn her husband at his Langata residence. Accompanied by one other member of the burial committee, Fred Ouma, Siranga found Wambui out. Her son Tiras Waiyaki was there but informed the delegation that he had no authority to speak. He said that Dr. Julius Gikonyo Kiano would be the person to speak with, but Dr. Kiano would not, he reported, be back from Mombasa until the following day. Siranga and Ouma returned to Ochieng's house at Ojijo Road. Over just two days, One Ojijo Road—Joash Ochieng' Ougo's residence near the National Museums of Kenya—had become an active base of clan operations as well as the focal point of widespread interest and attention among Kenyans.

While Siranga and others were discussing matters at One Ojijo Road, word arrived that Idalia Awino and Julia, sisters of SM, along with two daughters of

Joash, had been refused permission to view the body at the City Mortuary. Siranga proceeded to the Mortuary to make inquiries and found confirmation of the allegation. Wambui had, he learned, left instructions with the morgue attendants and at Kilimani police station to this effect. There was distress, tumult, at Ojijo Road.

That evening, Dr. Kiano, having returned earlier from Mombasa than previously announced, led a delegation to One Ojijo Road. Kiano was accompanied by Dr. Josephat Karanja, then a member of Parliament for Mathare, Nairobi, and two brothers of Wambui and one Mrs. Buliro. They journeyed to Ojijo Road to open what they later referred to as conciliatory discussions.

Omolo Siranga received the party and assumed the chair of the discussions, which revolved around the need to coordinate the funeral arrangement. Siranga's group stuck to their intention that the burial would be at Nyalgunga, while Dr. Kiano's group pleaded that they did not have a mandate from Wambui to discuss that specific commitment.

Further meetings among the negotiators were held on 23 December at the Devon Hotel in Nairobi, at Dr. Kiano's house the same day, and later in the evening the same day at SM's house at Langata. Wambui's negotiators held their ground. A direct appeal to Wambui, involving a visit the next day to Langata by Joash Ochieng', Magdalina (SM's stepmother), Julia (SM's sister), Siranga, and one Philip Rang'enga, also failed to persuade the widow on the issue of a Nyalgunga burial. Nor did another meeting the following Monday, 29 December.

Meanwhile, on 28 December, Voice of Kenya (VOK) radio carried the widow's announcement that the body of S. M. Otieno would be buried at their Ngong farm on Saturday, 3 January 1987, following a viewing and a service at the All Saints' Cathedral. But then, the same day, 28 December, VOK carried S. M. Otieno's brother's message that the burial would take place on 3 January 1987 at Nyamila village, in Siaya District, Nyanza Province. Nyamila, Otieno's birthplace, and Ngong, his residence for a number of years, are some four hundred kilometers apart.

House Number One, Ojijo Road, the Nairobi residence of Joash Ochieng' Ougo, is a roomy brick and stone compound located right behind the National Museums, close by The International Louis Leakey Memorial Institute of African Prehistory. The house "belongs" to Joash Ochieng' Ougo, but is the property of the Kenya Railways Corporation. Over the days before and after Christmas, it became the headquarters of the clan association, the Umira Kager, which assembled there for meetings every evening. Initially, Ojijo Road served as a rendezvous for all the mourners who could not make it all the way to the Karen suburbs to the Otieno residence. But then as word filtered across Nairobi that Wambui had locked her gates on SM's Luo kinsmen, Ojijo Road became the alternative funeral gathering site for mourners and various hangers-on.

As weeks passed, House Number One came to be inscribed, within Luo thought, everyday speech, and activity, as an historical landmark, part of a noble Siaya landscape extended to Nairobi.[8] For six months, it replaced Kaloleni as the tumultuous core of Luo activity in urban Nairobi. House Number One was the place of great public assemblies, and the place to meet and be seen. Rural people, on coming to Nairobi, asked to be taken to "our place" where "it was all happening."

Day and night, crowds of Luo milled about, exchanging views of the issues at hand, recounting the immediate history of events following SM's death, wailing, arguing, organizing a consensus about what to do next. One Ojijo Road became the site of a momentary "republic" within the Republic of Kenya, a theater of oratory and a college of colloquy, a site of mourning, a reservoir of rhetoric, and a command post. By week's end, such Luo nationalists as the archaeologist Dr. John Onyango-Abuje, trained at the University of California, Berkeley, had evolved a clear and simple message which declared unstintingly and defiantly (*gimieno wach*) that Silvano Melea Otieno, the son of the Umira Kager, would be buried at Nyalgunga and nowhere else. The committee chair, Omolo Siranga, announced on 29 December that an Umira Kager meeting at One Ojijo Road had resolved that the clan should directly proceed to take over the funeral arrangements, irrespective of the widow's intentions and actions.

The *Daily Nation* newspaper of Nairobi quickly reported that a dispute had developed over the plans for removing Otieno's body from the City Mortuary, for a public viewing, and for the burial. The dispute pitted the widow, Virginia Wambui Waiyaki Otieno, whom the press conventionally referred to as a "Kikuyu lady," against Joash Ochieng' Ougo, the deceased's brother, and Omolo Siranga, head of the Umira Kager clan which joined Joash in claiming the corpse of their Luo kinsman (*wodgi*) as one of their own and as their rightful property. On 29 December, the *Daily Nation* reported that announcements of plans for Otieno's burial had been halted by the Voice of Kenya. In the days that followed, court orders and injunctions blocked the plans of the widow and the brother for their respective 3 January 1987 ceremonies.

Between the various positions and statements broadcast on radio, published in the press, and mouthed in the streets, Joash Ochieng' Ougo was reported to have written to the Superintendent of the City Mortuary, urging him to bar Wambui from removing SM's body. On 29 December, Wambui filed a suit in the High Court seeking, *inter alia*, a declaration that she was entitled to claim her husband's body and perform a burial ceremony and that she, as SM's widow, commanded priority over Joash Ochieng' Ougo, and over any other person claiming to be the latter's representative.

So began a long and complex train of legal activity which pushed two lawyers, John Mugalasinga Khaminwa for Wambui and Richard Otieno Kwach for the clan, to the center of the stage, giving a new dimension and force to the struggle for the corpse, whose ultimate object was the repossession of the whole of SM: body, memory, history. Where for a week the comings and goings at One Ojijo Road and Langata — the little republics — gave form to the unfolding chronicle of dispute, Wambui's suit in the High Court, filed by Khaminwa on 29 December, restructured and repositioned the chronicle. From 29 December 1986 to late May 1987, the struggle between clan and widow would come to be defined substantially by the comings and goings of counsel and witnesses before the law courts of the Republic.

The next day, 30 December, Wambui's lawyers, John Mugalasinga Khaminwa and Samwel Kinuthia filed, on her behalf, a twelve-paragraph plea in High Court.

The plea, heard by Justice Frank J. Shields, asked the court to declare that she was entitled to claim the body of her husband and bury it; asked the court that Joash Ochieng' Ougo and Omolo Siranga be restrained from removing the body from the City Mortuary; and pleaded that Ochieng' and Siranga be restrained from burying Otieno's body at Nyalgunga in Siaya District or elsewhere in Kenya.

Justice Shields, an Englishman, quickly granted Wambui an *ex parte* order permitting her to collect the body of her husband from the City Mortuary for burial at Ngong.

Immediately upon notice of Justice Shields's decision, Ochieng' and Siranga, through their lawyer Richard Otieno Kwach, began preparation of a counter-injunction, which was filed on 2 January 1987, asking the court to nullify its earlier order and to restrain Wambui from collecting the remains of Otieno from the City Mortuary.[9] Before Justice Shields, Richard Kwach pleaded that Shields set aside his injunction of 30 December and that he issue an order restraining Wambui or her agents from burying Silvano Melea Otieno anywhere other than at Nyalgunga, Otieno's rural birthplace in Alego, Siaya District. Kwach then argued that Otieno was a Luo, and being a Luo, Otieno must be buried in accordance with Luo customs and traditions.

By the time Kwach went before the High Court requesting the counterinjunction, a wider cast of interested people had mobilized itself around Ochieng' and Omolo Siranga. They included Barrack Angoya Onyango, who claimed to be the chairman of a long-moribund "Alego Ragar Association," as well as Philip Rang'enga, secretary of another long-moribund body, the "Ugenya Association." Both individuals claimed to represent strong constituencies from the communities of Otieno's birth. "Ancient" locational politics of western Kenya came out of the past — the 1940s[10] — and into the ferment at Ojijo Road, and into the meetings at which Richard Otieno Kwach received instructions from his clients.

On 5 January 1987, Justice Shields issued his ruling on the plea for a counter-injunction. It made short shrift of Kwach's line of argument concerning S. M. Otieno being a Luo and therefore subject to the customs and laws of his Luo homeland.

> He [Otieno] was a metropolitan and a cosmopolitan, and though he undoubtedly honoured the traditions of his ancestors, it is hard to envisage such a person as subject to African customary law and in particular to the customs of a rural community.[11]

On matters of law, Shields found that Wambui, being Otieno's widow, was the person entitled to be Otieno's personal representative and therefore the person entitled to the custody of the body, including the authority to remove the body from the City Mortuary and to arrange for its burial. Turning to the subjects of his 30 December injunction — Omolo Siranga and Joash Ochieng' Ougo — Shields found that neither individual had any legal right (*locus standi*) in the matter of the burial of Otieno's body. This would remain the case, he pronounced, even if Otieno were to be buried according to Luo custom. Shields stated that the law[12] of Kenya recognized that only the legal personal representative or next of kin of a deceased person could be permitted to remove the body from the mortuary for burial. Justice Shields, for his part, recognized Wambui as that next of kin.

Kwach immediately appealed to Kenya's highest court, the Court of Appeal, to review Shields's High Court finding. But then Wambui announced to the press that she would bury her late husband at Upper Matasia on 10 January. Responding to this announcement, Richard Kwach, with instructions from Ochieng' and Siranga, asked the Court of Appeal to restrain Wambui from burying Otieno pending the hearing of the appeal of Shields's judgment.

The next day, 6 January, a Court of Appeal panel—with Justices J. O. Nyarangi, H. G. Platt, and J. Mugo Gachuhi sitting—was convened. Kwach's appearance was brief. The next day, 7 January, the Court of Appeal ruled that the body of Otieno should not be buried until after the court had made its ruling on Kwach's original appeal (of the Shields decision). Stated their Lordships:

> It is the practice of this court to preserve the *status quo* until the hearing of the appeal so as to preserve the subject matter (Mr. Otieno's body) and avoid the appeal being rendered nugatory (invalid).... In this application, the controversy concerns where the body should be buried. It is feasible for the body to be preserved in the City Mortuary and it is unreasonable and unnecessary to risk exhumation.... The body shall remain in the City Mortuary until a further order.[13]

On 9 January 1987, Kwach filed his memorandum of appeal, in which he argued that Justice Shields had, first, "erred in law" in granting the injunction against Ochieng' and Siranga without an *inter partes* argumentation from Kwach; second, "misdirected himself in law and in fact in holding that because of his education, marriage, association and professional success, Otieno had thereby lost his tribal identity and could not be governed by or be subject to the

Wambui Otieno at a press conference at her Langata residence, showing a court order that permits her to bury her husband.

customary laws, traditions, and culture of the Luo"; third, "erred in holding in effect that only the respondent [Wambui Otieno] is entitled to claim the body for burial and that neither of these appellants (one of whom is the deceased's brother) nor Umira Kager, the deceased's clan, has any claim whatsoever over the body"; fourth, "erred in law and gravely misdirected himself in accepting only the evidence of the respondent [Wambui] and rejecting the evidence of the appellants on the critical question of what the deceased's wishes were with regard to where he should be buried"; and, fifth, "gravely misdirected himself in holding that since Otieno was married under the Marriage Act, he automatically ceased to be governed by or subject to the Luo customary law or any other relevant laws of the land."[14]

The next day, 10 January, Kwach began his oral argument before the Court of Appeal, urging a retrial on the grounds that Justice Shields of the High Court had totally disregarded Luo customary law in his judgment. Kwach argued that Justice Shields had only heard Wambui Otieno's side of the case through her lawyer Khaminwa, and had not given Kwach his chance to interrogate Khaminwa's evidence, or to make his own case concerning Luo customary law. In Kwach's view, Justice Shields merely accepted Khaminwa's assertion that the customary law was "primitive." Kwach pressed the argument that with a proper legal hearing Luo assessors should have been summoned by Shields to hear the matter pertaining to Luo customary law. Kwach pleaded: "We should have been given a chance to prove our evidence."[15]

In response, John Khaminwa, Wambui's counsel, argued that Justice Shields had ruled properly, and that there was no reason for the High Court to consider the reach of customary law because

> ... customary law does not apply in the Otieno case. ... This matter does not fall into the arena of the traditional or customary law at all. And I repeat ... an emphatic nooo! ... This is a matter purely governed by common law. Under the written law, Mrs. Otieno is the first next of kin. Section 160 of the Succession Act stipulates that she has that right ... Customary law is out![16]

On 12 January, the Court of Appeal panel issued its ruling. The Court set aside the Shields decision in the High Court which empowered Wambui to collect and bury the body. Two issues drew the attention of the Court of Appeal. The first concerned the way in which the High Court heard the evidence.

> Given the nature of this case, one would hardly think that justice can be done without hearing both sides. Actually there are very few cases where justice can be done without hearing both parties.[17]

The second issue focused on the point of greatest dispute between the two advocates, Kwach and Khaminwa. This concerned the relevance of "Luo customary law." "The question that lies at the heart of this matter is whether or not the deceased is subject to the Luo customary law."[18]

With moment, the Court of Appeal panel ordered a full trial to be held by the High Court, with a different judge handling the proceeding. The Court of Appeal also ordered that Wambui "be restrained by injunction from burying the deceased anywhere other than Nyalgunga Sub-location until trial of the suit by the High Court or until further order."[19]

On 14 January 1987, two days after the Court of Appeal ordered a full trial of the dispute in the High Court, Wambui filed, through her lawyer John Khaminwa, an injunction in the High Court which sought to restrain the Umira Kager clan from collecting her husband's body from the City Mortuary. Wambui spoke to the press in her late husband's office at Uni-Afric House, declaring that she had been forced to file for the new injunction as a consequence of the celebrations in the street by the people of the Umira Kager clan after the Court of Appeal ruling.

> None of these people dancing in the streets and being carried shoulder-high as if they are in an election campaign care about my late husband. Not even his own brother, Ochieng'. . . . It pains me and my children to see my husband treated like dirt by people he did not know. . . . [20]

Reminding her listeners that she also had a clan, she declared:

> I am a Muceera in Kikuyu and Kapitei [sic] in Maasai. They should not think I am alone. I can also call my clansmen to come out and demonstrate in support as they have been doing. . . . Every woman in Kenya should look at this case keenly. There is no need of getting married if this is the way women will be treated when their husbands die. [21]

# 1

# One Body, Two Funerals

When I arrive in Nairobi everyone is talking about the dead Luo. He has already been embalmed twice, but if he remains unburied much longer he will have to be embalmed again. . . . Other than the initials S. M., I never learn his Christian name. But everybody knows what you mean when you say "Otieno" or "the dead Luo," and everyone has an opinion on where his body should go.[1]

The contest for control of the remains of SM—as his friends knew him during his life and at death—moved through seven legal settings over the next five months. The struggles within the court were accompanied by large demonstrations in the streets of Nairobi, calls by one side and the other to take the body by force from the City Mortuary, as well as by an avalanche of correspondence and commentary in the national press. The fate of S. M. Otieno's body, the rights of the disputants, and the prospective reverberations of the various possible outcomes, became subjects for serious comment at funerals held throughout the country during the litigation.

While the President of Kenya, Daniel Arap Moi, did not speak directly on the case during the period in which it was before the courts, a number of his ministers, members of Parliament, and important public figures positioned themselves on one side or the other. The struggle was concluded only by a final judgment for Joash Ochieng' Ougo and Omolo Siranga handed down by the Court of Appeal, Kenya's highest court. S. M. Otieno was finally buried by court order not on his Ngong farm in the Nairobi suburbs but rather in the land of his kinsmen at Nyamila village in Siaya on 23 May 1987, just a few days more than five months after his death.

## A Court of Law, A Court on Trial

From the end of December through May, the question of who would bury the body of S. M. Otieno, and where that burial would be, produced an immense public debate in Kenya—within the courts, in the streets, in clubs and bars, and

11

in scholarly seminars—concerning the risks and liabilities of "intermarriage between tribes"; the nature of the body as material property; the appropriate
authority of "custom" and "tradition"; the relative standing of statutory, customary, and common law; the meaning and force of bonds of intimacy between
husband and wife; the worth and legitimacy of "modern" social practice; the
rights of women within marriage, as widows, and before the law; the meaning of
death and the purposes of interment; the idea of "home" as the only appropriate
site of burial for a Luo individual; the tenacity of Luo identity; notions of the
"backwardness" of the Luo in a "modern Kenya"; and the form of Luo participation
in national life. What S. M. Otieno intended as to his own burial arrangements,
and what he actually said to a number of witnesses, became a centerpiece of
debate on a wide range of issues both in the court and across Kenya. And—
whatever SM's intentions—the case elaborated itself as a laboratory for the study
of the production of history and the sociology of power in contemporary Africa.


## Speaking of Death

The question of S. M. Otieno's own wishes, with the debates over the meaning
and veracity of statements that witnesses claimed to have heard uttered by SM,
reveals a curious proximity, yet palpable tension, between orality and literacy.
SM, as a lawyer, understood the power of the written word, and the litigation
over his remains is thick with references to letters, documents, and contracts. Yet,
from 1979, the High Court transcript of testimony reveals, SM had been telling all
and sundry about his intentions as to burial, his declarations were all oral, and
all were represented as powerful, affecting, and memorable oratory.

The venues of SM's many orations varied, from table talk at SM's house in
the presence of Rahab Wambui Muhuni, 50, a cultivator from Location One,
Muranga, and also in the presence of Musa Muna, 50, a propertied neighbor in
Langata; to conversation with Godwin Wachira, a journalist, at the residence of
Dr. Kiano; to discussions with his neighbors as they toured their "estates,"
including herdsman James Ligia Ole Tameno, 70, in Upper Matasia, and Harry
Mugo, 38, land appraiser, along their boundary in Langata. SM also ranted on the
subject while in his car somewhere between Nyamila and Kisumu, in the hearing
of Mariamu Murikira, *alias* Mama Koko, 61, a kiosk owner, and also with Jane
Njeri Muchina, a vegetable hawker at Wakulima market, Nairobi. Sometimes
Otieno would "let it out" at the bar counter, as he did with neighbor Harry Mugo
at the Bomas of Kenya bar in the "SM corner" along with a recitation from
Shakespeare's *Julius Caesar*. Or he might elaborate on the theme of his burial at
the Dambusters' Club, as he did in the hearing of German-born Juta Johanna
Adema and her Maragoli husband Alfred Adema in 1983. Or he might talk about
it at one of his places of legal practice, as he did in the presence of Timan Njugi,
Onyango-Otieno, and Lee Muthoga at the Kenya High Court chambers; and he
spoke of it in his own offices, in the hearing of Alfred Adema and Edward Muni,
among others.[2]

It was an illiterate friend, Rahab Wambui Muhuni, who advised SM about
the need to put his intentions into writing, suggesting a substantial inversion of
the literate world in which the literate lawyer eschews the concreteness of writing

against the advice of one who knows not how to write. Otieno provided an answer to Rahab Muhuni's suggestion, "... he answered her answerless": Wambui would know how to deal with the matter.

A boundary between orality and literacy was constantly under scrutiny in the cross-examinations of witnesses before the High Court, but specifically by the counsel for the clan, Richard Kwach. At a number of points, with different witnesses, Kwach called on his interrogees to indicate why they had not written down what they had heard. Kwach saw the practice of writing and literacy as a means of testing the veracity of witnesses for Wambui. He asked each of Khaminwa's witnesses to SM's declarations if he or she had made a written note of what SM had been heard to say. Kwach's implication was twofold: such a declaration would be so extraordinary that a normal or responsible individual would preserve a material record of it; and such remarks, or remembrances, or claims, preserved outside the documentary fold could have but little standing.

Kwach found these difficult waters. Witnesses asserted alternative modes and standards of validation of their observations and memories presented as evidence. One witness, Ole Tameno, when challenged by Kwach, placed before the High Court the status and power of the elder, saying "I am telling the truth, the whole truth. I'm an old man, why should I cheat?"[3] Another witness, Jane Njeri Muchina, emphasized the value of the eyewitness account in answering Kwach's challenge: "It is you who is fabricating stories because you were not there."[4] And another, Mama Koko, went one further: "You are the one who is lying. You were not there and I was. Were you there?"[5]

The alleged statements of Otieno, transposed from conversation and oratory at many sites into the stuff and transcript of a legal proceeding, carried paradoxical messages. On the one hand, SM's apparent obsession with voicing his intentions transmitted an underlying message that he, SM, felt himself "a stranger at Nyalgunga"[6] and was "more at home in Nairobi," where he had friends like Godwin Wachira and Dr. Kiano.[7] Yet, SM could not bring himself to use the tools of the civic and professional world to mark the boundary between the arena in which he was "at home" and the arena in which he felt a "stranger." He did not, the record shows, inscribe as will, testament, letter, or contract any indication of a wish as to how and where his burial would be performed.

That SM failed to convey any uniform burial instruction opened up an important and continuing[8] national debate concerning the relative legal standing of the three juridical "codes" in use in Kenya: existing Kenyan law statutes, principles of common law carried into Kenyan practice from an English legal tradition, and concepts recognized as "customary law." Here, where the litigants saw clear legal ground for their respective positions in one code or the other, legal scholars and jurists were unable to affirm directly and simply that SM's life and death were, in the end, subject to but one code. Throughout the case there was a field of tension among three positions:

a) that SM's entire life was ordered in a way that indicated incontrovertibly that he had chosen to live outside the reach of "customary law" and, therefore, that the narrative of his life is all the evidence required to demonstrate what legal code shall be applicable;

b) that no individual can choose which code of law shall apply and, therefore, only judicial reason can establish the appropriate answer in those areas in which different codes overlap and contradict one another. In this sense, it is not the nature of the person and his life but the nature of the laws and their interpretation that shall govern; and

c) that, as a Luo, SM was subject throughout his entire life to the authority of "customary law" and that no issues other than the manner of his birth and the facts concerning the ritual establishment of his "home" have any relevance whatsoever.

The fact that there were two sides to the case, yet three fundamental positions operative within the litigation, provided enormous space for the organization of argument. The constitution of SM's life within the testimony of the court—the production of S. M. Otieno as a "modern" individual—was, for the widow's side, a line of presentation that they could not forego, given the anticipation that the brother and the clan would attempt to argue the applicability of "customary law." And, in one of the most developed areas of the case, the widow's witnesses and counsel attempted to establish that SM's "home" was not in the countryside but at his "matrimonial residence" in Langata, Nairobi.

There were difficulties—ironies really—within the statements of each side as they sought to assert the authority of a particular code. For the widow's counsel to assert that SM's home was where he resided in Nairobi was, by opposition, to assert the authority of Luo "customary law" in regard to the idea of burial at one's home and thereby to weaken the argument that "customary law" could not be applicable because of the life that SM lived. For the counsel of the brother and the clan to advance the case for the application of "customary law," they first had to establish through witnesses that there were "customary law" procedures and practices appropriate to this issue. At the same time, they opened themselves up to the question, to many questions, concerning the reach of these practices into the lives and deaths of many Luo who were buried where they died and not returned to their proper "homes."

The discourse on "home" had such broad salience for Kenyans that, in the aftermath of the litigation, "home" became—in everyday middle-class parlance in Kenya—"Nyalgunga," in the sense that one might say, "I am driving home to my Nyalgunga this weekend." Moreover, one notes, after the trial, greatly intensified activity across Kenya among members of the middle class to develop their "Nyalgungas," in an important sense reaffirming ideologically the notion of "home" contained in the litigation. In this sense, the conflict SM constructed within the contest in the court and in the street offered itself as a powerful oration to and among the Kenyan middle class on the importance of establishing a countryside home of quality and meaning.[9]

While within the struggles for SM's body, witnesses, jurists, and the public produced and invoked powerful texts on Luo and Kenya culture and past, the case produced realignments in political networks amidst public valorizations of "tradition" and the "modern marriage." Ideas about culture and the past were openly debated as to their veracity, appropriateness, and meaning. History and anthropology, as largely scholarly ventures in knowing and representing past and culture, were convened as open fields defined now through deeply interested debate within the examination of witnesses and within the arguments of jurists. While the jurists argued not only over the remains of SM but also over the inner

Joash Ochieng' Ougo (l) and Richard Kwach (r) leaving the Law Courts

and intimate meanings of life in Kenya in the 1980s, it may be argued that the court itself was on trial before the nation, its process and its language under the intense scrutiny of an engaged national public, as well as the admonishing glance of an international press.

The legal struggles for SM's remains were reported in the overseas press, including the *Washington Post* and the *New York Times*. The overseas press tended to view the SM litigation as either a struggle between "tribes" (Wambui, the Kikuyu widow, versus Ochieng', the Luo brother) or as a struggle between "modernism" and "traditionalism" (occasionally, read "tribalism"), missing the crucial role of the courtroom contest in the very constitution of ideas concerning the "modern" and the "traditional" in Kenyan life.[10] During the trial, the Kenya press at times reflected this same reading of the case as a reconvening of old, persisting struggles between Luo and Kikuyu in Kenyan national life, misreading the complex interests and intentions on both sides of the case.

## Layers and Layers of Debate

As more attention is given by scholars to the unfolding of the case for S. M. Otieno's body, so layers and layers of debate will develop over the intentions of the actors, the meanings of action and rhetoric, and the very "facts" of the case.[11] In works in progress there is already disagreement over the rendering of certain fundamental details, for example, whether Wambui Otieno brought the initial action against the clan before Justice Shields of the High Court or whether it was the clan that initiated the legal contest by completing the legal paperwork to collect the body from the mortuary.

Questions have been raised as well about the ways in which the story should be told: for example, in regard to the "appropriate portrayal" of the person and politics of Wambui Otieno within the court contest; or in regard to the effects of public displays of enthusiasm and zeal outside the court upon the proceedings within; or in regard to the role of the "state" in the final adjudication of the case.

The dispute between Wambui and the clan over the disposition of the remains of SM, with its reverberations across Kenya and beyond, presents itself as a tableau open to diverse and continuing interpretation. The present work is not the first such treatment, nor will it claim authority as a "final text"; indeed, it develops as simply another layer of discussion amidst the ferment that began in late December 1986.

That the contest for SM's body became the site and the moment for a great national debate over the meaning of culture, and over the place of national and customary law within the intimate lives of Kenyans, is not to assert that this was the first such struggle, the first such vigorous national experience centering on a corpse. The sudden deaths by apparent assassination of Pio Pinto, of C. M. G. Argwings Kodhek, of Tom Mboya, of J. M. Kariuki, unleashed enormous public demonstrations in Kenya centered on the funerals of the victims. Nor did the Otieno case in Kenya close a "genealogy" of public upheavals surrounding deaths in Kenya. The mysterious deaths of Minister of Foreign Affairs Robert Ouko and Anglican Bishop of Eldoret, Reverend Alexander Kipsang Arap Muge in western Kenya in 1990 constitute still another layer.

Further afield, the world has experienced the mass and heavily politicized funerals of fallen revolutionaries in South Africa in the 1970s and 1980s, the reburials of heroes of uprisings and revolts in eastern Europe, the extraordinary discourses surrounding the theft of the hands of Juan Perón from his grave, the proposed removal of Lenin's remains from Red Square to a common gravesite,[12] and the recent reburial of the remains of Salvador Allende in Chile.

Within contemporary American society, hardly a day goes by when one cannot find a prominent news story relating a struggle over a dead body, from the recent contest among several parties in the state of Washington to establish authority over the ashes of the late transsexual jazz pianist Billy Tipton, to the one-time threat of Imelda Marcos to spread her husband's ashes across the Hawaiian landscape if his then still-living body were not permitted to be returned to Manila.[13]

And this is clearly not a phenomenon of the twentieth century, for we know that across the world—and not only from having listened to discussions of Shakespeare at the "SM Corner" of the Bomas of Kenya bar—that the funerals of kings were moments of immense contestation over the past and future of the kingdom. Within a ruling which cleared the way for the appeal of the case to be heard in the Court of Appeal, Chief Justice C. H. E. Miller himself ruminated on the broader meaning of the case:

> I must say in passing and as an aside that for my part, if burial as such be the true cause of the unending wrangle, and particularly through this Lenten season, the matter might easily have been settled in the backroom or vestry of a church, and the body already properly and with deserved dignity laid to rest, instead of giving the incidental dirty impression of tribal dissension now apparently destined to run into March next year. With so much else to do, I pity the courts. It appears that there is truth in the classical saying, that when beggars die there are no comets seen.[14]

## A "Paper Worth Reading"

Around the events in the courts there was occasional discussion of whether SM was a party to the case or simply the subject. These discussions repositioned the question of the "speaking body," of the capacity of the corpse to form or turn the discourse on the meanings of its history, of its intentions. At the conclusion of the litigation, toward the end of May 1987, the law correspondent of the *Nation* newspaper in Nairobi noted that SM had died before letting the Law Society of Kenya know what paper, if any, he was to present in response to their invitation for a paper to go before their 1987 annual meeting. The journalist wrote:

> Did SM probably wish to write a paper like "Of the laws of Kenya and burials and all that"? We do not know. What we do know ... is that it is no simple topic to discuss ... In his death and during the hearing of the dispute, in the final submissions by counsel and in the judgment of the honourable judge, SM has written his paper worth reading and analysing.[15]

Through the contests over the accuracy and meaning of practically every detail offered up concerning SM's life, an extraordinarily conflicted person—or is it a "transcript" of a life—was resurrected from the body lying in a fully embalmed state in the Nairobi City Mortuary. One is alerted, through the relating of episodes by witnesses and their cross-examination, to the simultaneous fragility and power of memory. The struggle was, at one level, over the very nature of the person who could be resurrected or constituted in testimony and through memory, but also—at another level—over the authority to inscribe S. M. Otieno's "transcript." As each side attempted to anticipate and also establish the logic through which the justices would hear and read their argumentation, one sees memory shaped and organized into testimony.

## Many Books, Many Mouths

In a report from Nyalgunga published on 25 May 1987 in the *Nation*, Victoria Okumu described the scene of SM's funeral. She remarked that

> [b]oth international and local press were present to tell the world what was going on in Nyalgunga. They had all come to say goodbye to a great

son of the community, who by a strange twist of fate, made as many friends after death as he did when alive. The trial his corpse went through made him a darling to many ... such were the moments that escorted SM to his resting place below. The grey-haired lawyer will be seen no more, but no doubt he will live forever in the pages of many books and the mouths of many people.[16]

One sees an opening to further discussion here concerning the position of the authors of this study of the S. M. Otieno litigation, such as the present work pretends, or proposes, to be, among all the "authors" within and around the litigation who sought and continue to seek to impose their voices upon SM's life.[17] Who was SM, and what are the ethics and manners of unveiling a life? Is it enough to comprehend him as "taciturn," or "secretive," or a "resource to his family ... [who] always sends the money!," or "a genius at quoting Shakespeare," or to understand him by reference to an address to the Law Society not delivered or a last will and testimony unwritten (or suppressed by his widow)? Or is it too much beyond the realm of good taste and ethical practice, though possibly necessary to an understanding of the case, to seek a comprehension of a public discourse on the form and qualities of the marriage of Wambui and SM, a discourse that holds SM, the "Luo," the "good father and husband of a modern Kenyan family," to have been a man who formed an enduring relationship with a woman who had had, by the time of their marriage in 1961, relations with, and children by, other "prominent men" in Kenya? Or, how far does the practice of history involve engaging and challenging the standing of various self-representations of parties to the case — for example, Wambui Otieno's insistence both inside and outside the courtroom on attributing importance to her role as a leading actor and detainee during the Mau Mau war, a role inconsistent with what an historian's "transcript" would show: that Wambui had engaged in little political activity before 1959?

These are some of the pieces of the person that have come to constitute silt upon the authors' desks. One is confronted with the realization that, as one works to unveil the production of history and culture in and around the case, one operates oneself in potentially sinister ways within that very process.

## Lineages of Corpses

One may also recognize a deeper history of Luo corpses in eastern Africa, trailing back through the mass funerals of the political heroes of the independence period to the precolonial contexts of struggle for burial of the dead. Indeed, the contested corpse of S. M. Otieno had an antecedent, nearly three centuries ago, in the body of a Luo speaker that refused to be buried in Busoga in Uganda, one hundred fifty kilometers from SM's final resting place. In the late seventeenth or early eighteenth century, a group of Luo speakers arrived in south-central Busoga in Uganda. The leader of the group, also the reputed founder of the Bugweri polity, is today referred to by the name Kakaire. A source from Busoga relates that

[o]ne day Kakaire decided to go to Wangobo and improve his *mbuga* [capital, enclosure] there. As soon as he arrived he fell seriously ill and died suddenly. His people decided to bury him there in honour of his

first home. They made a very deep grave for his body, which they wrapped in wonderful bark-cloth, and then gently lowered it into the deep tomb. They left the grave uncovered until they could get all the things necessary for the burial ceremonies from Bunyoro [where he was purportedly born, hundreds of kilometers to the west]. Three days passed and the grave was still uncovered. On the fourth day, as the people were crowded along the edge of the grave, lamenting and wailing for their dead master, the sky suddenly darkened with thick black clouds; strong winds blew, making trees squeak mournfully, and great clouds of dust flew up into the air, blinding the people, who could hear nothing. At last the storm calmed down and the people were able to look around. To their dismay and great astonishment, they saw nothing of the dead body—it had disappeared during the storm. This discovery not only bewildered them more but also increased their bereavement. After eight days a large stone was found properly laid in the grave in place of the body which had disappeared. This stone can still be seen as a large rock. The amazing disappearance of the body affected the people of Bugweri so much that they decided against burying any of their dead chiefs at Wangobo.[18]

Other accounts of this episode relate that the body flew back to Bunyoro (in western Uganda), Kakaire's supposed birthplace. The progenitors of SM's Kager clan were, like Kakaire, Luo speaking, and they appear to have passed the same way.[19] The funeral ritual represented in this story from Bantu-speaking Busoga resembles in essential detail the funeral rite for SM's brother, reports of SM's behavior at which were to be much debated in the 1986–87 litigation.[20]

The renderings of the story of Kakaire's body with its variant accounts alerts us to the possibility that there is a deeper history of corpses of Luo in eastern Africa. Moreover, there is throughout the transcript of the case and throughout the debates beyond the courtroom an engagement with the past, and an inscription of history. From the discussion in the streets and bars of Kenya of the life histories of SM and Wambui, of the details of their marriages, and of the births and adoptions of their children to the testimony in court relating SM's declarations, the couple's accumulations of property, and Wambui's tense relationships with members of the Umira Kager clan, there is an overwhelming sense that *history—* its details, its motors, its contingencies—mattered, was, within and around the case, accessible to revision and inscription. Further, one senses that various participants—speakers and listeners at Ojijo Road and on the pavement outside the High Court and as witnesses within—saw themselves as participating in a more sweeping reconstruction and redefinition of the past. One curious piece of this is the inclusion, as appendices, within the published proceedings of the 1987 Nairobi Law School conference of separate genealogies of Wambui and SM extending back through many generations.[21]

## Reading S. M. Otieno

There are many lines of entry to the S. M. Otieno case. Our attention is drawn particularly to the popular productions of culture and history so extensively revealed in the court transcripts and in the debates in the press and the public surrounding the Otieno litigation. Our study of the Otieno case builds upon an extended period of research and writing in and on Siaya (the site of SM's final burial) in western Kenya, which led to several years of work on our coauthored book-length study of Siaya. SM died shortly after the Siaya manuscript had gone to the publisher, and the authors appended, on the recommendation of James Currey, the publisher—at the last moment and to the final galleys—a brief "afterword" on the case.[22] The afterword indicated how argument within and around the case recapitulated a number of points made in the book on, for example, the position of women, concepts of "home," urban migration, and the pressures placed upon urban residents to bury Luo dead in their rural homes.

For the moment, the specific interest in the Otieno litigation comes out of recent work in what we call "the production of history," an expression which we intend to encompass not only conventions and paradigms in the formation of historical knowledge and historical texts, but also—among other things—the forces underlying interpretation and the contentions, emotions, and struggles that evoke and produce historical texts and historical literatures.[23] One sees critical junctures, fissures, and contradictions located in the interstices between popular and expert representations of culture and history. It is evident that, in such litigious settings, knowledge is transferred and remade as it moves within argument, across debate, and between academic and popular discourse.

On this issue, we take a position different from that of David Parkin in his *Cultural Definition of Political Response: Lineal Destiny among the Luo*. Where Parkin observed, or argued, that the Luo of Kenya are marked and affected by the overarching condition of "stifled cultural debate," in our study of the Luo of Siaya and in other "Siaya locations" in Kenya, including Parkin's Kaloleni site in Nairobi, we have observed that "the struggles over knowledge of past and over ordering culture and society are exceedingly rich."[24]

To an extent, it is possible to see the production of culture and history on each side of the Otieno case as organized in social practice. And one seeks to relate the close reading of text—now raised, out of literary criticism, to a high art in certain branches of historical and anthropological scholarship—to an analysis of the social relations of the actors/producers of an event/text.[25] One can also examine the Otieno debate as part of the broader practices of experts and the public in constituting new or reworked values in Kenyan national life, in this case constructing national culture through the struggle over a single body. One sees an opportunity to take up Sally Falk Moore's challenge to find ways of studying "historical changes as they happen."[26]

# 2

# *Orations of the Dead*

The full High Court trial opened before Justice S. E. O. Bosire on 22 January 1987. Mr. John Khaminwa, representing Virginia Wambui Otieno before Bosire, as he had in the various interlocutory proceedings that led to Bosire's courtroom, opened the case by arguing a set of related positions:

a) that Virginia Wambui Otieno, as Silvano Melea Otieno's widow, was in law entitled to bury her husband;
b) that Luo customary law had no application in this case;
c) that S. M. Otieno's very lifestyle precluded his being subject to African customs and customary law; and
d) that S. M. Otieno had expressed his wish to be buried at Langata, or Ngong', or Upper Matasia — but not Nyalgunga in western Kenya — to a host of individuals.

The question of SM's intentions, and of the import of his alleged instructions, constituted the first layer of the open, courtroom struggle over the control of his remains.

The living S. M. Otieno was widely recognized as one of Kenya's leading legal practitioners. He had been called to serve on a number of national boards and commissions and had maintained a substantial private practice to his death. Remarkably, he left his survivors no written instructions concerning the disposition of his remains. However, during his last years, SM had, according to a number of witnesses, given considerable voice to the question of his own burial. He had, as the record of litigation reveals, given many individuals a clear sense of his intentions and desires.... Only he had given distinctly different "instructions" to various relatives and acquaintances.

The statements of but three witnesses, among a considerable parade of witnesses, suggest how the dead body of Otieno was "made to speak." Moreover, they reveal the rhetorical and dramaturgical range of these recollected and alleged instructions. On the one side, in testimony before the High Court of Kenya, the widow Wambui recalled that her husband had once announced in her presence that:

21

If I died and you pass Westlands [in Nairobi] on the way to Nyamila, I will kick the coffin open, come out and beat up all those in the convoy and go back into my coffin ... because I have to die eventually.[1]

Five days later, the Nairobi advocate Timan Njugi was presented as a witness before the same High Court proceeding. Mr. Njugi recalled how, as counsel to the Miller Commission of Inquiry into the conduct of former Attorney General, and later Minister of Constitutional Affairs in Kenya, Charles Njonjo,[2] he had worked closely with S. M. Otieno, who was serving as a consultant to the Commission. Njugi recalled that, one day in early 1984, he and several others were seated in a Nairobi office awaiting Mr. Otieno's arrival. S. M. Otieno entered the office, greeted his friends, and, according to Njugi, announced:

Mussajjah, I've bought a piece of land in Kiserian (Ngong) [a short distance to the west of Nairobi]. ... I shall be buried at Kiserian and I have made this plainly clear to all parties that might be interested in my funeral. I shall be buried at Kiserian.[3]

On the other side, the High Court of Kenya heard from Mr. Albert Ong'ang'o, an elderly gravedigger and mason from Siaya District,[4] that a few years earlier — when he was completing the preparation of a grave at Nyamila in Siaya — Mr. S. M. Otieno, the distinguished Nairobi criminal lawyer, had stooped down over the edge of the grave and called down to him:

Albert, Albert, you have prepared my brother's grave. In case I die, you will also prepare mine next to my father's.[5]

These simple gambits concerning SM's intentions opened into a far larger and more complex struggle over the essential nature of Otieno's entire life, as if the character of his life, as constructed through witnesses and examination, held its own declaration of SM's intentions. For the widow, a considerable number of witnesses — including Wambui Otieno herself — offered stories or episodes that presented SM as a "modern" individual, a devout Christian, a person of the city rather than of the countryside, oblivious to the activities of his clan, hardly ever attending funerals in Siaya.

Khaminwa argued that Otieno had chosen a Christian way of life by choosing to marry Wambui under the African Christian Marriage Act. He argued that Kenyans were living in rapidly changing times and that the Luo, therefore, should not be encouraged to practice customs that were not conducive to this "modernity." He attempted to press the High Court that Wambui should be given her husband's corpse to ensure it be buried in "a civilized manner."[6]

Harry Mugo, a neighbor of the Otienos, was called by Khaminwa as a witness. Mugo, a land appraiser, purchased a property next to SM's in Langata, in the Nairobi suburbs, in 1982. Mugo reported that he and SM met frequently, both on their farms and at the Bomas of Kenya bar.

We met quite often. We had a problem with a bush which needed to be cleared and he used to walk along the common fence. At one time, he asked me if we could get into a joint venture to dig a bore-hole to irrigate our land. But I told him I merely required the land for just a little farming ... maybe keeping one cow or two for milking.[7]

Mugo described the setting for drinks and sociability at the Bomas of Kenya:

We used to meet at the Bomas of Kenya Bar and he called me neighbour. . . .
He and his wife used to sit at a place the bar's waiters called "SM
corner" at the end of the counter. Most of the time they were together. . . .
[A]s a neighbour and a good friend, he used to consult me on land
values. He had told me he was buying a plot at Ngong where he wanted
to concentrate on farming . . . Mr. Otieno was very widely read and we
would hold normal discussions while drinking. But particularly, he was
fond of quoting Shakespeare and together we would joke a lot.[8]

Mugo then shifted his discussion to the matter of death.

I remember when the former manager of the Bomas of Kenya, Mr.
[Hilary] Ochola died, Mr. Otieno said he missed him a lot as he was
liked by everybody at Bomas of Kenya, and quoted from *Julius Caesar*, a
play by William Shakespeare. The passage goes: "Cowards die many
times before their deaths; the valiant never taste death but once; of all
wonders that I yet have heard; it seems most strange that men should
fear; seeing that death, a necessary end, will come when it will come."
. . . I also quoted to him several passages and he would laugh.[9]

Finally, Mugo described a Christmas party in 1985 at his house, arranged to
introduce Tiras Waiyaki's new bride:

Our wives prepared the dishes and drinks. In all there were eight
couples, mainly neighbours. The first to arrive was Mr. Otieno, at about
6:30 p.m. As the others had not come, I decided to show him around my
farm. He told me he had nearly died at the Nairobi Hospital where he
had been admitted for about four days. Our discussion centred on how
slim life can be. I had slaughtered a sheep and a goat and he told me he
preferred mutton as he was allergic to goat meat. He said he had grossly
overworked and he was not in good health. He eventually had decided
to develop his land at Ngong so that if God took him, he would retire
there in peace.[10]

Wambui, in her initial testimony, also spoke of this time in 1985 when SM
had been hospitalized:

He was admitted to the Nairobi Hospital suffering from high blood
pressure. He repeated: "You know I would have died yesterday. My
blood pressure was 180/110 and I hope you remember to bury me at
Langata. If you do not get consent, then it should be at Upper Matasia."
For one year until his death, he repeated this.[11]

A week separated Mugo's testimony before the High Court from Wambui's, yet
at many other points they also connected closely. Where Mugo talked about SM's
intentions to improve his farm, Wambui had remarked a week earlier:

He started improving the farm at Upper Matasia. He cultivated
the whole of it and planted livestock feed. I helped him paint our house
as I had been taught when I was a detainee. He supervised the farm
personally.[12]

Throughout the testimony of Khaminwa's witnesses, SM is presented as a
man not only wrapped up in the practice of law, and in an active sociability
amidst parties and bars in Nairobi, but as a man actively involved in land
speculation, finance, and agriculture. Indeed, it was such a discussion of SM's

financial dealings that Wambui set forth as the context for citing the "kick the coffin open" declaration.

> On December 7, last year we went to our Kiserian farm and later to Upper Matasia. At 6 p.m. two visitors called. They were Ms. Wambui Muhuni and her son Peter Kenneth Mwangi. We offered them tea and while we waited for it, Mr. Otieno and Peter, who works with a financial institution, chatted. They were discussing a loan he [SM] had taken from the East African Building Society which he thought he had overpaid. He was enquiring on the aspects of paying interest on compound basis. He had intended to write a letter to demand back his money. If he got it back, he intended to build a nice home since he wanted to practise law for three more years. After the discussion, my late husband addressed Ms. Muhuni as "Musajja" — (a real man) and said: "If I die and you pass Westlands (in Nairobi) on the way to Nyamila. . . ."[13]

Through the examination of Wambui, Mugo, and other witnesses, Khaminwa reconstituted SM from the corpse in the Nairobi morgue. SM's life was accounted by the books he was said to have read, the conversations he was said to have had, the friends he kept. Words and meanings were placed in his mouth by a broad array of witnesses, including his widow, a son, a neighbor, a lawyer, a scientist, an appraiser, a farmer, a vegetable hawker, a kiosk operator, and office workers. Piece by piece, an image of a person almost whole was constructed through day after day of witnesses, examination, cross-examination, and summary argument. SM, in this construction, was a man involved privately and profession-ally in a world far removed from his birthplace at Nyamila in Siaya. In his mode of living, in his spoken intentions, SM was presented as an individual who lived his life outside the reach of Luo custom and tradition.[14]

In response, Richard Otieno Kwach, representing Joash Ochieng' Ougo and Omolo Siranga, summoned an array of witnesses whose cumulative argument was that Otieno should be buried according to "Luo custom," which involved no other result than burial in Nyamila beside his father's grave. Kwach's witnesses presented a perspective directly opposed to that produced by Khaminwa's wit-nesses. SM could not, according to their construction of the man, throw off the traditions, responsibilities, and laws of his birthright. Though he had married not a Luo but a Kikuyu, though he had not built himself a *dala* [a residence] in the Siaya countryside, his home was at Nyamila where his placenta had been buried at the time of his birth.[15] Indeed, Kwach's witnesses scripted an extensive ethnography of "Luo custom" governing:

a) the meaning of "home" for a Luo;
b) the fundamental distinction between a "house" and a "home";
c) the appropriate rituals requisite in the burial of a male such as S. M. Otieno;
d) the position and role of "the Luo widow" in respect to the burial ceremonies of her husband; and
e) the metaphysical circumstances and existential effects relating to the relatives of S. M. Otieno were his corpse to be buried in ways other than prescribed by "Luo custom."

Like his colleague John Khaminwa, Richard Kwach summoned a very diverse array of witnesses, including businessmen, artisans, a gravedigger, a brother of

Joash Ochieng' Ougo (l) with Omolo Siranga

the deceased, a stepmother of SM, a sister, and a University Professor of Philosophy. Omolo Siranga, a businessman in Nairobi, an official of the Umira Kager Welfare Association and Ger Union, and codefendant with Joash Ochieng' Ougo in the case before the High Court, was called by Richard Kwach as a witness for the clan. While much of Siranga's testimony under Kwach's examination referred to efforts of the clan to reach an accord with Wambui Otieno in the days following SM's death, Siranga presented his reasons for opposing burial on the Otieno lands in the Nairobi suburbs.

> I am coming for Otieno's body to be buried in accordance with Luo customs beside his father's grave. ... Otieno never set up a home there (Upper Matasia) in accordance with Luo customs. ... Upper Matasia is Tiras Waiyaki's home and in accordance with the Luo customs, a father cannot be buried in his son's home.[16]

Under cross-examination by John Khaminwa, Omolo Siranga took the opportunity to extend his discussion of "the Luo customs."

> The customs of our grandfathers. In terms of burial, a Luo over 12 years can only be buried at home. The clan takes the responsibility of the burial. His wife is even not allowed not only to bury her husband, not even to touch his body after he has died. The children become members of the clan after their father's death. The customs do not allow them to decide or point out where their father should be buried.[17]

Under questioning by Richard Kwach, Joash Ochieng' Ougo, SM's brother, also presented argument for burial at Nyamila:

Because, according to Luo customs and traditions, Mr. Otieno should be
buried at Nyamila. He has been the head of the family since my elder
brother died ... Simon Odhiambo. Thirdly, he had clearly said he
wished to be buried beside the grave of our late father and fourth, if he
is buried at Upper Matasia, the clan will curse me and I will have no
voice among my clansmen.[18]

The witnesses and Kwach all argued that SM had not asked his father to perform
the rites that would have established for him a home at a site other than his
birthplace. This being the case, while he had houses and property elsewhere, his
home, and his place to be buried, was nowhere else than Nyamila in Siaya.

Subtleties lay within the various testimonies on his life; and the arguments
of counsel and witnesses were in considerable disagreement over the meanings
and intentions of a vast number of things that SM was reported to have said and
done during his life. For example, counsel for the widow Wambui asserted that
Albert Ong'ang'o, the gravedigger, had simply lied about the incident at the
brother's gravesite or, being elderly and also well down in the grave from where
SM spoke, did not hear SM correctly, given that SM had made clear to so many of
his Nairobi friends and to members of his immediate family that he wished to be
buried at his Ngong residence.

But counsel for the brother and the clan said that the point of SM's statement
at his brother's grave was not that he wanted to have his body buried at
Nyamila—there could not have even been in SM's mind any alternative to
Nyamila—but that he simply wanted the gravedigger Ong'ang'o to know that he
should be the one to prepare the grave. And, for the brother's counsel, SM's
alleged declarations to his colleagues, friends, children, and his wife were either
the fabrications of the witnesses or just the kind of joking about things that
occurs every day in conversations among friends.

## Wambui and Otieno

Kwach: You regard your husband as personal property?
Wambui: That is an insult.[19]

In her evidence, Wambui produced a select and detailed etching of S. M.
Otieno as the man and husband whom she knew for some twenty-five years.
Hers was a portrait of an educated man who, after attending Simenya Primary
and Maseno Secondary Schools, proceeded to Bombay University. It was while in
India that Otieno made some of his lifelong friendships. An independent and
republican India in the 1950s provided contexts for Kenyans to gather and
socialize in ways unknown in the colonial Kenya of the day. SM became close to
Dr. Josephat Karanja, who was to become independent Kenya's first High
Commissioner to London and later Vice-Chancellor of the University of Nairobi,
Member of Parliament for Mathare Valley, and then Vice-President of Kenya—
and then fall into disgrace and political oblivion. And, in India, SM became close
to Virginia Wambui's brother Munyua, who qualified as a doctor, was elected to
the Uhuru Parliament in 1963, became an Assistant Minister up to 1966, and then
served as Minister of Foreign Affairs of the Republic of Kenya from 1974 to 1979.

And SM formed a strong friendship with Wambui's brother Mugo, who became a judge of the High Court of the Republic of Kenya.

It was, according to the recollections of Wambui and others, in Mugo's office . . . or Munyua's . . . that Virginia Wambui Waiyaki and S. M. Otieno first met. A relationship developed from this first meeting and was translated into a Christian marriage in 1963. S. M. Otieno was at the time a young man beginning a career as a lawyer, having opened his own independent practice. In 1964 he was appointed Deputy Town Clerk of Kisumu—according to Wambui, by President Jomo Kenyatta himself—and there he served for sixteen months before returning to Nairobi as an Assistant Principal Legal Counsel for the East African Community. SM served in this capacity until 1969 when he resumed his independent, private practice of law. He prospered over the years, was called to serve the Republic in important consulting capacities, and became a "prominent Kenyan."[20]

Wambui's testimony, and her statements outside the courts, presented her late husband as a hard-working, "busy" individual, but one who was also a good husband to her and a good father to her children and foster children. He was, for Wambui, a philanthropist, having adopted the six children of Richard Arina as his own after the death of their mother in 1966. Richard Arina, a Luo and a former District Commissioner, had apparently died without resources a year earlier. And Wambui recalled an S. M. Otieno who stayed close to his hearth, where he read Bernard Shaw, the Bible, Shakespeare, a bit of Perry Mason. He watched Kenya football on television, preferring to see the game in the comforts of his home, because he thoroughly disliked the hooliganism at the Nairobi City Stadium.

He was, from Wambui's testimony, a strong Christian, an occasional worshipper in church and a most generous donor to churches in Kiambu and Murang'a. SM's children were baptized in church. And SM demonstrated his "modernity" by naming one of his sons Jairus, after his father Jairo—naming him so when the patriarch was *still alive.* Wambui and SM maintained a modern language code within the family. They spoke English, "a slight Kiswahili," and no Dholuo within their abodes. At a younger age they frequently danced outdoors, and SM dutifully paid the expenses of Wambui's golf later in life.

The Otienos were well set up in the realm of property.[21] The Otienos jointly owned their Langata residence, the farms in Kiserian and Upper Matasia, and another property noted within the case but never identified by location.[22] Wambui did not refer to any part of his Siaya patrimony as a component of their collective, or SM's sole, property holdings. Additionally, Wambui had her own property holdings in Mombasa, Naivasha, and Kikuyu.

Wambui recalled that SM cared for his father Jairo in health, enhancing the old man's situation by building a semipermanent home for him. And SM cared for his father in sickness by taking him in during 1976 and 1977 when Jairo came to Nairobi for medical treatment. And, in 1977, SM and his son Jairus drove the old man back to Nyalgunga. SM dutifully went to the burial of his father in 1978, and to the unveiling of a cross over the grave a year later. Additionally, following Wambui's testimony, SM attended the funeral of his nephew George Michael Oyugi in 1982, and also the burial of his brother, Simon Odhiambo, three years later.

According to Wambui, SM was eminently accessible to both his brothers and sisters, excepting that some of them were prone to quarrel over SM's money. SM was generous, surrendering his patrimony in Nyalgunga[23] for the son of his stepsister Felgona Akinyi. Felgona's son was named "SM," and S. M. Otieno "did not want anyone named after him to be destitute."[24]

Wambui represented SM as a dormant member — nevertheless Number 18 — of the Ger Union, a corporate association that is part of the Ugenya moiety. While SM had a wide network of friends from among his Umira Kager kin — including Otieno Ombajo, Luke Odembo, Hilary Ochola, and Dr. William Ouko — for Wambui, SM carried a higher profile as a Kenyan, having been the Uasin Gishu Assistant Treasurer of the Kenya African Union (KAU) way back in 1945. He enjoyed friendships with Kenyans from around the country, Walter Midamba, Mr. and Mrs. Muna, Dr. Julius Gikonyo Kiano, a former government minister, and Josephat Karanja wa Njuguna, who would rise to the office of Vice President.

Wambui's portrait of SM presented him as a prominent member of the legal profession, with memberships in the Law Society of Kenya and the International Bar association. Above all, Wambui etched Otieno as a man of integrity:

> Mr. Otieno had his own ethics. He was for the truth and that is what he stood for.[25]

Curiously, it was Justice Frank Shields of the High Court, in his initial rendering, who constituted in a few words the very S. M. Otieno that Wambui "produced" through days of testimony before the court. As quoted earlier:

> He was a metropolitan and a cosmopolitan. ... It is hard to envisage such a person as subject to African customary law and in particular to the customs of a rural community.[26]

## Bomas of Kenya

The Bomas of Kenya Centre was built as a cultural rendezvous in the late 1960s. The Bomas experiment in the Kenya of the day was cousin to the extensive and transformative campaign of *authenticité* in Mobutu's Zaire, a program that was sweeping Black Africa at the time. In the Kenyan context, Bomas was an attempt by the state to provide a venue for African cultural expression in Nairobi, a city whose cultural landscape was then dominated by the British Cultural Centre and the adjoining National Theatre. Those were the days when the "new Africans," led by Seth Adagala, sought to introduce African theater, African dance, and an African presence within the National Theatre. Failing to penetrate the close-knit British hegemony that defined the National Theatre's functions and programs, but also failing to attract that great mass of Kenyans — *wananchi* — to come to the citadel of British culture, the cultural nationalists "won the day" when the state created Bomas.

Bomas was set up as an educational museum for children and adults complete with Kenyan huts — with distinct Kamba, Luo, Kikuyu, Turkana models. Bomas had a resident theater company, and a dance company whose first director of choreography was Mrs. Barbara Wasow, from Chicago, Illinois, in the United States.

Over the years the Bomas has had three clienteles making use of its facilities: schoolchildren on weekdays, the *wananchi* and their families on weekends, and the well-heeled African elites from the Otiende, Karen, and Langata surrounds who have turned Bomas into their neighborhood pub in the evenings. SM and Wambui were active, visible patrons within this third group. According to Wambui's testimony, it was here that she and SM would go for his evening beer, there to meet people of his kind, and there to recite Shakespearean texts at — according to several witnesses — the end of the bar called "SM's Corner."

SM also became close with the management of Bomas. Again, according to the evidence of Wambui, the late Hilary Ochola, Director of Bomas of Kenya, was both a neighbor and a friend, and this was given corroboration within the litigation by SM's sister, Mrs. Idalia Odongo. Another acquaintance whose name was dropped by Wambui in support of her argument that Luo men could be buried away from their *dala* was "Od-Billo," Robert Olunga Obilo, an Alego Uhanya man and the Bomas security officer.

In all its contradictions and paradoxes, Bomas is, and was, a site of cultural production. Founded as a new national site for the promotion of African culture, the day at Bomas was segmented in accord with the emerging class system of Kenya itself, with *wananchi* occupying and using the site at one time, the prominent and wealthy at another. For the well-heeled Kenyan, Bomas was also a familiar and convenient facility for wedding receptions, because of its large amphitheater and ample parking close by the models of African huts.

Here, at the most visible setting in a Kenya involved with the promotion of "traditional Kenyan culture," the zone of sociability was full of Shakespearean recitations. Curiously, such individuals as SM and Wambui found comforts and comrades at Bomas that they, like many of the Kenyan elite, could not find amidst the Western theater tradition of the National Theatre complex or the European fare of the nearby Norfolk Hotel. Every evening, the old dichotomy of "Western" and "traditional" was made, if not more problematic, more complex. If Frank Shields were correct about SM's "metropolitan and cosmopolitan" lifestyle, it was also true that SM implemented it within a site of organized revival of a "traditional African culture" that Shields saw as alien to the Otienos. The struggle for SM's corpse was, in an unspoken way, the search for resolution and understanding of such prevalent contradictions in Kenyan society as marked the used landscape of Bomas. Situating SM's orations at the Bomas bar was to make concrete and dramaturgical this larger search.

# 3

# *Silences of the Living*

*This is a case where silence speaks louder than words.*

—Richard Kwach[1]

A powerful layer of debate rose to the surface amidst the open discussion of the moral ground of Luo burial, and this concerned the rights of women within marriage in Kenya and within the Kenyan nation. For some Luo women, Wambui Otieno's case offered a chance for their assertion as individuals and as spouses. But for others, Wambui's claim was perceived as ultimately threatening to a woman's fragile security in her countryside household.

The various voiced positions of Wambui, the widow, and her counsel, may be construed as moving along a continuum, and the shifting terrain of argument reveals much about the challenges faced by women within litigation in Kenya. Wambui first announced that she was burying her husband at their farm. When this was blocked, she—or her counsel before the court—asserted that she was following her husband's wish to be buried at the farm. Again, when this simple position was answered, she and her counsel were forced to reposition their case in terms of a more complex argument—but one that at first appeared not so difficult to mount—that her husband had lived outside the locus of operation of Luo customary law. Challenges to this led Wambui and her counsel and her witnesses to develop an elaborate argument that the Otienos lived and raised a family within a "modern marriage" that gave her absolute rights to her husband's property, including his physical remains, both within Kenya statutory law and in broader English common law (which has continued to have some standing in Kenya courts since independence).

After Justice Bosire's High Court ruling, Wambui called a press conference at her Langata residence and declared:

> We have parted bitterly and he [Ochieng'] should forget that his brother ever had a wife known as Wambui Otieno. I have gone back to Kikuyuland.[2]

Two days later Wambui was met by reporters outside Saint Andrew's Church in Nairobi. She announced that she had become a "born-again Christian." And

Rev. John Gatu (l), Rev. Timothy Njoya, and Wambui Otieno outside Saint Andrew's Church, Nairobi

Wambui reported that she had told church leaders that "this time [referring to a likely appeal], I am going there [to court] with Jesus."[3] She had more to say about intimations that the clan would proceed to grasp SM's entire estate and the possibility that she would go, after all, to Nyalgunga for the funeral so as to permit the clan to complete all the ceremonies relating to SM's burial.

> My word about going to Nyalgunga is final. Property is not as important as my husband whom they are fighting for. They have called me all the names, including saying that I am "a man and a half." But my word is final. Let them take the property if they want but I am through with them. Luos will be the same whatever you do to them.[4]

## Churches and Churchmen

Wambui's February announcement that she had been "reborn" should not necessarily be read as a retreat from the political sphere of women's aspirations in Kenya, in which she had been so involved for decades. The new churches of "reborn Christians" in Kenya, along with a number of church leaders, were at the time becoming an important voice of opposition to some state policies in a setting in which free expression was increasingly under assault by the forces of state security.

The trajectory of church-state relations in post-*Uhuru* Kenya has been tortuous. In the 1960s observers of Kenya saw church leaders in close cooperation with the government, but in the 1970s a souring of relations was under way, with Henry Okullu, an important figure—as Vicar of the All Saints' Cathedral—remarking that the state was "hell-bent on regimentation." Since the early 1980s, the picture of tension and struggle has been filled in by numerous incidents in which church leaders have felt it necessary to speak and act boldly to defend, from state involvement, what the churchmen reckon as their spheres of spiritual work.[5] From the late 1980s, state activity has been increasingly surveilled, critiqued, and challenged by church leaders, and they have found themselves threatened and cajoled by political figures associated with the government and party.[6] In moving toward an identification with activist churches and new forms of opposition to the state, Wambui was, in one sense, positioning herself simultaneously in opposition to the "clan" and all it represented and in opposition to the state.

This coupling became still more explicit in late May 1987. One day after the Court of Appeal had made its final decision, Wambui, the widow, boldly moved her position, angrily announcing that she and her children definitely would not attend the burial in Siaya, but going further still:

> As far as I am concerned, that is the end of the road. I have now discovered that women are discriminated against in Kenya. There is discrimination in Kenya, contrary to the United Nations Convention for the Elimination of the Discrimination Against Women which Kenya ratified in 1984. . . . The judgement was very bad. I have been denied the right to bury my husband. I will take the matter to the International Court abroad.[7]

Wambui's positions, from December through May, constitute something of a continuum. What is suggested is an "economy of constraint" that confronts women before the law in Kenya, as well as within marriage.[8]

Most profoundly, neither counsel saw it functional to relate, beyond the briefest iteration, that Wambui Otieno was respected as one of the leaders among Kenyan women—through the National Council of the Women of Kenya—as well as one who carried and energetically claimed the credentials of a vigorous and radical fighter for national independence in the 1950s. Nor did they relate that her marriage to S. M. Otieno had the stuff of national mythology, with a record of participation in protest movements and union organization, that her self-crafted, public life history held that she had served a year of detention in Lamu Prison, having left prison in January 1961, to marry SM shortly thereafter.[9] Where a Kenyan public held that Wambui left prison and married Otieno, observers may glibly note that Mzee Jomo Kenyatta left prison to negotiate Kenyan self-government and independence . . . a divergence of experience and consequence that may elaborate its own further meanings.

Eight years before Otieno's death, Wambui related her thoughts on her "intermarriage" to fellow woman activist, Chelagat Mutai, who had been a student leader, an elected MP for Eldoret South, a fiery backbencher in the 1975–78 Parliament, and a political prisoner, then a reelected MP, and subsequently a political exile in the early 1980s, and who in 1979 was working as a reporter for *Viva* magazine:

> I was not bothered by his tribe, though this very issue was to cost me much in later life. I cared only for an assurance from him that I was free

to continue my public activities. He has given me, as he did then, wonderful love and support and I do not mind telling you that in the 1969 election he spent ten thousand pounds on my bid for the Langata seat. ... I had not realized at first that inter-tribal marriages are so detested, especially ones between a Kikuyu and a Luo. It amazed me because this was the only thing that made me lose the 1969 election. In 1974 I knew the score; I had not divorced my husband, so I could expect nothing from the electors. ... If two people have a basic affection, and a willingness to understand each other's shortcomings and the patience to work out solutions, any marriage can work, be it inter-racial or intertribal. Personally I do not stand many ceremonies of my husband's people which I regard as archaic, but apart from that our attitudes are the same. ... Kenyans must practice what they preach: that we are all united as one people, that we are above petty belief in tribe and custom, that we shall give leadership to those of ability. I should dearly love to see such a Kenya.[10]

Wambui campaigned for Parliament, served as treasurer of the International Women's Conference just two years before the Otieno litigation, having been active in national women's organizations in Kenya for a number of years, while maintaining close ties with prominent feminists in other countries. All this personal history was largely excluded from the litigation.

Both within and outside the litigation and throughout the duration of the case, the intimate relations of SM and Wambui within their marriage were exposed to public view, as the one side sought to impugn Wambui as a witness[11] and as the other side sought to enhance Wambui's status as a "modern wife" duty-bound to organize the rites as her husband (or herself) would have wanted. As the contest spread out from One Ojijo Road and Wambui's Langata residence to streets, taxis, bars, markets, clubs, schools, and hospitals, a "whole" family history was exposed to the public and became centered in public debate, including discussions of Wambui's sexuality.

The silencing of the "transcript" of Wambui Otieno, the disappearance of her person behind the litigation—accompanying the constitution of the person of S. M. Otieno out of his corpse in the Nairobi Mortuary—was, it could be argued, jointly transacted by both parties to the case, their counsels, and witnesses. Within the production of the case, Wambui was immobilized by the very positions that the anticipated juridical discourse (the good wife, the good husband, the good marriage, the modern family) imposed upon the practices of counsel and witnesses. As her husband's dead body was invested with life, so Wambui in pressing her claim for his remains became socially dead. Her social and political capital nil, Wambui came to recognize the complexity of organizing, as a woman and in respect to the rights of women, an effective position within legal contests in Kenya.

One might imagine that Wambui Otieno, symmetrically to the crowds supporting the case for burial in western Kenya, could draw on Agikuyu hordes to support her position, and also count on women across Kenya. At one point in the public remonstrations concerning the body of her husband, she said that she could bring out her legions just as Umira Kager were bringing out theirs. In fact, Wambui Otieno never mobilized the *manambas* (turnboys) and the unemployed to her cause, available though they were, and are, in Nairobi.[12]

## Burying Mary

In initially presenting her claim to SM's remains as reasonable and normal, Wambui could have alluded to the death and burial of one "prominent" Luo woman. Mary Ackoro, 31, died and was buried in Nairobi in March 1982. In fact, Mary's burial was also contested, but largely outside of public view. The contest was conducted within the family premises, a maisonette located in a block at Golf Course estate right behind the mortuary where Otieno was later to lie for over five months. The Ackoro dispute pitted Mary's husband, the engineer Pius Gumo Ackoro, 40, against his uncle, Anyango Sewe, and his clan, the Alego Ulafu clan.

Pius Ackoro was orphaned early in life, while a student at Saint Mary's Secondary School, Yala. Having lost his parents, Pius had felt ill at ease with his rural uncles and spent most of his vacations from Yala—and also while a student at University College, Nairobi—with friends, godparents, and other amenable relatives in Nairobi. As a graduate engineer, Pius moved easily within the nascent Luo middle-class world of Nairobi in the early 1970s. A prominent member of the football discussion groups at Kaloleni, Pius had married "well," into the family of "Major" Ogola, like SM an Umira Kager man, who worked as a real estate officer with Tysons Habenga Ltd. The marriage of Pius and Mary, daughter of Major Ogola, was celebrated in Nairobi.

Pius was highly visible in Nairobi among a set of professionals—"the engineering boys" to their friends. These young men often spoke of the pressures to build a *simba* (bachelor's house) in Siaya. But for a number of reasons, including the poor relationship with his paternal uncles, Pius had no *simba* at Alego Rawa, his father's home in Siaya. When Mary died, however, his uncle arrived accompanied by Pius's aunt, Athieno Nyamayoga, wife of Okola Skoch[13] of Liganua. For two weeks they urged a burial at Rawa. Telephone messages from all sorts of rural relatives poured into Nairobi from Ndere, urging a Rawa burial for Mary, and urging the Alego men to talk to Pius.

Pius, however, had decided that he was going to bury his beloved wife at the Langata Mortuary, and no amount of persuasion—and there was considerable pressure applied—would move him. Pius's argument was that his uncles had been unsupportive of him in his young years and had thus made him disenchanted with the whole notion of Rawa. Thus, he declared, he had decided not to build his *simba*. But he intended, at a later date, to build his *dala* (home, enclosure) in Alego. Therefore, for the time being—"it could take twenty years," he said—he would have Mary buried at Langata. Pius built a very elaborate mausoleum there, and sealed it airtight, as a "temporary" burial place for his wife. Family and friends occasionally speculate as to whether the body will be disinterred and returned for burial in Siaya.

## The Nyamodi Funeral

The *Weekly Review* reported, in the 20 February 1987 issue, that the Member of Parliament for Gem, Grace Ogot, had said that "women wanted to see some changes in the traditions and that widows should be respected." These words were attributed to her in the extended report of remarks made by several speakers at the funeral of Dr. Zachariah Ogutu Nyamodi, at Alego Nyadhi in Siaya. The Nyamodi funeral in February 1987 became the setting for wide discussion and anguish concerning the delay in the burial of S. M. Otieno.[14] Dr. Nyamodi's widow Veronica, the Managing Director of Kenya Industrial Estates, was said to have appealed "to members of the community to review age-old traditions and customs governing widows and bring them into tune with modern times."

Oginga Odinga also spoke at the funeral and was reported to have said once again that

> the attitude that members of the Luo community can only be buried in their ancestral homes was parochial and lacked a cosmopolitan outlook. . . . [T]he Luo Union (East Africa) had encouraged Luos to buy property and settle in major towns such as Nairobi, Mombasa, Kampala, and Dar es Salaam.[15]

Immediately after the Nyamodi funeral, the National Council of Women of Kenya (NCWK), under the chair of Professor Wangari Maathai, began a petition campaign that set as its goal one million signatures to call for immediate legislation to revise the Law of Succession Act so as to assure that no woman in Kenya would ever again be deprived, as Wambui Otieno had been, of her rights to a husband's deceased body.[16]

The petition campaign was reported to have gotten off to a fast start. But within days, Grace Ogot—MP for Gem, Assistant Minister for Culture and Social Services, and one of Kenya's novelists—and others had begun to make announcements dissociating themselves from the campaign.[17] Mrs. Ogot was reported to have taken umbrage not so much at the goal of the campaign as at the use of her photograph in the campaign literature without her permission.[18]

Indeed, Grace Ogot was seen by many observers of the case to be moving away from early support of Wambui based on an expression of women's solidarity toward a position more in consonance with that of her Luo constituency in Gem in Siaya, as well as with her subordinate and "graceful"[19] status in the male-dominated political arena. A letter from Mrs. Ogot, published in the *Weekly Review* on 6 March 1987, attempted to dissociate her from the earlier *Weekly Review* report of her remarks at Dr. Nyamodi's funeral. She wrote:

> During my brief speech as a close relative to the widow, Mrs. Veronica Nyamodi, I took a contrary view to that expressed by Mzee Oginga Odinga. I thanked Mrs. Nyamodi for giving her beloved husband a decent burial at Nyadhi Village among her people. This had enabled the family and all relatives whom Dr. Nyamodi had loved and assisted in various ways to be close to their son during his last journey. Secondly, I reminded all married women to always remember that the husbands they loved had a mother, father, sisters and brothers and the extended family who also loved him, and all were entitled to share the joys and sorrows of the family. Finally, when commenting on Mrs. Nyamodi's appeal to the plight of widows, I comforted her that, as she is a highly-educated woman and a trained lawyer by profession, we could work together and initiate discussions with our people with the view to bring about changes in some of the outmoded customs affecting widows and their children.[20]

Grace Ogot's letter of correction was a carefully worded construction of a position. It was a piece of a collection of efforts by Mrs. Ogot and others to evolve an influential and "progressive" politics in a setting that permitted scarce space for maneuver. In one voice, Mrs. Ogot's reiteration of her Nyamodi address directed an appeal to Wambui Otieno and those adamant in support of her case. Her letter was also a plea for careful reflection—perhaps not evident in the mass petition campaign—on the appropriate path to reform of laws and customs relating to the rights of widows.

As one closely examines Wambui Otieno's testimony on Luo culture, one recognizes the relatively indistinct boundaries and continuities among various descriptive accounts of African culture, traditional society, and custom, from the early writings of European women in Kenya—such as Karen Blixen (Isak Dinesen) and Elspeth Huxley—who were critical of what they perceived were patriarchal institutions, and the later writings of feminist scholars trained in the West such as Achola Pala Okeyo, Patricia Stamp, Kathleen Staudt, Luise White, Regina Smith Oboler, and Audrey Wipper, among others, and such testimony as offered by Wambui Otieno, along with her statements outside of court.[21] Among other things, the interplay of colonial and postcolonial discourses signifies some of the ambiguities and contradictions inherent in the enterprise of Africanist scholarship.[22]

So where Wambui's articulated position may have been read as developing along feminist lines,[23] many influential women in Kenya chose other roads than the one they would have walked arm in arm with her. Paradoxically, after the Court of Appeal ruling in May 1987, a number of Kenyan women went to court and, arguing from the Otieno precedent, got judges to enjoin their husbands by "traditional marriage" from taking new wives by civil marriage or, more dramatically, interrupted church weddings of their customary-law husbands to new brides, fully armed with injunctions from the High Court—hardly the outcome of the modernizing agenda that Wambui and her counsel sought within the litigation—demonstrating more clearly the complexities of organizing women on a wide front in the Kenya of the 1980s.

## The Silences of Jurisprudence

In his presentations before Justice Bosire, Richard Kwach attempted to construct a very strong case against entrusting a widow with the authority to arrange the funeral of her spouse. His argument—to assemble it from a number of fragments from throughout the litigation—rested on a crudely evolved, yet popular, notion that, as women married and formed households in many different locations, geographical chaos would be introduced into the burial and remembrance of the dead.[24] While the rhetoric of this argument is empty of anthropological formulations relating to marriage and residence, it draws upon, without citing, broad reservoirs of knowledge of specific cases in which migration complicated the death and burial of a Luo individual.

Pamela Anyango (known as "Monday" among her friends) was born in Ugenya. She was a daughter of Professor B. A. Ogot's sister. Pamela attended Butere Girls' Secondary School before proceeding to Britain for specialized studies.

While in the UK, she fell in love with and married Omondi Okungu, an Alego Kaugagi man and graduate student in London. They had children, returned to Kenya, and divorced.

Pamela became a "prominent Kenyan," operating successfully in the business world and in management consultation. She had a heady feminist agenda and a number of achievements, including entering the East African Safari Rally — celebrated as the muddiest automobile competition in the world — as co-driver with her equally liberated friend, Mary Orie-Rogo Ondieki. When Pamela re-married, she became one of three concurrent wives of an equally visible Luo man, Horace Ongili Owiti, who was the General Manager of Coca Cola in Kenya. In 1983, Horace Owiti ran for election to Parliament in Gem constituency, Siaya, and won. His election was, however, contested in court by Otieno Ambala, and Owiti found himself facing a by-election in Gem. Pamela threw herself furiously into campaigning for her man. It was during this flurry of political activity that a lorry hit her car at Luanda, in western Kenya, killing her.

The question was immediately raised as to where Pamela would be buried. The Kaugagi clan, Omondi Okungu's people, led by the philosopher Dr. D. A. Masolo, claimed her body as she was "our wife," and urged Omondi to press the case. Meanwhile, Horace Owiti was preparing to bury his wife at his Gem home. Pamela's two teenage daughters, Omondi's children, wished — so it was said — that their mother be buried at a "neutral site," at Siaya town where Pamela owned both a house and commercial property. There were visits, polite enquiries, negotiations, among a considerable spread of interested parties. Omondi Okungu and Horace Owiti came to a gentlemanly agreement, that Pamela would be buried in Gem, with Owiti carrying authority over the arrangements. The Kaugagi clan quietly detached themselves from a claim to Pamela as "our wife," and various other issues were settled. Pamela was buried in Gem, as agreed.

Yet, a converse happenstance could be equally arresting, and could serve to invalidate Kwach's general argument concerning the position of women in the organization of Luo funerals. Francis Otieno Pala, one of SM's neighbors from Otiende and a fellow patron of Bomas, also died during the "season of Otieno" — in April 1987. Francis, Frank "Owadgi Anyango" ("the brother of Anyango"), had, like SM, attended Maseno Secondary School, where he was the School Captain in John Khaminwa's class of 1955. He proceeded to Makerere in Kampala for a Bachelor's degree and then on to Columbia University in the United States, where he received a Master's degree in Literature and Librarianship. Upon his return to Kenya he was the first University Deputy Librarian and then was appointed head of the Kenya National Library Services.

A man of "culture" both in the Luo idiom and in the idiom of university academe, Frank had married first from the African diaspora and then married, successively, three Luo women: Zilpa "Zippy"; Alexandre "Alex"; and Margaret. In April 1987, while SM's corpse was lying in an embalmed state in the mortuary, Francis went home to Seme, Kombewa, to attend the funeral of a cousin. On his return journey he met the fate so emblematic of the world of the other-described and self-described "Kenya elite": death by road accident. A trailer wiped his life away on the highway at Molo, west of Nakuru.

Funeral arrangements for Francis Otieno Pala were discussed and finalized at his Otiende house, close to Bomas. In Nairobi, the Seme community recognized

Margaret as the wife and widow around whom the funeral arrangements would be planned. They also recognized Margaret as *mother* to all the children of Francis by previous marriages. But when Francis was taken home for burial at his *dala* at Seme, Kombewa, all three wives—in this case disregarding Francis's diasporic experience—formally assumed their positions as wives number one (Zippy), two (Alex), and three (Margaret) during the funeral activities, although both Zippy and Alex had in "real life" been divorced by the Western method. The explanation for the "wifely presence" of Zippy and Alex, Francis's previous spouses, involved a well-understood reiteration of Luo logic: a woman always retains the right of return to the husband of her first nuptual conjugation— *chwore ma ne ohange*—therefore, the woman of the first nuptual conjugation should be present at the burial of her husband. In this case, Zippy, Alex, and Margaret each recognized the solemnity of a distinct marital relationship with Francis.

This knowledge, this practice, was of course available to both Kwach and Khaminwa.[25] Khaminwa might have drawn upon knowledge of this practice to raise questions about his adversary's notion of "the migratory nature of women," to demonstrate that women could and did, even in a Luo setting, command arrangements of funerals.[26] That Khaminwa chose not to look into this deeper realm of knowledge of funeral practice—risking the simple view of another "prominent Luo" gone to his burial place in his western Kenyan *dala*—is further evidence of the way in which law produces an economy of practice that constrains evidence marshalled before the court.

For those in Kenya who saw—in reference to SM's remains—different scenarios from the one transacted in full public view in the courts and streets of Nairobi, cases such as that of Pamela Anyango and Francis Otieno Pala were full of meaning and importance. Yet within the court practice of the counsels Khaminwa and Kwach, such cases as these were withheld from view. The silences of the counsels were, essentially, jointly enacted. Khaminwa, for his part, could not countenance opening to view a precedent in which burial at "home" in Gem or Seme preempted burial at the site of a "propertied interest" through the application of Luo notions of "home." And Kwach could not, on his side, allow the court to inspect cases where such clan claims as the Kaugagi one to "our wife" were subordinated to an emotional concern to support the wishes of the surviving spouse.

Moreover, as the case developed, Khaminwa could not further his argument by presenting an exemplar of Luo traditional practice in what would be seen as "a humane and modern context," while Kwach could hardly admit to variable circumstances and negotiated solutions in the application of "the Luo customary law."

In his opening remarks to a Nairobi conference on the S. M. Otieno case, Professor J. B. Ojwang, the chairman of the Department of Private Law of the University of Nairobi Law School, saw the dispute as entailing

> two basic questions: (a) Who had the legal right to bury the remains of the deceased? (b) At what place ought S. M. Otieno's remains to be laid to rest?[27]

While the courts in their practice structured the dispute between the two parties as commensurate and reciprocally opposed (one body, two claimants), the case was, as structured by the litigants around critical silences, largely nonreciprocal and incommensurate. Through the litigation, the Umira Kager clan sought to establish the position of its own authority over its subjects—and by extension over all Luo speakers—by application of notions or principles of "customary law," while the widow Wambui was seeking to establish her own rights and powers as a woman (and a wife and a widow) before the law of the nation. Yet within the court neither side spoke to its own fundamental program.[28] Each party suppressed the nonreciprocal elements of its own position and the courts chose not to recognize the underlying (one might better say the overlying) and very different issues at stake for each side. And the attorneys and witnesses, in their practice before the court, reinforced the critical silences composed by their adversaries. The jurists, as well, along with the practices of the courts, chose not to recognize the essential, and nonreciprocal, struggles constituted by each party to the litigation.

One is, here, given the opportunity to look more closely at the constitution of argument—the manner in which argument was constituted through indirections, allusions, and direct statements, as well as out of silences. One is challenged to comprehend the field of tension between "voice" and "silence" in the case. The thick case record may permit some degree of scrutiny of the ways in which these "silences of the living" were organized as each side, and as each side's witnesses struggled to anticipate what the court would hear—rather along the lines of Luc Boltanski's recent investigation of letters of denunciation written to the editors of *Le Monde*.[29]

The exploration, through close reading of cross-examination along and across the "boundaries" of testimony, and of the responses of the witnesses, brings into much clearer relief the tactics or strategies of the two counsels as they assembled their cases within the court proceedings. In one lovely example, the widow's counsel John Khaminwa tried to lead the gravedigger Albert Ong'ang'o into admitting that Luo funerals rest on superstitions concerning "spirits and ghosts of dead people," but found his witness exceedingly cagey. Abandoning that line of examination, Khaminwa proceeded along other tangents, including attempting to lead the witness to admit that his testimony had been rehearsed with counsel and other witnesses. Eventually, Khaminwa took the cross-examination of Ong'ang'o in a different direction and found the tables turned on himself.

> Khaminwa: Now, this illness you are suffering from, do you think it has anything to do with Mr. Otieno's death?
> Ong'ang'o: It might be because I was okay at home. But when I arrived in Nairobi, I got a strange illness.
> Khaminwa: Then let us pray to the Almighty God.
> Ong'ang'o: Go ahead and pray for me so that when I leave hospital, I will be able to accompany the body of Otieno back home to bury him there.
> Khaminwa: I put it to you Mzee Ong'ang'o, that Otieno never told you he wanted to be buried at home.
> Ong'ang'o: May I ask you a question?
> Khaminwa: Go ahead, Mzee Ong'ang'o, you are at liberty.

Ong'ang'o: Have you ever stopped at the home of Otieno at Nyalgunga
[at Nyamila in western Kenya]?
Khaminwa: I haven't.
Ong'ang'o: Then how can you be talking about a thing you don't know
about? Give back our son so we can go and bury him at home! You can
join us on the way to Nyalgunga. I will take care of your stay there![30]

## "Home" and "House"

In saluting you, let me also sing
in praise of
Ooko, Bwana
Luke my brother
The one who took me to his *home*
in Rawila [Uyoma, Siaya]
Salutation to my brother-in-law.
Dear friend!

In Luke's *house*
We had a good time
With skilled *fundis* [artisans], my dear
brother!
For the son of the Lake took me along
Until I reached his *house*
In *Bwore* [Nairobi],
the faraway Sojourner's *house*
My best friend!

Let us also cheer son of Willy
Ogada, oh dear in-law,
Son of the Lake received me as I arrived
At *Kapango*, the place of rented houses,
in *Bwore*, Sojourner's abode,
Son of the Lake received me as I arrived
At *Kapango*, the place of rented houses,
in *Bwore*, Sojourner's abode,
My dear friend![31]

The song of George Ramogi anticipates by fifteen years the confrontation in
the High Court over the meanings and implications of "home" and "house."
Rawila, Uyoma, is here accepted as "home," whereas Kibera, Nairobi, is signified
as *Kapango*, house of the transient sojourners, *jopango*.[32] It is in the tension,
within statements and cross-examination, over these simple and fundamental
words "home" and "house" that one sees most clearly the *work* of counsel upon
the production of texts in the litigation. In cross-examination, John Khaminwa,
lawyer for Wambui Otieno, appears to have sought to force a slip, an admission,
even inadvertent, on the part of one of his adversary's witnesses, that S. M.
Otieno's residence in Nairobi was his, or even a, "home." For example, in cross-
examining Omolo Siranga, Khaminwa asked:

And you also knew he [SM] had a home in Nairobi?
Siranga: I knew he had a house in Nairobi.
(A loud burst of laughter from the gallery and the body of the courtroom
missed this answer, forcing Mr. Khaminwa to ask the question again.)
Khaminwa: Did Mr. Otieno have a home in Nairobi?
Siranga: In Nairobi, we have houses and not a home. Even when it is
fenced and has a gate, it is still a house.
Khaminwa: Are you saying he (Otieno) had no home in Nairobi?
Siranga: Yes.
Khaminwa: Is this in accordance with Luo customs or what?
Siranga: Yes.
Khaminwa: What is a home in accordance with Luo customs?
Siranga: This is the place where an uncle or a father takes you to point
out where you should build. You go to that place with your wife and
first son and put up a small structure. Your son builds a small hut called
*simba*. You sleep there with your wife and then it becomes your home.[33]

Khaminwa had a similar encounter with Japheth Yahuma, a witness for
Kwach:

Khaminwa: You said you went to Mr. Otieno's home in Langata?
Yahuma: Not home but house. Yes. I went there and Mr. Otieno and his
wife slaughtered a sheep for us.
Khaminwa: Were you impressed by the home?
Yahuma: Not a home, a house!
Khaminwa: Who told you about this?
Yahuma: A house is a house and a home is a home.
They are two different things. I was not told what to say. These differences
are very clear!
Khaminwa: Bishop Yahuma, if you were staying in Nairobi and you met
a friend while you were walking towards where you are staying, what
would you say when asked where you are going?
Yahuma: I would say I was going to my house!
Khaminwa: Not home?
Yahuma: No, house!
Khaminwa: I put it to you that you are telling lies. ..."[34]

Richard Kwach, counsel for the brother and the clan, appears to have made
his witnesses exceedingly sensitive to Khaminwa's tactical interrogations concerning what is a "house" or a "home." For example, in recounting his movements in
the hours and days immediately following SM's death, Omolo Siranga related
that Joash "came to my house"; "I got in touch with him [Joash] at his Parklands
house"; "he [Joash] had told me he had been to S. M. Otieno's house in
Langata"; "... [we] went to inform other society members and the general clan
to meet at Mr. Ochieng's house at Ojijo Road."[35] But there were also slips: for
example, Siranga used the word "home" twice in referring to the Otieno residence at
Langata before again referring to her residence as a "house".[36]
In an essay prepared for a Nairobi Law School conference following the
burial of SM, the Kenyan linguist Duncan Okoth-Okombo has explored the
semantics of the court discussion of "house" and "home" within the multilingual
and multicultural context of the litigation wherein difficulties arose for various
participants in translating and articulating the distinctive meanings of "house"
and "home."

[H]ere we have the crucial distinction between "home" as an English word and its Dholuo correlate *dala* (or *pacho*). For the definition of *dala* must of necessity contain an indication of how it comes into being. Since establishing *dala* is a ritual that involves at the very minimum the man who is to be the head of the home, his eldest son, his wife, and his own father (or an appropriate representative from his *anyuola* [minimal lineage]), it cannot be a personal affair. That is, a man cannot just *"feel"* that the building in which he lives is his *dala*. Thus no matter how much one "feels at home" in a given *ot* ("house") one cannot just declare it *dala* ("home") without the appropriate ritual, which is reducible to such essentials as may be prescribed by the consulted elder or elders.[37]

Okoth-Okombo extends his discussion into the distinct situations of the various participants in the case, noting that whereas John Khaminwa may have "understood the word 'home' only in the English sense," other witnesses may have "understood the word 'home' only in its Dholuo sense since they received the advocates' questions in translation and were, in all likelihood, unaware of the English meaning," while others such as Richard Kwach, Omolo Siranga, and Joash Ochieng' Ougo were very aware (even as they slipped into contradictory usage as noted above with Siranga) of the significance for Luo custom and for the airing of the case before the court of the distinctions between English and Dholuo meanings of "house" and "home."[38]

That there is still a more complex story behind the arguments relating to the meaning of *dala* in Luo thought and action is suggested by the observations of such early scholars of the Luo as E. E. Evans-Pritchard who argued that *dala* is a "Bantu word" adapted into Luo speech, the "original" Luo word being *pacho* (pl. *mier*).[39]

This constructed and imposed tension between the sense of witnesses responding freely and witnesses extensively prepared for the semantic implications of prospective lines of questioning is a further reminder of the particular quality of a court transcript, in which composed and tactical speech is rendered more powerful by the apparent naturalization of question and response. The point here is not that court testimony is thereby unreliable by means of its extensive "scripting" but that there is a process of production of text — court testimony and other — that may be unraveled through attention to the ways in which assertions and arguments are naturalized, knowledge combed, and silences constructed.

# 4

# Living Bodies and Their Knowledge

> "Professor, we are the people
> And you are the loaded,
> Our white men.

> Mwalimu, sisi ni *raia*
> Na nyinyi ndio *tajiri*
> *Wazungu* wetu."[1]

In his ruling of 2 April, Chief Justice Miller cited Shakespeare's *Julius Caesar* in remarking that "when beggars die there are no comets seen."[2] Silvano Melea Otieno was, indeed, the harbinger of comets, and at numerous points throughout the litigation, lawyers, judges, and witnesses focused attention upon the lives of the privileged in Kenya.

Miller's remark was a broad, concise, and unwittingly brilliant commentary on the historiography of Kenya since the beginning of the colonial period, in which scholars—historians and other social scientists—have largely focused attention on the elites, on those individuals and groups who somehow, sometime, moved beyond the condition and circumstances of the *raia*, the ordinary people.[3] Where studies have drawn attention to colonial and postcolonial activities of the "underclass" such as slum building, beer brewing, and prostitution, their authors have sought to define and describe the process by which select women and men attained higher social and economic status within the periphery of capitalism through accumulation and property speculation.[4]

What is lacking is the history of the *raia*, the ordinary people whose lives become momentarily important to observers only when they drop over and die as a consequence of unemployment, hunger, social neglect, and homelessness, as happened to the Oxford-educated, but nevertheless derelict, Samuel Chweya Ayany of Alego Agulu, another Umira Kager man scavenging the Kibera slums of Nairobi in 1987; or when they narrate their experience to the evangelically motivated and sympathetic ear of a writer like Marjorie Oludhe Macgoye listening to the voices of the poor at the fragile shelters of the old people of *Mji wa Huruma*, a charitable almshouse in Nairobi.[5]

In the constellation of lives that constitute the Kenya of the colonial and postcolonial eras, there are not only the faceless and nameless *raia* and the

Crowd control outside the Law Courts

prominent and privileged, such as the Otienos; there are many who live seemingly uneventful lives as artisans, women working their rural lands, peasant farmers, transporters, laborers—whose lives marshall the interests of historians and other record-keepers only as they educate their sons all the way to Harvard, as with Onyango, the artisan employee of the Railways Corporation and father of Hilary Ng'weno, the very successful Editor in Chief of the *Weekly Review*, or Wangoi, the cultivating mother of the Oxford-educated lawyer and human-rights champion, Gibson Kamau Kuria. Even then, recognition most often comes not to the struggling *raia* who produced those who achieved visibility and prominence, but rather to the achievers themselves.

The decade of the 1980s in Kenya was marked by the realms of controversy that surrounded two men, Charles Njonjo and S. M. Otieno. Through the close observation of the courts at work, Kenyans came to learn about these two lawyers, one the former Attorney General and confidant of President Jomo Kenyatta, and of Daniel Arap Moi for five years, and the other the noted Kenyan criminal lawyer. "Ordinary Kenyans" were exposed to quite extraordinary views of the private domains of these mighty individuals: what they ate, what water they drank, how they consorted, how they talked about their world, how they used — and mixed with — their servants. But these views of the prominent and privileged extended to include portraits of the lives of *raia*, through revealing the work, lives, voices, interests, attentions, and opinions of the *servants* of the "rich and famous."[6] In the setting of commissions and courts, the so-called *raia* were able to "view" themselves through the dramas of the legal system.[7]

Two ordinary individuals assumed central positions within the litigation surrounding S. M. Otieno's corpse. One, Albert Ong'ang'o, a gravedigger, was brought by the clan as a witness to S. M. Otieno's "oration" said to have been given at the grave of his brother, Simeon (Simon) Odhiambo, at Nyamila. The other, Mama Koko, a casual cook in the Otieno household, was produced as a witness for Wambui Virginia Otieno, as John Khaminwa, Wambui's counsel, sought to document the tensions between S. M. Otieno and his rural kin at Nyamila. While invoking conflicting positions on the litigation, Ong'ang'o and Mama Koko were both presented to the court as "ordinary folk." Separately, they were represented, and represented themselves, as individuals with diverse and relevant artisanal skills, experience, and observational talents. Their own histories, as occasional servant and as career artisan, came to play critical roles within the litigation. Their very witnessing, their language before the court, their physical presence, offered eloquent critique of the Chief Justice's adage.[8]

## Cooking for the Otienos

This puzzle of 48 years ago testifies to the dramatic settings even an ordinary life negotiates during its passage. . . .[9]

Mariamu Murikira, known popularly as Mama Koko, was an occasional cook to the Otienos. According to her own account she was born in 1926. Mama Koko belonged to that category of the *raia* who have made Nairobi their home, and who — through service — make the elite of Kenya comfortable in Nairobi's suburbs without insisting on writing their own history of service.[10] She owned a food kiosk in Nairobi, sold food to workers at times, visited Wambui both as friend and as reachable servant. And she traveled with the Otienos from time to time.

The very transience of Mama Koko's labors and associations painted her as a somewhat shadowy figure. The court public occasionally laughed at her own, or the counsels', representations of her profession, for it moved along uncomfortable boundaries of the moral and lawful, the achieved spectacular and the lived ordinary. In his cross-examination, Richard Kwach, for the clan, attempted to redraw Mama Koko's life as one closely involved with what he expected the court to see as the dark side: provisioning magic and engaging in prostitution. Equally, in closing his cross-examination of Mama Koko, Kwach attempted to establish Mama Koko's domain as a "world apart."

[I]t would be better if you stuck to your kiosk and medicine business.
(Mr. Kwach sat down with a flourish.)[11]

Then, in his closing argument before Justice Bosire, Kwach situated himself
directly within the discourse on Mama Koko's life and social worth, declaring,

I would like to go on record that I have never eaten in a kiosk.[12]

Mama Koko may have had a dark and shadowy side—the crowds on the
sidewalk outside the court reveled in such rumor—but all this was not clear
within the work of counsel *inside* the court. Whatever ambiguity surrounded her
life outside the court, Mama Koko had her "rendezvous with victory"[13] inside it,
for both lawyers were interested in the fact that Mama Koko happened to be with
Wambui and SM at Nyalgunga during the burial of SM's nephew Oyugi and then
again at the funeral of Simeon Odhiambo, SM's brother.

According to her testimony, Mama Koko cooked meals for the Otienos at
Nyalgunga; she reported preparing only food brought along by the Otienos from
Nairobi; she saw Otieno drinking water from a source which they had carried in
their car from Nairobi;[14] she had knowledge that SM had driven to Kisumu to
sleep at a modern and comfortable hotel rather than at Nyalgunga; she "overheard"
SM and Joash Ochieng' Ougo arguing over accusations that Wambui was a
prostitute; and she was, with many others, witness to a declaration of SM's
intention as to his own burial:

I asked him [SM] why he could not build a house at Siaya so that we
could be visiting him. He replied and said he could not build a house
there because he has his own land at Ngong and that was where he
wanted to build a house.[15]

Who was Mama Koko? Mama Koko stood at the intersection of a number of
important processes and problematics that ran through the litigation and through
Kenya society. She herself was married "outside," to Mfahaya Jumbe who came
from the Comoros Islands. She was urban and urbane, struggling to comprehend,
survive, and succeed through struggle in the spaces left open, disdained, or
created inadvertently by the prominent, privileged, and wealthy. She was
"successor" to a Swahili-speaking, urban Kenyan world which has been traced
back to the 1910s by both Janet Bujra and Luise White. She, with women and
men who preceded her, learned *new* languages: not just Kiswahili but also
Oluluyia, Ol Maa, Ruhaya, and Gikuyu[16]—and used them to "accommodate" in
manifold ways the newer immigrants to the urban areas.

Such women recognized the salience and force of Haya, Akamba, and Maasai
spirit possession practices and cults, along with magic and medicine from western
Kenya and syncretic Islamic practices including spirit mediumship (*upepo*) from
the Kenyan coast.[17] Such individuals as Mama Koko were able to survive and
sometimes prosper through service—spiritual, sexual, and material—to a pool of
urban folk that included unemployed young men seeking work, and young
women moving into hawking and prostitution. They have helped, and profited,
from services provided to the importune bride anxious for a pregnancy, the
scientist wife of a Nairobi University don, she with a Computer Science degree
from Northwestern University in the United States, anxious for wealth; to the
self-made transporter terrified by the fact that his wives will not stay faithful in
Majengo, Kakamega, when he is driving far into Rwanda and Southern Sudan.

Women such as Mama Koko possessed the intelligence of urban Nairobi, their knowledge ranging from good culinary expertise to political insight about city-council and national elections. These are the women who made the politician Tom Mboya, who captured the votes for him in slumland Gikomba and Muoroto in Starehe constituency, and who first made Virginia Wambui into a leader of the Nairobi Peoples' Convention Party Women's Wing in 1959.

At still another level, Mama Koko signified friendship between sister and sister, and also across class, ethnic, and gender lines to embrace S. M. Otieno on the "simple" basis that he was a "good man." In being close by Wambui on an on-and-off basis, in being Wambui's confidante, she was also serving effectively as her conscience, alerting Wambui to the possibility that "there but for the grace of God ...," perhaps further cementing Wambui's alliance with SM? While the programs of the litigants, counsels, and courts constructed Mama Koko (and Albert Ong'ang'o) as "other" to Wambui and SM, it was the testimony of a "Maasai from Ngong," James Ligia Ole Tameno, 70 years old, that spoke books concerning the nature and scope of "difference" between SM and Wambui, on the one hand, and the ordinary people, *raia*, who surrounded and served them, on the other:

> Mr. Khaminwa: Now, when Mr. Otieno showed you where he wanted his grave to be, what did you say?
> *Mzee* Tameno: I didn't say a word. He was a lawyer and I'm a *mzee*. What he said was final![18]

Mama Koko's appearance in court, at the behest of John Khaminwa for Wambui, reminded the court that there is worth in being ordinary, that there is value in the witness, experience, and opinion of the *raia*.[19] In challenging Mama Koko in his summing up, Richard Kwach—as noted above—chose not to examine what she said, but rather attempted to depose her testimony by attacking the ordinariness of her social status—perhaps a belated recognition that it was her station as a member of the *raia* that would give unique authority to her evidence as a witness.

Yet Kwach would not be charitable even in this concession. In his summary argument before the Court of Appeal panel, Richard Kwach returned again and again to the question of social status and moral worth. It could be a most complex argument, for on the one hand he argued:

> My learned friend [Khaminwa] said a new class of intellectuals has emerged since independence but I haven't seen any. Who is the witness who came to represent this urbanised class of Kenyans? A lot was said about him. I don't think such a cosmopolitan and metropolitan person would be operating a kiosk and selling vegetables. That class of people is as elusive as a mirage. You see it and it disappears.[20]

While, on the other hand, Kwach readily admitted that such a person did exist, as exemplified by *Kwach*, who could say he had "never eaten in a kiosk." Also, in centering his own personhood as a sign of class, Kwach could say, "If you would like to know about me, don't ask my gardener."

Paradoxically, it was Kwach's "ordinary witness," Albert Ong'ang'o, as we shall see, whose testimony was empowered by its very ordinariness. His testimony ultimately drove a crucial nail into Khaminwa's case in Justice Bosire's court.

## Ong'ang'o and Odera

On Friday, 13 February 1987, Justice S. E. O. Bosire of the High Court delivered his judgment in the S. M. Otieno case.[21] The final text of the judgment contains extensive comment on the standing of various witnesses and their testimony, including that of two men: Albert Ong'ang'o, 79 years old, a gravedigger from Alego, Siaya, and Professor Henry Odera Oruka, a member of the Department of Philosophy, University of Nairobi, 42 years old. While Ong'ang'o and Odera Oruka were both witnesses for Ougo and Siranga—that is they advocated burial in the countryside—the ways in which they presented themselves and the ways in which they were viewed within the practice of the court offer further openings to the study of the ways in which knowledge, expertise, is seen to attach to the body. We may look at two passages within Bosire's text:

> The Umira Kager Clan comprises a large number of people. Even if I were to accept what Professor Henry Odera Oruka said, that the clan sages take the decision, who is to decide that a particular person should be called upon to give direction with regard to burial as required? To my mind it will be idle to say that the clan takes a decision as to where and how a deceased person is to be buried. A line must be drawn somewhere to show who are involved in making the crucial decisions with regard to burial.[22]

> Albert Ong'ang'o, a mason in Siaya District and a cousin of the deceased, also testified that the deceased did intimate to him that he wished to be

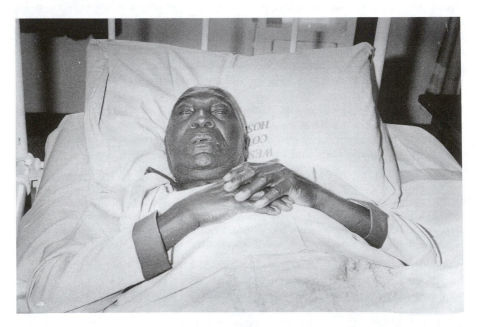

Albert Ong'ang'o, a mason, giving testimony before the High Court at Westlands Cottage Hospital

buried next to or near his father's grave. Ong'ang'o was at the time cementing the grave of the deceased's elder brother, Simon, who was then awaiting burial. The witness testified that the deceased expressed his wish in the following words or words to that effect:

> "Albert, Albert, you have now prepared my brother Simon's grave. In case I die prepare a grave for me next to that of my father."

Those words were spoken to the witness, so he said, when he was inside the grave which was under construction. The court moved to Westlands Cottage Hospital where the witness was admitted, having had a prostate operation, to receive his evidence. He testified as he lay on his back in his hospital bed. In spite of being in that condition he had no difficulty expressing himself. He impressed me a lot. He appeared candid and truthful. I had no reason to doubt his testimony.[23]

The juxtaposition of these two individuals, one the elderly gravedigger Albert Ong'ang'o, the other the youthful Professor Henry Odera Oruka, challenges one to readdress issues of expertise and authority in the production of knowledge. While we read Bosire's commentaries *within* the practice of a court, our reading of these testimonies, along with our reading of Bosire's "reading" of the testimony of these two witnesses, draws us toward a number of arguments.[24]

First, the testimony of each of these two men does not stand outside its performance. And the performance does not stand independently of the programs of counsel to construct and deconstruct authority within the practice of the courts. For Bosire, the very context of the examination of the gravedigger in Westlands Hospital "speaks for itself." The very body and posture of the elder contributed to making his words appear candid and truthful.

For the witness Odera Oruka, the erect and formal posture of the sprightly and energetic philosopher was not sufficient to affirm the authority of his testimony. An extensive transcript of his career and his scholarly work was adduced in prefatory questioning by Richard Kwach, the lawyer for the clan. In his introductory questions to his own witness, Kwach drew out that Odera Oruka is "of Nairobi University," a "professor of philosophy," "of the Kenya National Academy of Sciences," "a holder of [the] B.Sc. degree in philosophy and science from Uppsala University, Sweden," that he "co-authored a number of articles," that he has taught "for sixteen years" at the University, that he has been Chairman of his department "for six years," and that he has "researched on African customs and traditions in Kenya."[25]

In cross-examination, Wambui Otieno's counsel, John Khaminwa, drew out that Odera Oruka's research had mainly focused "on rural areas," that he has interviewed "some sages, wise men," that "some of them were interviewed by students," that his research covered Siaya, South Nyanza, and a bit of Kisumu," that "the local community" determined "who qualified" as sages, that "about ten students" were involved in the research, that "the students . . . would ask the community who the sages were, interview them and ultimately the students would decide the best of the sages" — "subject to his [the sage's] approval!"

In discussing the value and credibility of these two witnesses, Bosire appears to have seen the essential quality of Ong'ang'o's testimony as fully embodied in the person as represented before him: elderly, infirm, prostrate. And the Judge appears to have regarded Odera Oruka's testimony as contingent on the status of an array of credentials, histories, and arrangements outside his body. Through examination and cross-examination, with various interventions by the judge, we are confronted by two distinctive modalities through which the person, represented by these two men, has been constituted before the court and its broad national audience.

Second, the testimony, within performance and within the program of legal practice, was silently but powerfully valenced by other significant factors, most importantly by the meanings attached to the ways in which the two lives were "grounded" within western Kenya. Here we may see the category of "man" disaggregated into two distinctive cultural fields: Ong'ang'o's authority drew on his age, but also upon his manual work and ability, and with reference to his connection with the earth of the grave and to the dead. Unspoken, his relationship to the dead was multiply expressed, through the site of the hospital, through his sickly appearance, through his remembrance of being at the graveside, through his represented voice from the grave, and through his association with the disposition of the corpse of Simon Odhiambo (S. M. Otieno's brother).

Odera Oruka's authority drew on the privileges conferred by the scientific method and on achievement in and through the academy. While his research work was based in Siaya,[26] Odera Oruka was grounded not in the material world of western Kenya but rather in the world of the academy. He was presented, and represented himself, as vigorous and active, as organizing teams, groups, and elaborate research methodologies.[27] But the very meaning and force of Odera's body dissolved into an elaborated mastery of his profession.

Kwach and Ong'ang'o were, on the other hand, situating Ong'ang'o's testimony differently. He was presented as one, as whole, in the world, his life and his discourse uninflected by the contradictions of speaking of one world while trying to live in another. In his cross-examination, Wambui's counsel, John Khaminwa, attempted to unveil contradictions in Ong'ang'o's life and testimony, but the gravedigger in his responses, as we have offered in the example above, cleverly unveiled the contradictions in Khaminwa's practice and knowledge.

Third, the program of litigation, by which counsel "managed" this testimony and its performance, anticipated different and yet simultaneous "readings" by the court. Bosire made clear that it was the infirm body and its presentation of a voice which gave authority to the story that Ong'ang'o intended to tell. He did not choose to enter and examine the text of Ong'ang'o itself, to evaluate its inner meanings and logic. But, with Odera Oruka, he was drawn into discourse over the meanings, logic, and practical implications of the professional representations of "Luo culture" and "Luo philosophy." To reiterate Bosire's stand:

> Even if I were to accept what Professor Henry Odera Oruka said, that the clan sages take the decision, who is to decide that a particular person should be called upon to give direction with regard to burial as required? To my mind it will be idle to say that the clan takes a decision as to where and how a deceased person is to be buried. A line must be drawn somewhere. . . .[28]

In a sense, Odera Oruka himself—through Kwach's piloting—forced the court's examination into the deeper evaluation of his report. Odera Oruka related that he drew knowledge of "Luo culture" and "Luo philosophy" from "sages,"

. . . wise men who are able to explain beyond the basic common beliefs in customs. Persons recognised by the community. . . .[29]

Clearly, Odera Oruka applied a different validation criterion than did Bosire in respect to Ong'ang'o's testimony before the court.

Fourth, the testimony, and its performance, was connected to broader "readings" beyond the court, addressing other parties and other issues which had no direct and immediate place in the formal setting of the court. These materials can be read more deeply by Kenyans and other observers as touching and evoking critical elements of the ways in which person, gender, and society are constituted. We have noted how Bosire convened a different "reading" for Ong'ang'o than the reading he gave to Odera Oruka. From our vantage point as removed observers, we may play with the testimony in different ways than Bosire himself could have; for example, we may compare the manner in which Bosire "read" the elderly gravedigger with the way in which another authority, the philosopher Odera Oruka, "read" his sages. We may observe, for example, how Justice Bosire situated Ong'ang'o's words within the material facts of his infirmity, maintaining Richard Kwach's *embodied* rendition of those words as he had organized Ong'ang'o's testimony from his hospital bed. We may note, through closer reading of his extended testimony, how Odera Oruka disembodied the voices, the words, and authority of his elderly sages, abstracting them from the material contexts in which they had spoken. For Odera Oruka, the very practice of philosophy, in his hands, obscured these material facts of his interviews.

Odera Oruka began his research with the view that his sages would pass on to him *knowledge* which they would have learned from older sages, and there was further obscuring by virtue of the use of student interviewers carrying formulaic methodologies to the field. By advancing one frame of authority, that of the scholar and the scholarly apparatus, Odera Oruka and Richard Kwach obscured the very elements of the work of the sages that would have given their texts authority within Bosire's court in the sense in which Bosire had chosen to read it.

It would be a mistake to see Ong'ang'o and Odera Oruka as occupying symmetrical and opposed positions.[30] Odera Oruka has committed himself to an academic revival and valorization of a cultural tradition, the recapture of a "traditional world" through which only the trained and expert reportage of the sages can provide access. To do so he has appropriated the tools, and adopted the habitus, of what would be taken to be the "modern world." While arguing the case for the repertoire and standing of "traditional authority" and bringing into parlance the ideas of a "traditional world," Odera Oruka has entered fully the world that Wambui Otieno, her counsel, and witnesses claim to have been the world that S. M. Otieno inhabited as a "modern individual" living far from, and outside the bonds of, "tradition and custom." He has become "civilized" — *Ng'ato molony*!

With the Otieno case, the debates may still be more complex, for the participants themselves — whether within the courtroom or far removed from it — were recognizing the different positions taken, and at the same time defining and interpreting the substance and meaning of difference. Such analysis and interpretation took place at any number of sites, and people sought to make the case their own, even if there was little information about the case actually available.

## Liganua Erudition

The Otieno litigation entered the world of Siaya in western Kenya by means of the Swahili service of the Voice of Kenya, which daily provided an early-morning summary of the previous day's deliberations as reported in the press. In early 1987, the Otieno case filled the conversations and debates of rural people in the tea shops and along the cattle-trade routes of Siaya. People carried into the markets their own "readings" of the case, extrapolating on what they had just heard over the radio or, more commonly, on what was reported to them as having just been heard. The discussions took on different shapes and were far from predictable or monotonous.

An example of one extended discussion in a Liganua cattle shed in February 1987 involved Albert Ongwama, the local veterinarian who was spraying Mama Rosbella's cattle herds against ticks, and Christopher Ochieng' Oganga, a retired police sergeant. Christopher presented himself that morning as particularly expert in analysing the adversarial postures of the participants in the court contest, for he himself had served as a prosecutor in the course of his police duties. Christopher's analysis focused on the way in which the bench "heard" the proceedings. For Christopher, the bench would not wait to consider the entire proceedings at the conclusion of the case. Rather, he saw the court adjudicating the merit of each argument within each day's proceeding,[31] with points scored for or against the two adversaries, Kwach and Khaminwa. Christopher's analysis was not exceptional, for rural discourse on the case was commonly organized around whether and how "Kwach defeated Khaminwa yesterday but Kwach should watch out because today Khaminwa might surprise him" ... as if the litigation were a boxing match being scored round by round.

Christopher Ochieng' Oganga's analysis, and that of the rural public, was to accentuate the roles and qualities of the two lawyers, as opposed to the content of their arguments or the structure of their cases. For example, there was broad agreement that both lawyers had "hard mouths" — *dhogi tek* — that they could twist words, peddling rhetoric without due regard to the truth of what was being said. Indeed, it was accepted by Christopher and his audience that the lawyers had no substantive dispute as to the law, or at least were not arguing on the basis of law or code, but rather they were engaged in a wrestling match of words. They were tweaking meanings out of the speakers, the witnesses, translating, deriving, and imputing meanings not intended by the speaker. Christopher, and those who saw the case proceeding by these practices, termed these two lawyers as *okil kamaloka*, "lawyer," the "word-twister."

But that morning Albert Ongwama had a different perspective. Albert's discussion of the case, like that of some others in the western Kenya countryside, assumed that the proceedings of the High Court were identical to those of the Location Tribunals that they had participated in or witnessed during the colonial period. While Christopher saw the case wholly in terms of the performance of the lawyers, Albert saw the lawyers as essentially transparent. For Albert, it was not so much what the lawyers said, or how they said it, but rather what the witnesses said to the judges that was critical. In the Location Tribunals of colonial days, Albert had extensive experience of standing face-to-face in the open court at Boro, arguing his case directly with Senior Chief Amoth Owira of Alego in the chair, with assessors (known as "judges" by the local people) like Mtanda and Lukas Ngure on the side, and Magere, the court messenger-cum-the chief's *éminence grise*, perched on the edge waiting for instructions to extort or punish.[32] Albert asserted that morning in February that what it took to be a witness in the court was courage, the ability to look the judges right in the face (*kwaro wang'*), and to convince, by one's strength and one's clarity, that what one was presenting was the truth.

In this learned discourse in the Liganua cattle shed, Albert Ongwama submitted that the older people involved in the litigation—Albert Ong'ang'o, Yahuma, and the others—would do well, for they knew how, from way back, to conduct themselves at court. He had seen these very individuals confront Chief Amoth at Boro, he affirmed. Albert's concern, however, was over what he saw as the younger, inexperienced witnesses who were being summoned by Kwach: people like Omolo Siranga and Professor Odera Oruka. Were they familiar with the court, it was asked? Could they withstand the bullying of the judges? The chief's tribunals were well known for such bullying, such testing of the truth and seriousness of an individual's presentation to the court.[33] Could they tell the truth? Could they present what they tell as truth? In effect, could they really swear through *mbira*, the traditional oath, to tell the truth?

The question of truth, and swearing before the court, was particularly important. Albert argued, and the mothers at the shed concurred, that

> these Africans do not fear the Bible. They can hold it aloft in court and swear by it, but it has no ancestral curse upon them so they cannot be bound by it. This explains why young men lie in court with impunity. If they understood *mbira*, then they would fear it and they would be bound to tell the truth.

Nor was this concern of the Liganua folk isolated, for the market "experts" on the Otieno case at Bondo expressed the same fears at this time.[34]

The discussion that morning then shifted to a middle ground between the positions of Christopher and Albert. The two principal discussants and the group around them agreed that a proper "coaching" of the witnesses must have been done by Kwach and by Khaminwa so as to produce effective testimony. But how well would the coaching work out, they asked? The outcome, they agreed, would be known when the day's proceedings were presented over the radio the next morning in the news bulletin.

## Gagging Class

Juridical practice, and the social constitution of argument among people in the streets, clubs, bars, law chambers, and courtrooms, unearthed, mediated, and also transformed the discussion of certain critical conflicts in Kenya. Most particularly, the court contest appears to have constructed a grand silence around lowly voiced, yet heavily conflicted ideas concerning community and equity among Kenyan Luo.

For a start, there appears to have been an effort, beginning with leaders of the Umira Kager clan but also extending out among other Luo leaders, to silence the voice and opinion of Oginga Odinga at gatherings, meetings, and funerals in which support for the brother and the clan's position in the litigation was developing. Odinga, the great patriot if not living patriarch of the "Luo nation" of Kenya, privately expressed strong support for "long-time comrade Wambui Otieno" in her ordeal.

Secondly, neither side appeared interested in disclosing and centering the explosive tension emergent in Kenya between relatively wealthy urban residents and their poorer urban and rural affines and kin.[35] Wambui Otieno's counsel clearly saw no value in an argument concerning the importance to many urban citizens, like the Otienos, of protecting their hard-won wealth from the claims of country cousins.[36] People could and did speak of the morality of immense expenditures on funerals in Kenya. As noted in *Siaya*,

> The funeral is a focal issue in Kenya Luo consociation. The vast majority of voluntary, mainly polysegmentary associations in the towns function most effectively as funeral associations. The turnout for a meeting is itself instructive. A typical clan meeting, characteristically called to discuss the issue of *harambee* for a primary school building (for example, of the Umira lineage) will, "to save money", cloister itself in a two-and-a-half metre by three metre room in Gorofani estate, Nairobi, and conduct its business for a full three or four hours. Perhaps ten or twelve people will attend. But comes a funeral and a licence becomes affordable, and the entire Umira family will turn up at the house of the bereaved on one or more of the seven or eight days when the inevitable collection of funds for funeral expenses takes place. Such funeral gatherings, whether to honour the high or the low, are pivotal in drawing people together.[37]

Neither Khaminwa nor Kwach chose to consider such an expenditure as, essentially, a transaction between those possessors of wealth and their poorer kin. Nor did either counsel bring into view the lowly voiced ambivalences among many Luo between the prioritization of programs of collective and private expenditure in education, development, and business and the great cultural project of countryside burial.

Thirdly, Richard Kwach, counsel for the clan, and several of his witnesses, spoke throughout the case in a totally uncritical manner about "prominent Luo," as if it were an unproblematic category.[38] Indeed, in both his cross-examinations and his arguments concerning precedents for Siaya burial, Kwach constructed the category of "prominent Luo" as an essential and meaningful category.[39] In cross-examining one of John Khaminwa's witnesses, Charles Machina Ngari, Kwach attempted to demonstrate that "prominent Luo" were not buried in Langata Cemetery in Nairobi (after Ngari had pointed out to the court that a number — "90 per cent of the names appearing under 'O' are Luo" — were buried in Nairobi.)

> Kwach: Is there a name of a prominent Luo in your register?
> Ngari: We do not keep records of prominent people. Those in the register are those who are accorded a decent burial by their next of kin.[40]

A related silence concerned the history of Luo burial practices. The counsel for the brother and the clan, with witnesses, sought to construct Luo beliefs relating to death and practices of burial as ancient, perduring, and authentic. In so doing, they produced an ethnography both normative and static. John Khaminwa, the counsel for Wambui Otieno, sought to portray such Luo beliefs and practices as antiquated, out of touch with the realities of the "modern Kenya nation." Khaminwa would find no value in revealing to the court that Luo death beliefs and burial practices were flexibly changing to new circumstances. And the counsel for the brother and the clan would have also seen it within the defendants' interest to present Luo beliefs and practices as relatively unchanging, of having value and power because of their antiquity. At several points in his presentation of his case, Richard Kwach referred to the poetry of Okot p'Bitek. He quoted one part of p'Bitek's *Song of Lawino*:

The ways of your ancestors
Are good,
Their customs are solid
And not hollow
They are not thin, not easily breakable
They cannot be blown away
     By the winds
Because their roots reach down into the soil.
I do not understand
The ways of foreigners
But I do not despise their customs.
Why should you despise yours![41]

Kwach could have as easily invoked the authority of Edmund Burke on this point: "Never entirely nor at once to depart from antiquity."[42]

## Wambui as Pim

During his examination of Wambui, John Khaminwa asked, "When you were married to Mr. Otieno did you consider him as a Luo?" Wambui replied,

No. I did not consider even whether he was a leper, a poor man or whatever. All I know is that we were young people who had met and fallen in love.[43]

But in reading their final judgment on the Otieno case, Justice Nyarangi intoned,

Otieno was born and bred a Luo and as such under Luo customary law his wife on marriage became part and parcel of her husband's household as well as a member of her husband's clan.[44]

Wambui's representation of herself and of her marriage, spoken with emotion and conviction, could not have been more thoroughly opposed to the cold, judicial, and consequential representation of that identity made by the Court of Appeal. Yet Wambui's portrait of her husband and of her marriage, in which she attempted to position the S. M. Otieno household as distant from and uninvolved in the world of the Umira Kager, was itself in stark contrast to Wambui's keen intelligence on the subject of SM's patrilineage. It was Wambui, in both Khaminwa's examination and Richard Kwach's cross-examination, who provided the court with a detailed and annotated map of the social world of Jairo Ougo[45] — the father of her late husband and of her court adversary Joash Ochieng'. In and out of court, Wambui constituted herself as the widow of a man who had long ago ceased to be Luo, but in exercising her expertise on this issue she substantially constituted herself as a Luo citizen. When John Khaminwa asked, "Is it true that

SM was one of the three sons of the late Jairo Ougo and his wife Salome Anyango as stated in affidavit?" Wambui replied,

> No. My late father-in-law had five sons. ... There was Isaya Ougo, Simeon Odhiambo Ougo, Silvano Melea Otieno, Joash Ochieng' Ougo and another one who died when Mr. Otieno was still young.[46]

Luo familiarly recall *pim*, the woman who imparted history, wisdom, knowledge to the children of the *dala*.[47] *Pim* is recalled as a woman who came into the household from a social and sometimes geographical distance. Often an outsider, *pim*'s entry into the household as a widow, or new bride, offered protection, food, friendship, a renewed position in life. In some instances, she came from an "enemy lineage" and thus the designation *nyar wasigu*, daughter of the enemy. But in time, *pim* learned the lore of her new household while bringing the intelligence of the wider world to her new folk.

In preparing for the responsibility for care, nurture, and instruction of the younger children and maturing girls, the *pim* accumulated knowledge about the family, the clan lands, lineage disputes, uterine jealousies (*nyiego*), the heroic past, and fields of silence, fear, and anxiety of everyday importance to the lineage. As the respected older woman of the household, "graduated" to the station of *dayo*, *pim* assumed the role of teacher, passing on to the children broad sections of this corpus of knowledge, interlaced with folk stories and songs, as the children fell to sleep in the *siwindhe* (dormitory). Her role, her knowledge, protected her from social death, from neglect and starvation because of infirmity.[48]

Wambui's evidence in court revealed that at age 51, she, a grandmother, had in essence become a Luo *pim*. Everyone associated with the Umira Kager position reckoned that Wambui had achieved such a status, that, while as SM's widow she would not be remarried, she would be given *ndawa*, tobacco or a cigarette to graduate — in Professor Odera's words — into clan widowhood, which aligns with the old category of *pim*.

It appears not to have been the intention of any party to the case to construct Wambui as an authority — in the tradition of *pim* — on the lineage of Jairo Ougo, SM's late father, but that is exactly what the evidence of Wambui herself, and of other witnesses, amounted to. It was Wambui who revealed knowledge of a brother to Ochieng' who had died in Tanganyika in 1941, and was buried there. It was Wambui who told the court of the earlier marriage of SM's stepmother, Magdalene, and about the latter's subsequent widowhood and remarriage to Jairo in 1944. It was Wambui who brought knowledge to the court about the division of family land in Nyalgunga by the patriarch Jairo to his sons. Wambui likewise unraveled material exchanges, signals of familyhood, between SM and his brothers extending back to 1956. And it was Wambui who detailed acts of generosity between her late husband and his young nephew, the other "SM," son to SM's stepsister, Felgona Akinyi.

Wambui brought to court knowledge of the Jairo Ougo family spanning nearly half a century, though she had been married to SM for only half that period. The knowledge she presented may have challenged the foundations of her, or her counsel's, overall argument. Could S. M. Otieno have been all that distanced from the world of Nyalgunga if Wambui were repository to all this intelligence? But the revelation that Wambui had acquired over many years a unique and extensive knowledge of Nyalgunga would hardly have been useful to Kwach's side either. Wambui could not be a "rebel"—Kwach's word—and still take an interest in the detailed workings of the Jairo Ougo family. In this sense, the valediction of the Justices of the Court of Appeal rings true in a double sense. Having married a Luo, Wambui "became part and parcel of her husband's household as well as a member of her husband's clan."[49] And, in time, she became a special resource in the transmission of Umira Kager history and culture to another generation of Kenyans. She was, in this sense, *pim*, constituted through the elaboration of extraordinary expertise and experience some four to five decades after what many Luo regard nostalgically as the time in which *pim* disappeared from their world.

## "Wambui as *Pim*": The Jairo Ougo Lineage[50]

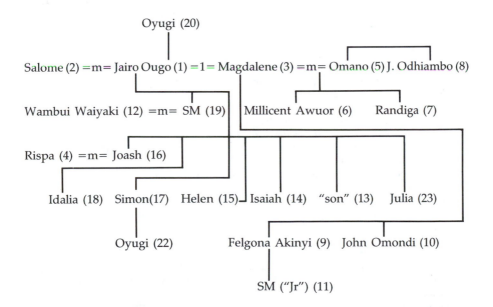

=m= married
=l= levirate relationship

*Annotations from Wambui's Testimony*

1. Jairo Ougo, church elder from 1913, teacher, owner of two plots of land, Alego Central Nyalgunga/1983/1994; husband of Salome Anyango and, by levirate, Magdalene Akumu, with six children by Salome and two by Magdalene. Wambui "washed, dressed, and buried" him. Wambui and SM visited him at Simenya in March 1965.

2. Salome Anyango, wife of Jairo, mother of SM, Joash, Idalia Awino Odongo, Simon Peter Odhiambo, Helen Akoth (Mrs. Ogutu), Julia, Isaiah Ougo, and another son who died at a young age. Salome died in 1941.

3. Magdalene Akumu, a woman from Alego Komenya, widow of Omano, levir of Jairo Ougo in 1944, mother, with Jairo, of Felgona Akinyi and John Omondi.

4. Rispa, wife of Joash Ochieng' Ougo, received personal party invitation from Wambui, referred to by Wambui as *Nyieka* "co-wife" in the letter.

5. Omano, first husband of Magdalene, father of Millicent Awuor and Randiga, deceased during World War II, leaving her a widow; he owned a plot of land, Alego Central/ Ujwang'a/1603; brother of John Odhiambo.

6. Millicent Awuor, daughter of Magdalene and Omano.

7. Randiga, son of Magdalene and Omano.

8. John Odhiambo, brother of Omano, who committed a fraud: falsifying a colonial identification card, trying to pass as son to Omano so as to inherit land plot Alego Central/Ujwang'a/1603 (trying to cheat Magdalene's children out of it). Took for himself clothes sent by SM for his father Jairo.

9. Felgona Akinyi, stepsister of SM, mother of twins, including SM ("Jr"), separated from her husband.

10. John Omondi, stepbrother of SM, watchman, and unemployed.

11. SM ("Jr"), son of Felgona Akinyi, a twin; SM granted SM ("Jr") his share of Nyamila plot 1983.

12. Wambui Waiyaki, widow of S. M. Otieno, "living as man and wife since 1961," married 17 August 1963, mother of nine children and six foster children.

13. "Son," male child of Jairo and Salome, died at a young age.

14. Isaiah Ougo, son of Salome and Jairo, had two children, died in Tanganyika in 1941, buried at Mwanza. Eldest brother of SM.

15. Helen Akoth, daughter of Salome and Jairo, married to Ogutu, lives in Siaya but keeps a house in Nairobi where her children stay.[51]

16. Joash Ochieng' Ougo, son of Salome and Jairo, litigant, received a letter from India written by SM in 1956, fought with SM at their Kisumu residence in 1963, and at other times they had disputes over money.

17. Simon Peter Odhiambo (also "Simeon"), son of Salome and Jairo, tried to induce SM to buy a commercial plot in Siaya town, died in 1985.

18. Idalia Awino Odongo, daughter of Salome and Jairo, lives with her husband at Ngei Phase II, came frequently to the Otienos up to 1985 to get vegetables from Wambui's *shamba*.

19. Silvano Melea Otieno, son of Salome and Jairo, husband of Wambui, died in 1986, corpse subject to litigation.

20. Oyugi, father of Jairo Ougo, moved into Alego from Simerro Ugenya, settled on land belonging to his uncle, Oluoch.

21. Oluoch, uncle of Oyugi.

22. George Michael Oyugi, son of Simon, died at Kenyatta National Hospital in Nairobi in 1985. Wambui and SM attended funeral.

23. Julia Akoth Aroka, daughter of Jairo and Salome, sister of SM, lives in South Nyanza near Lambwe Valley.

# 5

# *The Productions of Culture*

The struggle for SM's body brought into an organized dispute setting the entire moral ground of Luo beliefs about death and Luo funeral practices. Beyond the description of rituals and customs, witnesses for the brother and the clan were brought into court to unveil the *meanings* of death and the purposes of burial for the Luo. Under cross-examination by John Khaminwa, the chief counsel to widow Wambui, Mrs. Idalia Awino Odongo, sister of SM, put forward the view that

> [i]f Luo adults die and are buried outside Luoland, everybody in his family, including children, will be in problems. ... [E]vil spirits will follow even us who are married. The whole family will be affected. ... Even in the Bible, there is a parable of the demons which descended upon swines and they went and drowned in the river.[1]

The evidence of Johannes Mayamba was a large and important contribution to the High Court on "Luo ethnography." Mayamba, sixty-six years old, was the husband of six wives. He was part of the small, "rural nobility," *Jo Monyalo*, of Yogo village, and he was, as well, a member of the Kager Kogolla clan, chairman of a KANU sublocation, an adherent of the Church of Christ in Africa (*Johera*), and, it was whispered to one of the authors at Rang'ala market during the period when Mayamba was giving evidence, a potent *jabilo* (apothecary and manipulator of powerful medicines and magic).

It was to Johannes Mayamba that Richard Kwach turned for detail on, first, the nature of a "home" in Luo custom; and, second, the nature of Luo burial customs. In regard to *goyo ligala* (home building), Kwach opened the presentation with a question: "How does a son build a home?" Mayamba then replied:

> A son puts up a home when his father takes him where he intends to build it. He is accompanied by his father and his eldest son. The son carries a cock, dry grass and firewood. His father just carries his walking staff and the first born son carries an axe.
> Kwach: What happens when they reach there?
> Mayamba: When they reach the spot, *mzee* shows his son where to light

59

the fire. He is then asked to tie the cock near the fire and they start building the house.

Kwach: For how long does he stay in that house before he can be joined by his wife and children?

Mayamba: For three days; he sleeps in that house with his son.

Kwach: What happens after that period?

Mayamba: He must have built another house in those three days. His wife can't stay in the first one.

Bosire: For the three days, is the wife allowed to take them food?

Mayamba: Yes.

Kwach: If a man wants to build a home and his father is dead, who plays his father's role?

Mayamba: He has to look for his father's brothers.

Kwach: And what happens if a man sets up a home but dies when his parents are still alive?

Mayamba: He has to be buried in his father's compound.

Kwach: Can he be buried in his own home?

Mayamba: He can't because there is a *magenga* (funeral fire) which a father cannot warm himself by in his son's home.

Kwach: Is it possible for a man to build a home without the knowledge of his father and uncles?

Mayamba: No, he can't.

Bosire: If both parents are dead can the father's peers gather at his son's home?

Mayamba: No, they still have to go to his father's home.[2]

As one can see, Mayamba's testimony is a jointly enacted one, with Kwach's interrogation very much a part of the ethnographic exposition. Together, they produce the feel and authority of a certain and prevalent form of ethnographic text. There is an unproblematized sense of the continuity of a knit of customary activity across time and across numerous contexts. There is an implicit theory of authority, that "custom" carries with it an order, a coercive power, a predicated outcome. Significantly, Bosire's interventions and questions indicate that he himself was drawn into the language and implicit theory of this ethnographic mode.

The ethnographic production centering on the examination of Mayamba in the High Court continued into the "examination" of Luo burial practice.

Kwach: When a man dies, some ceremonies are performed, can you elaborate this to my lord?

Mayamba: If it is a woman, women wash her body and dress it, fit the body in a coffin and call her brothers-in-law to cover the coffin.

Kwach: And in the case of a man?

Mayamba: The funeral fire, *magenga*, is lit.

Kwach: How long does it burn?

Mayamba: In the case of a man, four days but in the case of women, three days.

Kwach: Is there a rite called *terro* [sic] *buru*?

Mayamba: After the burial, a cock is slaughtered for in-laws of the deceased at the funeral fire. The next morning, people come with cows for slaughtering.

Bosire: What is it intended to do, guard again evil spirits?

Mayamba: This is a custom started by our great grand-fathers.

Bosire: I'm sure he doesn't know what he is saying!

Mayamba: That is our custom. When *magenga* burns for four days, the sons of the deceased have to stay around the fire. Their wives sleep in the house of the deceased.

Kwach: Why do they have to stay separately?

Mayamba: If you sneak and sleep with your wife, your son has to die and your wife will never be proper again. That is why elders ensure the custom is adhered to.

Kwach: If a man dies away from home, how is the body admitted in the home?

Mayamba: The body is received through the *mbuga*, a space cut through the fence to admit the dead. But this has been discarded with the coming of Christianity!

Kwach: You knew the late SM Otieno?

Mayamba: Yes, he is of our clan.

Kwach: His wife told this court that he expressed his wish to be buried in Ngong.

Mayamba: That is not true. He could not have told her alone. He could even have told his brother, Joash.

Kwach: Is it possible for a man to be buried in his son's home?

Mayamba: Never. It appears Otieno had shown his son where to stay. He cannot, therefore, be buried there. It is impossible and against Luo custom.

Kwach: What is the reason behind a man not being buried at his son's home?

Mayamba: Because he will haunt the man's children demanding to know why they allowed him to be buried there. That is why you see madmen around (prolonged laughter).

Kwach: We have evidence that Otieno died without either building his own home in Nyalgunga or his son's hut.

Mayamba: Even if he had built a son's hut there, his late father's compound is there. That is where his placenta was buried.[3]

As if burial at the home of the father were not a sufficient concern of Mayamba's testimony, the witness suggested that there is even a code, a style, for burial within the framework of Luo custom. Mayamba explained to Justice Bosire:

We buried Ofafa in a tie and he has been haunting us. He screams that the tie is choking him.[4]

For the brother and the clan, proper countryside burial sustained ancient and core values of being Luo and sustained the Luo person in life and also in death. The funerals of SM's forebears were recalled as substantiation of the countryside burial tradition. In his summation, the counsel for the brother and clan, Richard Otieno Kwach argued that

it is my submission that my clients are not a group of cannibals. They want to carry out a time-honoured custom which we believe in. The witnesses called have testified about these customs. Their belief in them and what would happen if they did not carry them out. Professor Oruka has told us that if a child named after a person who has died falls sick, *manyasi* is prepared to cure him or her. This consists of some soil from the grave of the person who [*sic*] the child is named after. My lord, it would be a long distance from Siaya to Upper Matasia if there is a need to save a life in this manner. ... My lord, my learned friend asked you to strike down as repugnant some Luo customs. That would be a draconian measure and will offend the tribe. My lord, you need evidence of atrocity before you can strike them down as being repugnant to justice and morality.[5]

Witnesses and counsel for the widow sought to bring attention to the numerous burials of Luo corpses, including some of SM's own late kin, that had occurred far from countryside homes.[6] And they sought to present Luo funeral practices as archaic and outside the fold of Christian belief. In cross-examining Joash Ochieng' Ougo, Khaminwa attempted to do just this:

Khaminwa: Can you tell us how you will be cursed if you let your brother be buried in Nairobi?
Ochieng': Wherever I go, my clanspeople will spit on me and say I am *Bure* (nothing). The spirit of the dead will follow the whole family of Jairo as he was head of the family.
Khaminwa: What will happen then?
Ochieng': I will not be able to sleep properly because wherever I go, there will be ghosts haunting me for having let my brother be buried elsewhere other than at home.
Khaminwa: Is it not strange that you as a Christian believe this?
Ochieng': No. This is because it is fitting with Christianity.
Khaminwa: And you are ready to do anything to ensure that Otieno is buried at home?
Ochieng': Yes. That is why I am in court.
Khaminwa: Would you still be haunted by these spirits and ghosts if the court decides to allow Mrs. Otieno to bury her husband in Nairobi?
Ochieng': Oh yes.
Khaminwa: Can you not explain to these ghosts and spirits that it is not your fault?
Ochieng': No. This is because you cannot catch these spirits or talk to them.
(prolonged laughter from the audience.)

In his summation, John Khaminwa, for the widow, argued:

It has been emphasised to your lordship that Luos are never buried outside Luoland so that Umira Kager clan can have an opportunity to exercise these rituals to remove fears of being haunted because death can destroy them. My lord, this is not what a court of law should enforce. It is contrary to public policy and Christian beliefs. Your lordship is fully aware that whoever causes death by witchcraft must face the consequences. Witchcraft is no defence. The fact that the Umira Kager clan believes in ghosts, spirits and demons and that they fear that their son will kill them or that their wives will be unable to give birth is not sufficient to warrant this court to give them the body of S. M. Otieno for burial. It is neither here nor there. In my submission, it would be outrageous that such myths should be given a legal basis in our courts.[7]

## Mayamba and Ochieng'

Johannes Mayamba's extended testimony across several issues of concern to the Otieno case was echoed by a number of other witnesses. Many, however, revealed not only a weak grasp of the "ethnographic mode" but also only vague notions concerning the nature of "custom." Joash Ochieng', a core individual in the management and development of the case for countryside burial at Nyalgunga, remarked that "one of the rituals we will comply with is praying for four days after we bury him."[8]

A number of observers knew that Christian prayer arrived powerfully in Nyamila only around 1924, via the very patriarch, Jairo Ougo Oyugi, whose grave established the projected site for SM's Nyalgunga burial. Old Jairo built the Nyamila Church in 1924. Ochieng', within his testimony before the High Court, was clearly involved in an instant "invention of tradition."[9] Prayer at the graveside was, therefore, a development that came only after the reception of Christianity into Nyamila. Six decades of practice, and the pressure of the court situation made such prayer "customary practice" in the testimony of Ochieng'.

Still another "customary practice" he cited involved the levirate. Ochieng' argued before the court that since Wambui was past childbearing age she would not be taken by a new husband; rather, instead of marrying her, a step-brother "can give her a cigarette. . . ."[10]

Probably, Ochieng' meant to say "tobacco" but perhaps more accurately Ochieng' was reflecting the Kenya of the post-1954 era, when the British American Tobacco Company (BAT) introduced cigarettes to the African masses.[11] But there  was another meaning lying beneath the surface of Ochieng's "misstatement," in that in this decade a "cigarette" meant a "fuck" and this may have been exactly the meaning of the levirate that Wambui Otieno and her sons most wanted the court to recognize. And it was perhaps the meaning that the crowds at One Ojijo Road and at the High Court wished to see mobilized and imposed upon Wambui the widow. The murmurs from within the crowds announced many "volunteers" for the deed.

Ochieng' was equally inadept in explaining another "custom," stating in one instance that *tero buru*, originally the practice of a mock fight against a neighboring enemy clan after the burial of an adult male,[12] was, in this assertion of Ochieng', conducted "to chase away demons."[13] Ochieng' was not alone in these missteps. Kwach, in his summary, also deformed "custom," sometimes misstating his witnesses' expositions, in other instances oversimplifying a description of "custom," but throughout his case clearly working on a premise of a reified and concrete and perduring Luo "custom."

Within the litigation, an ethnography of Luo death beliefs and rituals was constituted through the statements of counsel and witnesses. Yet also, in testimony, through cross-examination, and by summary argument, Luo burial practices were deconstructed. Luo core values were problematized. Implicit and hidden meanings were exposed and challenged. Concepts of the "modern," "traditional," and "Christianity" were constituted within the examination and cross-examination of witnesses.

Expert witnesses were invited to the court by both sides to participate in this intensive scrutiny of Luo culture; and more than sixty published authorities were referred to in argument.[14] The cross-examination of experts as well as the challenging of expert texts, and the juxtaposition of expert and nonexpert testimony, raised questions for the jurists and for observers concerning the relevance and authority of "modern" academic expertise in the representation and reproduction of "traditional" cultural practice. Expertise — ethnographic, historical, and legal — was continuously invoked, yet also continuously challenged. Indeed, in their final opinion, the justices of the Court of Appeal admonished John Khaminwa, the widow's counsel, who, they said,

> confessed before us that he did not really understand the Luo customary law. Needless to say, it was his professional duty to carefully study and understand the Luo customary law and, if he thought it was in the appellant's interest, to call evidence.[15]

But anthropological expertise on Luo beliefs about death and burial was certainly not excluded from the court's view. Indeed, the layering of assertions and arguments concerning expert knowledge, such as that from anthropology, opened to view some of the complexity of cultural debate within and around the Otieno case. John Khaminwa, Wambui's counsel, used anthropological monographs in a curious way. He argued that these monographs — during the trials he referred specifically to quite a number of works including ones by Leakey, Wagner, Hobley, Ochola-Ayayo, Snell, Hollis, Peristiany, Kipkorir, Welbourn, and Massam — presented a passing way of life not chosen or shared by S. M. Otieno:

> The Luos cannot continue with customs that tend to isolate them from the rest of the country. There are a lot of books written by people — anthropologists — on burials. In respect to these books, they refer to a society of the old order and do not refer to contemporary society at all. Some of the things said in these books — we are living in a modern Kenya — and we would find them unacceptable and not in keeping with us. ... The literature by anthropologists is no longer applicable in contemporary Kenya.[16]

This is not to claim that there was an organized suppression of knowledge on the part of counsel and witnesses. It may be that they actually *were* poorly informed on earlier Luo practices and beliefs. Needless to say, the model of "unchanging African tradition" — whether accorded great value or subjected to intense criticism — holds great power in Kenya and elsewhere, even when everyday knowledge and common sense provide alternative perspectives on the past and on change.

The static and normative portrayal of "Luo custom" was jointly enacted, and this ethnography from the court excluded knowledge of substantial change in burial and belief in this century, from a baseline source of 1905, which observed that Luo corpses were buried in a sitting-up position within their houses, to a later practice of Luo being buried in a reclined position with head facing in a specific direction, to the growing use of coffins more recently and the early reaction to coffins — that "they tended to suffocate the ghosts of our people."

While substantial portions of witnesses' testimony concerning the nature of Luo burial rites read as normative and static, the trial transcripts are also thickly illustrated with detailed information on the social organization of funeral practices, the ways in which individuals, families, clans, and associations undertake the practical arrangements of transport, mourning, and burial. One recognizes how the entire ritual of Luo death and burial rests profoundly upon carefully organized and orchestrated activities — activities in, also, a conflicted field — that the cultural architecture of a funeral is not handed-down, or simply given, tradition but rather a complex social construction. One sees in the Otieno case resonances with Geertz's 1957 treatment of a Javanese funeral, in which he attempts to situate an extraordinarily conflicted burial rite between what is held to be the correct mode of burial by Javanese tradition and what is held to be possible given the specific form of the political and social field in which the funeral was worked out as rite.[17]

### The Janeko of Nyamila

Early in her testimony before the High Court, Wambui Otieno reported what she represented as her late husband's reasons for not wanting to be buried at his place of birth at Nyalgunga:

> The first reason he gave me at the beginning of 1979 on our return from unveiling his late father's cross was that he never had a home in Siaya. He never intended to build one there and he never took our children there.
>
> The children do not speak Dholuo. He [SM] told me that if I buried him there, I would be a very ungrateful woman because he had sacrificed too much for me and our children. He said that burying him there would be like throwing him there because we would never go there to tend his grave.

Wambui Otieno leaving the court with her sons Munyua Otieno (l) and Patrick Otieno (r)

The access to the grave would almost be impossible. It would pose difficulties for us to look after it. He [SM] mentioned that he [SM] was the only person who was looking after his late father's grave apart from his only brother [Joash], who is never willing to part with a penny.

He also told me that there are some Luo rituals performed after the death of a husband to which he would not like us to be subjected, such as building a hut symbolising his home, where I would have to sleep the whole night with his body and a *janeko* (lunatic) would be paid to allegedly remove demons. . . . I would also have to wear my husband's clothes inside out and my hair and that of my children would have to be shaved. After his burial, elders in his family would sit down and nominate a man to be my husband. There would also be a goat and chicken to be slaughtered, but I don't know at what stage.

My late husband did not want either me or our children to be subjected to these rituals. I don't think I can go through that.[18]

In conveying her husband's words on Luo rituals relating to the burial and to the widow, Wambui Otieno's testimony had three edges: first, she placed before the court another text with SM's voiced intentions regarding his own burial; second, she set in words a sense of her own fears in regard to what would happen if the body of SM, and she herself, went to Nyalgunga; and third, she lay before the court a representation of Luo culture at odds with "modern, Christian, Kenyan life."

In her testimony before Justice Bosire, Wambui produced an "anthropology" of the Luo that cast the people of her husband's birthplace as "the other," different from urban, civilized people. To establish her rights in her husband's body through an argument of modernity and civilization, Wambui effectively co-opted the colonial discourses on "Africans"—in the particular instance, read "Luo"—that cast them as lazy, half-witted, primitive, obdurate.[19] At the same time, keen observers of the case would note Wambui's expert command of details concerning the Jairo Ougo family extending back decades prior to her marriage with SM, an indication that these rural people were real and tangible to her, anyway.[20]

Three days later, Jairus Michael Ougo Otieno, one of Wambui's and SM's children, testified as a witness for Wambui. Then twenty-three years old and a student at William Paterson College in the United States, Jairus stated, under questioning by Richard Kwach, that he had learned about the "burial customs" of the Luo people from things he had read. And in his testimony, Jairus, like his younger brother Patrick, extended Wambui's argument one step further. The sons of Wambui and SM tried to establish before the High Court that SM himself harbored these negative views of the Luo as the "other." Jairus claimed that SM had declared himself opposed to his being buried in Nyalgunga "because he did not agree with the people and their customs"; because the traditional customs obtaining in Nyalgunga were "primitive and uncivilized," and therefore young, modern people "wouldn't understand them." The young people who cared to respect SM's memory as their father would not understand the ways of the Nyalgunga folk because they were the ways of "lazy" people who lived in "simple structures" and "would not like us," the urbane, city people.[21] In his cross-examination, Richard Kwach asked Jairus:

Are the people like you?
Jairus: No.[22]

Young Patrick Otieno, sixteen and a half, not only confirmed his elder brother's evidence, but augmented the rhetoric on the "idiocy of rural life" by claiming that his father had said that the relatives in Nyalgunga had "starved" the patriarch Jairo Ougo "to death."[23] Not content with that, these country folk now planned to impose an extreme humiliation on his mother Wambui by subjecting her to a burial in which the Otieno nuclear family would have no say.

Wambui and her sons attempted to describe Luo burial ritual as primitive, crude, and brutal. Jairus presented his understanding of Luo burial ritual.

> I read about them and how they used to be and, therefore, I have a basic idea about them. ... When a man dies, the wife and children are not involved in the burial arrangements. These are taken care of by the clan members and the elders or surviving brother of the man. When the body is taken back home, the woman has to spend a night in the same room as the dead man. A *janeko*—described in the books as a lunatic—also spends the night in the room to chase away evil spirits or demons.[24]

The *janeko* discourse is a significant one. It merits some extended discussion, not only with reference to the similarity of the accounts of Wambui and her son—one purporting to relate SM's description of the ritual, the other reporting what was said to have been garnered from books—but also in respect to the ways in which counsel for the two sides handled such presumed "traditional Luo ritual" as the *janeko* account.

In his cross-examination of Wambui Otieno, Richard Kwach, counsel for the clan, sought to demonstrate that SM's alleged comments concerning *janeko* were at odds with Wambui's own experience of Luo funeral practices:

> Kwach: Yesterday you explained to this court the Luo customs and the Luo customary law as instructed by your late husband? ... You went into great detail about what happens to a wife when her husband dies? ... Did Magdalene [Ougo][25] sleep the whole night beside the body of her late husband during his burial?
> Mrs. Otieno: No, she did not.
> Kwach: Was there any chang'aa drinker or a lunatic hired to sleep in the same hut with the body and chase away the demons?
> Mrs. Otieno: All those so-called traditional rites were not performed during my late father-in-law's burial. That is why I am questioning the rites being talked about in the affidavit. None of those things were performed in the home.
> Kwach: Did Magdalene wear her late husband's clothes inside out?
> Mrs. Otieno: No, of course not.
> Kwach: Was any of her relatives, the sons, daughters and other children shaved their heads? [*sic*]
> Mrs. Otieno: No.
> Kwach: Was there any killing of a goat or a chicken?
> Mrs. Otieno: None of those things were done.
> Kwach: Were any of those rites performed during the funeral of Simon Odhiambo (one of the brothers who died in 1985)?
> Mrs. Otieno: None at all. Not when I was there.[26]

Kwach also called Professor Henry Odera Oruka of the Department of Philosophy of the University of Nairobi to explain "the rituals and customs of the Luo community in relation to burials, building of homes . . ."[27] On the one hand, Kwach sought to demonstrate that there were Luo customs of burial to which SM was subject and, on the other, Kwach hoped, via Odera's expertise, to place Luo rituals within the realm of the comprehensible and acceptable.

In his cross-examination of Professor Odera, Khaminwa tried to uncover what he saw as conflicts and contradictions between Christian and Luo beliefs and practices. And he did so through situating Odera, and then interrogating him, as both a Christian and a Luo.[28] Khaminwa attempted to draw Odera into the *janeko* discourse but substantially failed both to induce Odera to reproduce the discussion of *janeko* such as presented by Wambui and Jairus and to produce an authoritative text on widow inheritance that would substantiate a view of "a repugnant and un-Christian practice."

> Khaminwa: What experiences does a widow go through after the death of her husband?
> Odera: Traditionally, she is taken over by another man chosen as a husband for her by the elders. If she is of child-bearing age, she can get children with the man and name the children after the deceased. Otherwise, if she is past child-bearing, a brother or a cousin of the deceased can offer her *ndawa* (cigarette or tobacco) which signifies that she has been formally but not practically married.[29]

Nevertheless, in his summing up before the High Court, Khaminwa attempted to define Luo burial practices, as related to the court by Wambui and Jairus, as antiquated and repugnant.

> The question is, Was S. M. Otieno a person who would have liked to see such rituals performed in his funeral? My answer is no. These rituals are unchristian practices. They have been condemned by Christians. They are part of traditional religion and the late Mr. Otieno did not believe in them and would not have liked to see them performed in his funeral.[30]

What is perhaps most arresting about the representation of *janeko* and the manner of description and deconstruction of Luo rituals in the practices of the two counsels is that this quite elaborate discussion centering on the dark vision of the widow enclosed at night with the husband's corpse and the *janeko* was something that was largely invented within the litigation itself. There is no written evidence associating this practice with any Luo speaking group over the last century, and no recollection of its existence in some remote, earlier period—whatever Jairus's claims to have read about them "as a scholar."[31]

With respect to the levirate—"widow inheritance"—social practice and the ethnographical literature are consistent: there are examples of levirate marriages within kin groups. But, among Luo groups and over time, the detailed picture varies.[32] It is commonly said that the practice has been that younger women of childbearing age—*ria*—were situated in conjugal relationships with the levir,[33] whereas women past childbearing would, symbolically, share a room overnight with the levir, and would be given token presents in place of sex (as Odera notes, tobacco) the following morning.

But it is also commonly known that over the last twenty or thirty years, some of the widows of Christian marriages have not been inherited in any sense and have not been subjected to any levirate ritual. What is curious in regard to Wambui's expression of fear of the *janeko* and the lawyer Khaminwa's expression of revulsion concerning Luo rituals of burial is that Richard Kwach did not challenge the myth of the *janeko* either. Nor did he go beyond his cross-examination of Wambui's testimony on Luo ritual to reassure her that she would have nothing to fear concerning her situation as a widow of a Christian marriage.

What is clear is that the discourse on Wambui's fate as a widow was handed over to the crowds outside the courtroom who, exasperated with Wambui, began to insist vocally that there was indeed a Luo custom such as Wambui and her son Jairus had themselves described, that Wambui had to be inherited in marriage by her in-laws as part of the burial of SM. Wambui created the wild man, the *janeko*, within her testimony. In the streets, the wild man was constituted as Luo custom.

## The Widow's Shroud

Wambui's testimony opened another field of discussion that moved across boundaries from ethnographic literature, local knowledge, and talk in the streets. This concerned the clothing of the widow. Luo recall that at the beginning of the twentieth century, a woman would, on the death of her husband, ceremonially discard her outer skirt, *chieno*, the very same that she would have been given at marriage and that she was expected to wear at all times in the presence of her husband.[34] During the funeral she would replace the *chieno* with a new skirt, *okola*, made of banana fiber. The new skirt defined her as a woman in mourning, and she would replace the *okola* with a new *chieno* on being inherited by her late husband's kin.

By the late 1920s, this pattern of mourning dress had been modified. Women were wearing dresses and men were wearing shirts and shorts. It became "traditional" that, upon a man's death, the widow would wear *his* shirt and shorts for the duration of the mourning up to the time of her being inherited by her late husband's kin, when the levir would present her with a dress. By the 1960s, this practice of widows wearing their late husband's clothing was spoken of as, and felt to be, repugnant — especially among Christians and younger, educated widows.

In the late 1960s, widows such as Pamela Mboya and Joanna Argwings—Kodhek were to be seen wearing black mourning dresses at their husband's funerals, while rural Christian converts would wear white dresses and scarves, at least on the day of burial. Following the funeral, the widows would ease back rather imperceptibly into their everyday clothing. By the 1980s, Wambui would fit into the latter regimen without too much fuss; indeed, she did, wearing black throughout the elongated period of mourning.

Our attention here is upon the manner of a "cultural practice." Mourning dress has been invented, internally critiqued, devalued, and reinvented.

There is another sense in which clothing conveys meaning within the context of a Luo funeral. As Khaminwa and several of his witnesses asserted, up to the

Joash Ochieng' Ougo and a cousin displaying the clothing in which SM will be buried

1950s, some Luo were buried away from their homes in western Kenya, in Kilimambogo, or at the Kisumu mortuary, to give two examples. When Stefano Atieno was buried at Kisumu mortuary in 1937—rather than at his "proper home" at Liganua—the clothes he wore to the hospital became containers of meaning, symbolic carriers. The clothes became the message of death. As the relatives would be handed over the clothes of the deceased by the hospital authorities, the bereaved found all the information they needed to know. The arrival of the clothes was the equivalent of the latter-day Voice of Kenya announcement of a death and funeral.[35]

Wambui Otieno leaving the Law Courts with daughters and friends

Wambui's abstention from her late husband's funeral at Nyalgunga was read by many in Kenya as a triumph for her in one sense: because she was away, SM could not be ritually reconstituted into the domain of death through the rituals of being mourned and buried by the widow. So there was no *magenga*, no *tero buru*. S. M. Otieno, the child of Ougo, was buried alongside his father at Nyamila in Nyalgunga, but S. M. Otieno, the husband of Wambui, rests uneasily in a state of limbo, awaiting burial in Upper Matasia.

In December 1989, the Kenya press reported that Wambui had dug her grave at Upper Matasia, and that she had done so in case there were any doubt where she was to be buried. On 20 December 1989, the *Daily Nation* reported that Joash Ochieng' Ougo was calling on Wambui Otieno to cover her grave as she would be buried beside her husband in Nyamila village, Nyalgunga, in Siaya. In March 1990, the press again reported such an exchange, this time on the occasion of Wambui showing the completed gravesite at Upper Matasia.

## Rugby and Culture: "Tero Buru"

The youngest witness to appear before Justice Bosire was Patrick Otieno, the last child of the union between Otieno and Wambui. At sixteen-and-a-half years, he in a sense represented the post-*Uhuru* children of the Kenya elite: he was bright, articulate, an achiever—he already had attained six distinctions at his matriculation examinations and was waiting to proceed to college. In the press photos of the trial he could be seen as a tall young man, "mummy's boy," according to his age-mates, his clothes clean and well pressed.

While he sought to present himself and to represent his person as, simul-taneously, an Otieno and a Kenyan, the two counsels sought to represent him still more variously. John Khaminwa, Wambui's counsel, presented young Patrick before the court as an intelligent youth who could be relied upon to recall accurately what he had heard his father SM say about society, progress, life, and death. On the other hand, Richard Kwach, for the clan, sought to disparage Patrick precisely because of his youth. Kwach went further to argue that Patrick was ill brought up and impolite to the people of his father's ancestry on whom he had cast aspersions in his evidence. Both counsels were involved in a definition of where Patrick belonged: to Khaminwa, he belonged to a modern, progressive family, and stood as a model of the Kenyan of the future; to Kwach, Patrick belonged to a spoiled generation of brats, and his appearance before the court alongside his brother Jairus provided Kwach with a pretext for labeling Khaminwa's witnesses as inexpert, juvenile, and unworthy of a serious court of law.[36]

Outside the courtroom, in classrooms, at sites as diverse as Kenya High School in Nairobi and Kakamega High School in western Kenya, Patrick's age-mates followed closely the unfolding Otieno saga, and the role of their peer within the struggle. The boys and girls of Kenya argued endlessly about the case. The case became a favored topic for interschool debating clubs. And they took sides for or against Wambui, for or against the clan, and for or against Jairus and young Patrick. Many felt empathy and comradeship with Patrick. Many had themselves been orphaned, or knew of friends who had been orphaned through the catastrophe of road accidents, and so many young Kenyans then and now know parents and uncles who died suddenly and whose affairs fell into disarray. The S. M. Otieno story became their story. At Kenya High, those girls who favored a rural burial for SM came to acquire the nickname "Nyalgunga."

The youth knew the Otieno story as it came to them through television, radio, newspapers, teachers, parents, bus and *matatu* conversations, market talk, and gossip among house servants, but they also produced their own knowledge of the case. They surveilled adult (read "male") talk at their homes as they brought beer or tea to their fathers' guests; they eavesdropped on women's talk about the Otienos in the kitchens and backyards, and constructed, daily, meanings into this affair, about which, ostensibly, they had nothing to offer, being merely "children" in the eyes of the grownups, yet fully aware of the way in which this very issue of their own social worth had become, with Patrick's testimony, an issue before the court.

School playgrounds offered the youth of Kenya much-needed *space*—both physical and intellectual space—to rework their own meanings into the Otieno story. They hung onto the claim of their age-mate Patrick that he was "of the Kenya tribe" and did not come from "home-squared" or *gicagi*-squared, meaning "real, real home" in the countryside. They shared talk about country people, whom they refer to as *miro*—"country bumpkins." They joked about the material culture of the rural people: the notion of drinking water from *agwata* (calabashes), the *ugali* and *ngwaci* (sweet potatoes) that rural people ate, the *simsim* delicacies that they hated but were always treated to by their doting grannies from the countryside. They drew contrasts with the glasses, the motorcars, and the *sukuma wiki* (collard greens) that were signal articles in the material culture of urban people.

The school stage became another venue for this youthful reworking of the Otieno saga. Since 1987, schools like Agoro Sare in South Nyanza, Murray Girls' at the Coast, and Kericho Secondary School in the Rift Valley have presented dances entitled *Tero Buru* at the annual national Drama Festivals in Nairobi. These dances, a mix of every sort of recognized ethnic choreography, have been produced by the students themselves, a tribute to young Patrick's claim that there is indeed a Kenyan "tribe" out there to which he belongs.

Young people at the Impala Rugby Club—a facility on Ngong Road, Nairobi, frequented by the sons of the elite from Nairobi, Saint Mary's and Lenana Schools, with their sweethearts from Loreto Msongari and Kenya High—have composed their own song in *Sheng*, their new urban language, which draws elements from Dholuo, Gikuyu, English, Kiswahili, and Lingala. Entitled *Tero Buru*, the song, which was composed by this young set at the time of the litigation, is still sung and danced to—and still improvised into new textual form—before and after every match of rugby, that most English of Kenyan, and Kenyan of English, games. *Tero Buru*, the ever-evolving song, alerts one to the fact that the production of culture and history is not the monopoly of an adult world—no matter what Richard Kwach, and Professor Odera, with his sages, considered to be the canon. In this regard, the "S. M. Otieno saga," as the Kenyan press came to call it, is a largely unfinished story, still to be interpreted, reconceived, and told again in new voices in the future to the children and grandchildren of Patrick Otieno's age-group, *riika*.

*Tero Buru*[37]

soloist:      Mos, mos, mos Mama Milka
                    Slowly, slowly, slowly Mama Milka
reply:      Milka!
                    Milka!
s:      Milka Bonyo[38]
                    Milka Locusts
r:      Bonyo!
                    Locusts!
s:      Bonyo, Simsim
                    Locusts, simsim[39]
r:      Simsim!
                    Simsim!
s:      Simsim, waru
                    Simsim, English potatoes
r:      Waru!
                    Potatoes
s:      Waru chips
                    Potato chips

r:       Chips!
                    Chips!

s:       River Nyando[40] is not navigable.

r:       Tero buru! Tero buru!

s:       Hotel Sunset is very comfortable.[41]

r:       Tero buru! Tero buru!

s:       You ask for chicken, they give you the whole kitchen.[42]

r:       Tero buru! Tero buru!

s:       Gor Mahia is very powerfulu![43]

r:       Tero buru! Tero buru!

s:       Peter Dawo[44] is very wonderfulu!

r:       Tero buru! Tero buru!


s:       Agwata motuch ok nyal ting'o nyuka.
                    A perforated calabash cannot carry porridge.

r:       Tero buru! Aiiee, tero buru!

s:       Nyako molil ok nyal bedo chiega.
                    A dirty woman cannot be my wife.

r:       Tero buru! Aiiee, tero buru!

s:       Basin molil ok nyal luoko nyathi.
                    A dirty basin is unsuitable for a bathing infant.

r:       Tero buru! Aiiee, tero buru!

s:       Okapu moyiech ok nyal tingo mbuta.
                    A torn basket cannot contain Nile perch.

r:       Tero buru! Aiiee, tero buru!

s:       Glass motur ok nyal tingo toivo.[45]
                    A broken glass cannot contain the brew.

r:       Tero buru! Aiiee, tero buru!

Encore:     Mos, mos, mos.
                    Slowly, slowly, slowly.

# 6

# *The Constitution of an African State*

The court was but slightly exposed to the deep contests and struggles located within the Luo political community of Kenya and to the play of this case as an effort to restore unity to the Luo house. Oginga Odinga, the Luo and Kenya leader of the left, whose writings on the core values of Kenya Luo culture were clearly a centerpiece in the production of a case for countryside burial, was notably absent from the proceedings in court, and, as indicated earlier, Odinga was excluded from a range of public functions in which support for the brother and the clan were being encouraged.[1] Odinga was heard to have voiced in a number of settings that it was only since the 1940s that all this attention to burial in the countryside began. ... that before 1940 people were buried pretty much where they died. ... that somehow the present Luo interest in funerals is related to the accumulation of wealth in the cities ...[2] and that it is only with the legal capacity and financial enthusiasm of Luo for the purchase of property that the issue of where to bury a corpse would arise. At the funeral of Dr. Zachariah Nyamodi at Nyadhi, Siaya, in February 1987, Odinga was reported to have deplored the campaign for a Nyalgunga burial for SM, arguing that over a long period the Luo Union (East Africa), *Ker*, of which he was a founder and President, had encouraged Luo to move, settle, and buy property in distant towns and cities throughout East Africa.[3]

That the leader of the great chronicle of Luo movements in the twentieth century and supreme authority on Luo political values was to be separated from this movement introduced a range of contradictions into the political agenda of the Umira Kager clan. The fate of Odinga's voice leads one to consider how the battle for Otieno's body broke across old, well-established boundaries of solidarity and established a significant new ground for the constitution and invocation of broader political and social thought concerning both local and national culture and both given and produced history.[4]

The case and the debates around it have been seen by some as a next phase in the elaboration of an idea of a strong Luo nation within the Kenya nation, advancing its interests into every sector of life while defending itself against the oppressions and inequalities of a larger society. That the contest for SM's body was also a context between a Luo clan and a "Kikuyu lady" was somehow confirmation to many observers, and particularly to the foreign press, that once again ethnic or tribal conflict had lifted its ugly head in Africa. But the case, with Luo witnesses on both sides, and its subtleties, which the foreign press failed to capture, has the potential of revealing much about the various "republics of free discourse" within the "Luo nation."

There were great silences concerning wealth and privilege among Luo families, of the leveling, yet also impoverishing, functions of vast expenditures on funerals, and regarding the source and purposes of extraordinary pressures upon successful Luo in Kenya "to build a *dala*" [residence] in the countryside. ... These great silences themselves actually illuminate the differences in condition, status, opportunity, and interest among Luo in Kenya, whether in the city or the countryside. Was the Umira Kager clan's case for SM's body defined by these differences, as various parties struggled for interpretative power among several possible positions? Or did the source and power of the clan's case lie in the recurrent experiences of ethnic consolidation in which various and conflicting "republics of free discourse" find themselves challenged or suppressed? A first clue may lie in looking at a parallel and simultaneous "event," the struggle for the return to western Kenya of an ailing python.

### Omieri the Snake

During the campaign for Nyalgunga burial, the people of Nyakach in western Kenya organized a parallel campaign to bring their loved python Omieri from Nairobi where she had been taken for treatment for burns after her nesting place had been set on fire by persons unknown. According to one Nyakach resident, Zachariah Odera,[5]

> Omieri was part of the village life, roaming in the neighborhood where children would stroke her with their hands and no harm came their way. ... She was a good snake. She would visit the village and then go back to the lake. And then there would be rain, a good harvest and plenty of food.[6]

Residents of Nyakach appealed to the National Museums of Kenya authorities in Nairobi to return Omieri, both for the sake of its own recovery and for their own good fortune. The rhetoric of the Omieri campaign drew upon, and in turn fed and enriched, the campaign of the Umira Kager for the return of SM's remains. The campaign for Omieri was successful and she was transferred "home" for treatment at the Kisumu Museum.

On 23 May 1987, Mr. Ndolo Ayah, the sitting Member of Parliament for Kisumu Town (and from 1990, Minister for Foreign Affairs), in addressing the massive gathering at SM's funeral, drew the connection between Omieri and SM most explicitly, pointing out that for the last few months, the attention of the entire Luo community has revolved around three things: the Otieno court wrangle, Omieri, the python which was taken away from Nyakach in Kisumu District to the chagrin of the local people who believe that the serpent brings them good fortune, and the performance of Gor Mahia Football Club in a continental tournament. . . . [T]wo of these have been achieved for Omieri is back in Kisumu and Otieno has been buried in Nyamila and now it is Gor Mahia which the community is turning attention to in its prayers.[7]

But by August 1989, Omieri was dead, being treated with formyl for preservation and readied for stuffing and display, to be "preserved" in a

sealed blue container with a black top in a locked room. In cold dignity, her head points toward the lake which had been her home.[8]

In commenting upon Omieri (whose passing made the front page of the *Kenya Times*, the official newspaper of President Moi's ruling party, KANU), Zachariah Odera, among others, took the view that her period of exile in Nairobi may have been ultimately responsible for the illnesses that finally took her life. The *Kenya Times* reporter, Gray Phombeah, reporting from Kolal village in Nyakach, noted that in her exile Omieri

had been estranged from her legendary husband. For three months she missed her ancestral drinking water from River Asawo and the Odoro stream. . . . And it was a long time since she had last taken her traditional swim in the river.[9]

Soon after her death, the *Weekly Review* of Hilary Ng'weno, a physics major at Harvard with a Master's degree in mass communications from Columbia, as well as other Kenya papers, reported that there was great mourning among the Luo of Nairobi for Omieri, particularly among the Nyakach people residing in the capital city.

The Nyakach people in Nairobi were organizing burial arrangements for the python and raising money for the funeral, besides opening a condolences book at Kaloleni social hall. Museum officials . . . have also opened a book of condolences of their own at the Kisumu Museum.[10]

The *Standard* reported in February 1989, that

Mr. Oluoch Omollo [an official of the Kodul Welfare Society Committee] said in a statement the people of Nyakach had learnt with sorrow the untimely death of their "colleague." "Nyakach people are in mourning following the death of Omieri. We send her husband, Nyakach, condolence messages during this time," said Mr. Omollo. He said a fund had been launched and had raised over Sh.400 for the burial expenses.[11]

The lines of battle were now, once again, drawn—this time, between Nyakach burial by "the clan" and stuffing and display in the Kisumu Museum.

The struggles for Omieri, as a living and ill snake and in death, constituted a piece of a complex and ancient process of organization of collectivity and identity.[12] The world—encompassing the materials of the state, the Kenya Republic, with the realm of local and national football prowess, and the grassy and riverain habitat of a Nyakach python—was constantly addressed, redefined, and appropriated in the programs of collective political organization and cultural production connected with the Omieri case.

## Member Number 18

As with the campaign for Omieri, it is quite clear that "Luo ethnicity" was centrally involved in the struggle for SM's body and for Nyalgunga burial; it is not so clear how such "ethnicity" worked as a means of collective organization. One approach might be to see the problem of SM's body as, initially, a problem for the Umira Kager clan, of which SM was member number 18, and then only secondarily as a problem for the entire Luo speech community, of which the Umira Kager clan was but one corporate entity among many that served Luo constituencies in Nairobi and Mombasa.

There was more to this than one clan or lineage among many: the Umira Kager clan, in its experience over the past two hundred years, has most clearly exemplified a subhegemonic process in western Kenya of continuous expansion into and increasing control over once Bantu-speaking areas along the Luo–Luyia speech boundary.[13] Umira Kager carried a heightened sense (as against other Luo congeries) of ethnic solidarity and considerable experience in operationalizing it, and this was extended to the neighborhoods of Nairobi as large numbers of Luo speakers traveled and settled in Kenya's capital.

In the growing tension between the voiced positions of Umira Kager and those of Oginga Odinga, one may see another paradox, an asymmetry in which the informed historical sensibility brings Odinga to an inflexible position at odds with his own historical and political community while the experience of extraordinary change, coupled with an ahistorical discourse, promotes a different yet equally inflexible interpretation of history and culture on the part of Umira Kager, but one that still drives the formation of a new political constituency, far broader than the clan. One view is that in this shift the Luo supporters of a Nyalgunga burial were for the first time "liberated" from Odinga, with his working-class ethos and rural radical agenda. They thereby became more acceptable to the core of power in Kenya constituted in the office of the President, in the person of Daniel Arap Moi, and in the interests and resources of a male, polygamous, and patriarchal African national bourgeoisie.

Court discourse, as exemplified by the Otieno case, suggests that there is an "economy of the law" which will, in its logic, bring forth into the court's deliberations the most "telling" witnesses and experts, the fullest body of evidence, and the most expert argumentation. It is through the *practice of interest* — separate, collective, and conflictual — that the deliberations should produce a comprehensive exposition and examination of information.

Yet the close reading of the record of the Otieno case, when set alongside an understanding of the broader setting of knowledge, "telling," and argument in Kenya in 1986 and 1987, suggests that there are two "economies of the law" operating within and around the case. The first economy concerns the logic of what is brought into the court through the introduction of evidence, through witnesses, through cross-examination, and through summing up. The second "economy of the law" defines the reach of the case into the realms of knowledge and expertise in Kenya and the reach of expertise into the production of the litigation. If the case were in part about the nature of Luo culture, Luo "tradition," and Luo society in the past and the present, the litigants and their counsels were extraordinarily selective in the witnesses and experts they brought to the court.

The landscape of learning on Luo culture and society teems with scholars in the humanities and social sciences[14] who were accessible to the contestants, who could have been called upon to testify, but were not. Kenyan scholars have, over the past four decades, addressed many of the questions that came before the court: the place of "custom" or "tradition" in Kenyan life; the semantics of everyday Luo speech, related to such basic concepts as that of "house" and "home"; the rites associated with the construction of a Luo homestead; the ideal constructs of Luo marriage; Luo ideas concerning God, life, apothecary, healing, death, and the hereafter; the changing legal regimes in colonial and postcolonial Kenya.

So an observer of the Otieno case might well ask why John Khaminwa did not call on scholars of religion to testify as to the significance of Wambui Otieno's commitment to Christianity, and to open the discussion of the meanings and values of Christian ideas and practices concerning the treatment of the dead; or legal experts to discuss the legal and professional issues surrounding the intestate death of a learned advocate; or feminists to argue Wambui's rights as an emancipated woman. Equally, one might well ask why Richard Kwach did not call upon some of the statesmen of Kenyan and Luo academe—such as Professor S. H. Ominde and Professor B. A. Ogot, to draw from them testimony on the evolution of Luo cultural practice—or on ethnobotanists such as Professor John Ong'ayo Kokwaro to reaffirm the efficacy of *manyasi*, the herbal cure invoked by several of Kwach's witnesses.

In excluding such experts, and in separating their legal work from the research on Kenya's cultures that was then being conducted with high visibility by the Institute of African Studies of the University of Nairobi, both lawyers established a deliberate breach between existing and accessible academic expertise in Kenya and the program of organizing evidence and argument within the litigation.[15]

It is revealing to examine how this breach was constituted in the practice of the lawyers, and to look at the underlying logic of some of the decisions made by the counsels that had the effect of constraining the expertise brought before the court. In his arguments before the court, Khaminwa displayed and cited a number of tangential and obsolete ethnographic and anthropological texts. He did not bring before the court recent work in anthropology and cultural studies, nor their authors. Rather, it is clear, Khaminwa's goal was to demonstrate that, within "modern Kenya," custom, as contained in the older ethnographic and anthropological literature, was obsolete. Khaminwa would have found the more recent anthropological literature, which almost *de rigueur* problematizes the distinction between "traditional" and "modern," a difficult ground from which to mount his argument that SM was a modern man who would not countenance burial by Luo custom.

## The Education of Lawyers

S. M. Otieno went to Nairobi in 1950 after completing his school education at Maseno in western Kenya. Born on 20 February 1931 at Nyamila in Nyalgunga sublocation, he carried with him to the town not only the experience of a rural upbringing in what is today Siaya, but also a molding through missionary education. His first schooling was at Simenya Primary School and then he went on to the CMS Maseno Secondary School, also in western Kenya, where he was enrolled from 1943 to 1950, when he obtained the Cambridge School Certificate. His education included mandatory studies in English language and literature, which would, in Nairobi, "certify" Otieno as "educated." Which was not to say "civilized" or "modern," for these terms, by contrast, described a status of exemption from "customary law" under legislation passed in 1938, which made it possible, theoretically, for "detribalized natives" to be freed from *kipande*, the pass system, and the native poll tax. No Luo person had so far qualified and Otieno, in entering Nairobi, was to be recognized as a "Kavirondo native" at one level, as an "educated man" at another.

Otieno's immediate supervisor in Nairobi, in the job he got at the Law Courts, was Tiras Waiyaki (Wambui's father), grandson of Waiyaki wa Hinga, a Kiambu Gikuyu frontier warlord in the last century. Many of Waiyaki wa Hinga's descendants sustained their elevated status throughout the twentieth century. When Otieno met Tiras,[16] the latter had sons studying law and medicine in India. Indeed, Oginga Odinga, who appears at many points within the account of the S. M. Otieno case, but never in the court itself, had befriended Apa Pant, the Indian High Commissioner to Kenya, and the 1950s saw a number of Kenyans traveling to India for legal and medical education via scholarships arranged by Odinga.[17] SM studied at Bombay from 1953 to 1959. He did a Bachelor of Laws at the University of Bombay, and then moved to Elphinstone College in Bombay where he was called to the bar.

Otieno returned from India in 1961. He had a law degree, but it was only from India, not Britain, and the European legal community would not accept Otieno as a real "gentleman."[18] The culture that Otieno had returned with from India was a British legal formation, but twice removed. Cut off socially from the British jurists, Otieno fell in with Asian and African lawyers who would meet in Asian pubs in the evenings, quite in defiance of the laws and practices of segregation still in vogue. These lawyers, educated in India, were thrilled to hear one another quote Shakespeare and to discuss "war stories" from the universities and cities of India. Some "historians" at One Ojijo Road held that it was at one of these "joints," the Princess Hotel on Victoria (now Tom Mboya) Street, where S. M. Otieno is said to have met Virginia Wambui, who was then — it was asserted — working at the Hotel;[19] while others say that they met in Mugo Waiyaki's law chambers. And while some hold that they met in Nairobi in the early 1950s, others declare that they did not meet until SM returned from India.[20]

The poet Aloo Ojuka referred to Richard Otieno Kwach, lawyer for the clan, advocate of "Luo tradition," proponent of Siaya burial, as "the most Shakespearean of them all." There was something ironic about Richard Otieno Kwach emerging in the Kenya of 1987 as the "champion of tradition." Like S. M. Otieno and E. S. Atieno Odhiambo, Richard Otieno Kwach, who was born on 10 October 1940 at Simenya in South Ugenya, attended Simenya Primary School in present Siaya. Richard Otieno went on to Maseno, and then to Alliance High School where Carey Francis, who had taught his father at Maseno, was principal, and then on to the Law School at University College, Dar es Salaam. From 1967 to 1969, he worked in the attorney general's chambers in Nairobi, but in 1969 left Kenya for the United States where he studied communications and management at the

Universities of Pittsburgh and Michigan. He returned to work as a Legal Counsel for the East African Community in Arusha, Tanzania, until 1972, when he retreated to Kenya and formed a law firm, Masime, Kwach and Co., in Nairobi. In 1975, Kwach joined Hamilton, Harrison and Mathews, and then in 1986 formed Ndung'u, Njoroge and Kwach Co. Advocates.[21]

Until he achieved celebrity for his role as the counsel for the clan in the S. M. Otieno litigation, Richard Otieno Kwach was best known for his wide-ranging reading habits, not only of Shakespeare but also biography, for his suburban Nairobi existence complete with a son named Carey Francis Kwach, among five children (all boys), six Chihuahuas, and for the fact of a penchant for intellectual discourse at the Hilton Hotel sauna and the Nairobi Club.

Kwach, like his adversary John Khaminwa (counsel for Wambui), and unlike S. M. Otieno, had built an elaborate rural homestead, his *dala*, in Siaya. Ironically, on Friday afternoons, Khaminwa, who would rise to defend the modern family in

John Khaminwa at Haverford College

Kenya and denounce the effect of "tradition," and Richard Kwach, the lawyer of the clan who would nurture a representation of valued tradition before the court, would both leave Nairobi and drive upcountry to their respective patrimonies in western Kenya. SM would remain in the vicinity of Nairobi, according to Wambui.

For those of Kenya who observed Kwach, he was a lawyer in Nairobi for part of the week and a Luo in his *dala* in Siaya on weekends.[22] Eight years earlier, he had built his own "home" in Siaya: to get away from being called "*'wuod' Ugenya*" (son of Ugenya) and graduate to being called "*'ja' Ugenya*" (man of Ugenya).[23]

And where Wambui, her counsel, and witnesses argued that S. M. Otieno's interest in and knowledge of Shakespeare were attributes of a "modern individual" free of the reign of "tradition," Richard Otieno Kwach, "the most Shakespearean of them all," the learned jurist and exponent of the value and power of "tradition," traveled back to his *dala* on the weekends.

Within his practice of the case, it was for once difficult to distinguish between Kwach the lawyer and Kwach the Luo. For the supporters of the clan, these identities were no longer distinct but wholly collapsed. In a biting exchange with Wambui in the High Court, Kwach made this point himself:

> Kwach: And you said he used to read
> Shakespeare, did you say Julius Caesar? What
> else did he read?
> Mrs. Otieno: I said Bernard Shaw, a bit of
> Perry Mason . . .
> Kwach: And you said he watched football on
> television because of the violence at the
> City Stadium.
> Mrs. Otieno: Yes.
> Kwach: And you said because of all these
> activities he had severed his relationship and contacts with his tribe?
> Mrs. Otieno: You are too much of a Luo.
> Kwach: I too read Shakespeare but I am still a Luo.
> Mrs. Otieno: I said you are too much of a Luo.[24]

In public discourse at the time of the trial, Kwach was held to the highest standard of a "Luo warrior," and praise-songs that celebrated his courage, genius, and devotion to Luo culture were composed and recorded and broadly distributed across Kenya.[25]

John Khaminwa followed a somewhat parallel track to Kwach's, from a rural birth in western Kenya to a distinguished private law practice in Nairobi. Born an Isukha of the Luyia people in 1936 at Khayega in Kakamega, Khaminwa was educated at Musingu Primary School; like Kwach after and SM before him, he proceeded to Maseno Secondary School, and then he went to the Alliance High School. He did advanced study at Makerere College and holds a law degree from London University and a Master's in International Law from New York University. He opened a private practice in 1973, eventually forming Khaminwa and Khaminwa Advocates with his wife Joyce, also a lawyer.

By the time he was engaged to represent Wambui Otieno, Khaminwa had already established a name for himself as an attorney who would work on controversial and sensitive cases. In 1981, his firm represented Mary Nduta in a dispute between, on the one side, the brothers of Mr. John G. Mburu, an American university graduate and former Provincial Commisioner, and, on the other, Mburu's wives Agnes Ngami and Mary Nduta, along with his "concubine," Helen Omoka, who disputed the site of his burial.[26] Khaminwa was thrown into detention for a year, from June 1981, following his taking on the case of Mr. Stephen Muriithi, a former deputy director of intelligence in the police force, who had been forcibly retired from the civil service and posted to head a parastatal organization.[27]

As we extend our surveillance from Ong'ang'o and Odera Oruka to the lawyers Kwach and Khaminwa, we begin to see a web of experience, formation, and social practice — not congruent or identical, but certainly continuous — extending across the courts and law offices of Nairobi. One is alerted to what is perhaps an underlying sociology of power in which the litigation was, from one perspective, deeply immersed. The practices of the courts, and virtually all the participants in the litigation, constructed a wall between the work of the court and the lattice of power in the Kenya of the 1980s. The silencing of various authorities, which both protected them from the turbulences of the conflict for SM's remains and removed broad areas of knowledge and subtleties from the litigation, was part of this construction.

The interrelationships, alliances, and common histories of various parties to the case, and of experts and authorities outside it, were excluded from the court, yet were essentially involved with it at every turn. Many Kenyans attempted to stand apart from — or as some have remarked "above" — the fray, yet observers of and participants in the S. M. Otieno case attributed various motives and strategies to the figures "on the sidelines." For one, President Daniel Arap Moi made no direct remarks in public until after the case; but he was universally considered as having a specific outcome as an objective, and, moreover, the interest and the power to effect such a result. Given prevailing interpretations of the Kenyan regime's search for control in every arena,[28] it was widely held that the office of the President confirmed or forced the High Court's or Court of Appeal's rulings in favor of the clan.[29]

Experienced legal scholars spoke quietly about the many and significant jurisprudential errors of the justices hearing the case in the two courts; some attributed them not to the flaws of justice, or to a specific economy of the law, but to the discreet and channeled control of court decisions by political figures associated with the President's office. In private conversations, observers of the Kenyan Leviathan held, and continue to hold, views that the Kenyan state encouraged the conflict as a means of dividing Luo and Kikuyu opposition to growing presidential authority in Kenya. These offstage conversations are themselves difficult to unravel and critique, but they *do* show the way in which there were no boundaries in Kenya precluding connection with the case, that it had the capacity to "enravel" all and sundry.

Where it is difficult to document the ways in which the president of Kenya became "involved" in the litigation, it is clearer how others who stayed far outside it were at the same time thoroughly involved within it. At various points, observers cite Oginga Odinga, the essential Luo man — *JaLuo asili* — the one who never comes into court but whose words and presence invade the litigation and the broader conflict surrounding SM's corpse. The comradeship between Oginga

Odinga, the architect of a politicized Luo consciousness, and Wambui, who openly denounced Luo cultural practice, lay outside the litigation but underlay it in important respects, for it had much to do with the historic political alliance and the 1960s radicalism of Odinga and Munyua Waiyaki, Wambui's brother.

Lastly, the old lawyer networks of S. M. Otieno, connecting the dead body in the morgue to the living bodies of both counsels and to the jurists of the High Court and the Court of Appeal, were suppressed within the litigation. At a more intimate level, most of the legal experts — counsel and judges — shared experiences of interethnic marriage in their own lives, experience that was "withheld" from the litigation. One could say that the legal authorities were, in an important sense, presiding over the burial of one of their own.[30]

## The Unexpected "Man from England"

Curiously, William Shakespeare may play quite an important role in the unveiling of the underlying sociology of power at work in and around the case, beyond the fact that the bard might have scripted the struggle for SM's body . . . and beyond the observation that Shakespeare was extensively cited throughout the case. For Kenyans like SM, Kwach, Khaminwa, and the judges, Shakespeare constituted an extraordinarily important part of their intellectual formation. The recitation and citation of Shakespeare in bars, clubs, and meetings in Kenya, and at home, connotes achievement, status, separation from the masses, and it does so without the complex implications, dire risks, and responsibilities entailed in quoting from the literature on political economy, political science, and sociology. Shakespeare is more powerful anthropology for lawyers like Khaminwa. And Shakespeare becomes a "national literature" in Kenya, shared easily across the boundaries of ethnic differentiation. Shakespeare is for the professional elite of Kenya the absolute converse of Kaloleni, the throbbing, tumultuous, perpetually reinventing core of the Luo population of Nairobi.

It is important to note that the recitation and citation of Shakespeare among the legal professionals of Kenya is itself a subject of everyday storytelling, discussion, and social criticism in Kenya. During a mission to London with President Daniel Arap Moi in 1979, Minister of Water Resources Stanley Oloitiptip and Shariff Nassir, MP for Mombasa — so it is told — were taken on an excursion to the National Portrait Gallery. As they stood before a portrait of Shakespeare, the guide told Minister Oloitiptip that Shakespeare was England's greatest bard. "I see," said Oloitiptip. "Has he been to Kenya?" "No," said the guide. "Then he must come to Kenya," pronounced Nassir. Upon which Isaac Omolo Okero, SM's classmate at Maseno Secondary School and at the University of Bombay in India, who was at the time of the London visit Minister for Works, was heard to say:

> Wish not a man from England . . . I would not lose so great an honour as one man more methinks would share from me . . . O, do not wish one more! (Henry V to Westmoreland, *Henry V*, IV, iii)

Okero, replaying onto Oloitiptip and Nassir Henry V's exasperation as well as the notion of bringing another Englishman, Will, to Kenya, was heard to hiss beyond the hearing of his fellow parliamentarians, "Fools!"[31]

Shakespeare is pertinent here in part because some of Wambui's witnesses, her counsel, and Wambui herself saw SM's control of Shakespeare and his frequent use of Shakespeare in his everyday speech as sufficient proof of his being a "modern man," outside the range of control of the Umira Kager clan. But Shakespeare is of additional significance because the texts of Shakespeare have established themselves as an encoded discourse on status and power in Kenya which flows easily and effectively into and out of the court. It is privileged, uncensored. For SM, and for others among the professional elite of Kenya, the reverence for the classics — and Shakespeare — is to be understood not only in terms of their search for another intellectual mode distant from that of their homelands, and not simply as a mode that can be national and international, but also because Shakespeare and other classics have, as the immediate written products of an oral culture, resonance with an oral world of which they still are part and to which they are still substantially subject.

This in itself should not be seen as unusual. Scholars of early modern Europe affirm that even after the Gutenberg Revolution, in the era of Luther, the *oral* word was regarded as *primary*; the printed word, in the Lutheran pamphlets, was of course rendered back to orality for the consumption of the broad masses, while it is widely accepted that most written texts in early Europe were read not silently but aloud as another variant of orality.[32] As one inspects the world of lawyers such as SM, Khaminwa, and Kwach, one recognizes a host of difficulties in distinguishing oral and literate worlds, and in defining the one as the alternative to the other.[33]

S. M. Otieno, Isaac Omolo Okero, and others would have carried a knowledge of, and perhaps an interest in, Shakespeare from their Kenya schooldays to India, where Shakespeare was fully alive (and a formal higher education requirement) in the universities and in the theater.[34] We recognize here the edges of what might be seen as the development in the 1950s of a transnational professional class, exemplified by SM, Okero, and Indian friends both in Africa and on the subcontinent, with Shakespeare as a thread in the formation of this class, an embalmed remnant of which was fought over in Nairobi for 155 days.[35] One sees within the arguments concerning SM's person and his intentions, and more generally in Kenya, a notion of a "natural love of Shakespeare." In a recent paper, Jyotsna Singh has tried to unveil and deconstruct historically, within an Indian context, such a "natural love," stressing the politics of its construction.[36] She has argued that the legacy of the treasures of English literature in the former colonies testifies "to the far-reaching effects of the early colonial efforts in naturalizing their subject's allegiance both to Shakespeare and to the empire."[37]

There is an obvious paradox here in the assertion that a facility with such texts and knowledge as that of Shakespeare establishes one as a "modern man." The stuff of Shakespeare referents is ancient, arcane, and the medium is the spoken word in a judicial setting in which the written text establishes authority. Moreover, the deployment of Shakespeare — as in Okero's *Henry V* above — is effected along the boundaries of institutions and associations that are themselves taken as the fixtures of modernity.

There is additional paradox in Wambui's reference to SM's love and use of Shakespeare, for the play of Shakespearean wit among Kenya's professionals was, as much as anything else and quite specifically, a field of play for *men*,[38] and it was in the last analysis the web of associations of men — counsels, jurists, statesmen — that constrained and silenced Wambui's voice.[39]

## The Admonishment of Lawyers

As noted earlier, in their rendering of judgment, the judges of the Court of Appeal admonished John Khaminwa for his poor knowledge of customary law and practice of the peoples of Kenya. Curiously, two days after the judges of the Court of Appeal of Kenya issued the final ruling on the fate of S. M. Otieno's body, with its castigation of Mr. Khaminwa, Mr. Robert Stevens, then President of Haverford College in Pennsylvania, presented a degree of Doctor of Laws, *honoris causa*, to (in the words of Mr. Stephen G. Cary who presented Mr. Khaminwa for the degree)

> John Mugalasinga Khaminwa. . . . Distinguished lawyer, spokesman for human rights, articulate scholar educated on three continents, you have come far indeed from your modest Quaker roots in rural Kenya. In your achievements, you do honor to your parents and your teachers, who gave you knowledge, and through their example, illumined the values that now guide your life.

The honorary degree was awarded without reference to Mr. Khaminwa's role as Wambui Otieno's counsel, but was intended to bring attention to Khaminwa's courage during seventeen months of detention without trial in Kenya and to human-rights concerns in Kenya more generally.[40] On 19 March 1988, President Moi of Kenya raised the subject of the Haverford degree with a visiting group of senior Luo academics from the University of Nairobi:

> I cannot understand some people. Instead of rewarding someone like Mr. Kwach who has defended our culture, I hear that they have now honored the other person.[41]

The president shortly thereafter rewarded Richard Kwach by appointing him to the Court of Appeal. These few events stretching from the courts of Kenya to an American collegiate ceremony to the president's Kabarak patrimony suggest the complexity of the field of relations between lawyers and the state in Kenya. Lawyers, the legal profession, and the judiciary in Kenya since Uhuru were fundamental to the elaboration of both patriarchy and oligarchy in the country. The range of authority of the state was extended through lawyerly practice and discourse, as more and more Kenyans sought legal assistance and legal authority to support their progress through Kenyan society. Simultaneously, the very form and character of the authority of the state were refined and elaborated through the mediation of command and consent in ways both less visible and more powerful than with the program of the republic's parliament. It has been a truly Machiavellian terrain.

It is perhaps the very centrality of legal practice and lawyerly society in the elaboration of the Kenya state that produced an equivalent centrality of lawyers in the denunciations of the excesses of authority that have plagued Kenya from 1985 to the present. It may also be argued that Kenyan lawyers had, since 1985, constituted the nexus of the most important relations between the Kenyan state and governmental, commercial, and capital interests organized outside the country. It is notable that the *Nairobi Law Monthly* became from 1988 through 1990 one of the most popular periodicals in Kenya and the most important review of politics even as it performed the traditional role of such journals: the provision of authoritative law reports and jurisprudential analysis. It is not so surprising then that the government of Kenya banned the *Nairobi Law Review*, which it did in September 1990, enlarging the troubles faced by its editor Gitobu Imanyara.[42]

In early July 1990, the Kenya government again arrested John Khaminwa and placed him in detention as part of an attempt to intimidate lawyers in the course of their professional activities, to suppress the discussion of human rights, and to constrain the discussion of political pluralism in Kenya. After a frantic period for his family, friends known and unknown, with a concerted international effort on behalf of Khaminwa and other new detainees, Khaminwa came out of incarceration making strong representations against detention. He told a church gathering of "the harsh conditions in detention," saying his confinement had strengthened his belief in God.[43]

# 7

# *Owino Misiani's Lamentation, 1987*

**Side 1: *Otieno Waiko Nyalgunga***
**We must bury Otieno at Nyalgunga**

Jossy Owino Maka Willy Ka Jona
Okew gi Orongo Magunga
Wenda biro kelo ajema
> Jossy, I Owino, son of Willy and Jona
> Nephew of Orongo, the Harbinger
> My song may precipitate a crisis.
Piny ka apimo
Jos maka Willy ka Nyang'uny
Achom kure gi wuoyi?
Rateng' omin Ochieng' nindo
> As I contemplate the world,
> I Jos the son of Willy and Nyang'uny
> Where shall I head to with our son?
> The Black One, Ochieng's brother, lies dead.
Penj ma apenjo
Achom kure Jowadwa
Achom Ngong' ka Simba
Koso adhi Alego Nyalgunga?
> The pertinent question I ask is:
> Where shall I head to, my people?
> Shall it be to Ngong, the home of the lions
> Or will it be to Alego Nyalgunga?
Yawa ma winjo
Uyie to udwokwa ka mama
Dipo ka uwito kido e thim

Mondwa biro goyo nduru
>My agnates within hearing
>Please answer, my siblings, answer us back.
>You might dispose of our Culture in the wilderness
>And our women will wail against us.

Kisumo gi Siaya, gi South Nyanza, Jowadwa
Gini wawuoyoe e piny ngima
Jopiny da uwinjo wachwa.
>Kisumu and Siaya and South Nyanza, my people
>We are discussing this issue worldwide
>Countrymen,
>You should heed our discourse.

Ung'uonnwa
Ukel Otieno kuom ringi
Tabu ma uketo obedoego
Weuru sando chunye
>Excuse us!
>Bring Otieno home quickly
>The tribulations you are subjecting him to ...
>Torment not his spirit.

Un ka uparo
Tom maka Ounga, Ja Chula
Omin Akoth lowo otero
Janam ne wayiko e dala
>If you recall:
>>Tom [Mboya], son of the Lake Breeze, Man from the Island
>>When he died, brother of Akoth
>>We buried the Son of the Lake *dala*.

Kendo ka uparo
Agwingi omin Luka bende oweyowa
Chango watimo e ng'we yamo
Rateng' ne watero e dala
>And when you recall:
>>Argwings [Kodhek], the brother of Luka,
>>Also left us
>>We collected money like a whirlwind
>>And took the Black One *dala*.

To ma en mane?
Usando Otieno Jowadwa
Utame donjo Kar Mungu
We uru sando Wuoyi
>So why is this one different?
>You are persecuting Otieno, my people
>Obstructing his entry into God's abode
>Do not persecute Our Son.

Oyangi gi Makenzi bende ji odwokwa
Gin bende ging'eyo gigo pep
Weuru Otieno nindo

Oyangi and Mackenzie should also support us
They also know the whole truth
Leave Otieno to rest in peace.
Siranga
Ukony Ochieng' Jowadwa
Pole watimo e piny ngima
Mosuru Kwach gi nyasi
Siranga!
Help Ochieng' out, my people
The whole world sends condolences
Let us salute Kwach ceremoniously!
Wuoyi ka wakowo
Walamne Mungu mondo orwake
Mang'eny ma ulawo kuome go
Podi ubiro chando chunye.
As we escort our illustrious son
Let us pray to God to receive him
The extras you are still pursuing
Will only torment his soul the more.

## Side 2: Nyasaye Konywa e Thoni.
## God, tide us over this death

(Refrain)
Yawa
Wanayuag ang'owa e pinyni
Pinyni mar Jehova
Ong'eyo chalne te.
My people
Why must we wail, in this life?
This world belongs to Jehovah
He knows all its configurations.
Preacher's Text:
Kata da awuoyo gi dhok mag ji Kata Jomalaika, to waonge hera, wabedo ka mula
moywak, kata ka olang' ma igoyo (*Jokorintho Mokwongo* Sula 13, kare 1).
Though I speak with the tongues of men and of angels, but have not
charity, I am become as sounding brass, or a tinkling cymbal (*I Corinthians*, 13:1).
Rap: [A parade of leading Luo and where they are buried]
Dickson Oruko Makasembo wawito e Nyanza ka
Argwings Kodhek Ja Oremo, CMG
Thomas Joseph Mboya, Ja Rusinga
Dr. Robert Ang'awa, Ja Oremo
Owiso Magenge, Ugenya Masiro
Edward Onyach Halwenge, Ugenya
Owiti Ongili, Ja Oremo
Punde si Punde
Bende uparo Otieno Ambala, en kanye?

Charles Bengo Obinju, Kano
Samuel Aguko, wuon Omoro, Kano
William Barasa, Masiro
Joshua Abuya, Shirati
Kod Fanuel Aguko.
> Dickson Oruko Makasembo, We lost him, Nyanza
> Argwings Kodhek, man from Gem, C. M. G.
> Thomas Joseph Mboya, Rusinga man
> Dr. Robert Ang'awa, Gem man
> [Habil] Owiso Magenge, Ugenya Masiro
> Edward Onyach Halwenge, Ugenya
> Owiti Ongili, Gem man
> As the world turns:
> Do you recall Otieno Ambala? Where is he?
> Charles Bengo Obinju, Kano
> Samuel Aguko, son of Omoro, Kano
> William Barasa, Masiro
> Joshua Abuya, Shirati
> and Fanuel Aguko.

(Refrain)
Yawa
Wanayuag ang'owa e pinyni
Pinyni mar Jehova
Ong'eyo chalne te.
> My people
> Why must we wail, in this life?
> This world belongs to Jehovah
> He knows all its configurations.

Mr. Gumbe, Mayor, Karuchuonyo
Paul Mbuya, Rachuonyo
Otieno Oyoo, Kisumu.
> Mr. Gumbe, Mayor, Karachuonyo
> Paul Mbuya, Karachuonyo
> Otieno Oyoo, Kisumu.

To ok mago kende
Miyo pinyni en mar Jehovah
En ma ong'eyo gikone.
> And not just these alone!
> This world belongs to Jehovah
> He alone knows its *eschaton*.

# CONCLUSION

The Otieno debate is a brief but perhaps a most significant moment in the construction of a Kenya nation; but it is equally a powerful motor in that construction. The apparently simple act of reconstituting the person through argument out of the body at the Nairobi City Mortuary established a broad struggle for control of the interpretation of every conceivable detail of his life. The meanings of his body and his life were magnified in contest. The two sides agreed to the facts of where SM was born and where SM died, but all the rest was open to interpretation as to the meanings surrounding what he ate and where, why he slept in a car for four days, what his gestures conveyed, what his stories meant. Food bought from the kiosk exploded into discussions of the values of different sorts of food in Luo culture and in Kenyan national life and into considerations of the distinctions between values and behaviors posited as "Luo" and those posited as "Kenyan." Labels of identity were placed on the most basic of acts, whether this was "Kenyan," or that "modern," or this "traditional" and that "Luo." And these labels were also challenged and undermined. If one would bring methods of deconstruction to the close reading of the text of the case, one should also recognize that practices of deconstruction were extensively deployed within the case by the cast of litigants, witnesses, counsel, and jurists themselves.

The Otieno case is also a powerful conjuncture in the constitution and reconstitution of the Luo nation in that nation's varied arenas, from Nyalgunga to Langata; at its various levels of heightened consciousness regarding its internal authenticity, its rhetorical affirmation of identity through the resonating of custom and the valorization of culture; its own penchant for doing things the Luo way, "NyaLuoly"; its recurrent revamping of its own heroic tradition through the "media" of football and land litigations; its sustenance of diverse "republics of free discourse" within the Luo nation and broader Kenyan society; its redefinition of the meaningful geography of Kenyan life; its constant problematization of the role of the Kenyan state in diverse arenas of everyday life; its tendentious formulation of its locus and relevance to the Kenya state; and its persistent assertion of claims to citizenship in the modern world.

At another level, the Otieno case brings to the fore the eternal questions of personhood and agency, but does so in a fresh, new way. A key to the power of the body of S. M. Otieno in this struggle for the remains was that he, S. M.

Otieno, was both party to, and absent from, the litigation. A whole life was created in the court proceedings. Meanings and emotions could be attached to the body in death, and associated with it, retrospectively, in life. His interests and intentions could be located, cited, and relayed through the attributions, inferences, and declarations appropriated to his corpse—"the orations of the dead." SM's life, with its multiple voices and intentions, could be thickly and conflictually inscribed in death in ways that it could not in life.

Equally significant, the Otieno case brought into sharp relief questions of gender—and the entire notion of being *male*, of being a man. The court transcripts uniquely illustrate the fact that men, African men, appeared to organize their world—and were expected to organize that world—*publicly*: through orating Shakespearean learning at Bomas, a site of African cultural revitalization; through talking about mortgages, high blood pressure, and death across barbwire fences; through walking guests across their lands; through preparing their cars for the weekend trips to their "Nyalgungas"; through covering the club fees for their golfing wives; through helping a nephew or a friend at a difficult moment; through holding to rules of sexual abstinence at rural funerals; through adjuring on one's final resting place; and through voicing contemplations on the nature of one's own funeral.

Whether in the realm of daily living, or within the solemn confines of the courtroom, the male world of S. M. Otieno was constituted in such a manner that there appear to have been no constraints upon men: they pranced rhetorically across a broad field of issues, they authored judgments on culture and history, they asserted legal authority, they read the ultimate verdict on Otieno's final repose.[1] Men's voices were raised to represent society, Kenyan society. Whereas there were efforts to produce women's voices and authorize the witness of women—Virginia Wambui Otieno, Mama Koko, Idalia Awino—the justices of both the High Court and the Court of Appeal found "truths" in male voices that they did not find in women's. The histories of women—Wambui Otieno and Mama Koko—were scrutinized and subjected to critiques not experienced by male witnesses. One is alerted to some of the ways that discourse, be it feminist or other, appears at one moment to be free and at another to be subject to power and authority. One essential condition of this working of power is that male consensus in the Otieno setting appears to have been constructed and sustained in unconscious and in wholly unself-conscious ways. One may ask if male power and male power over women is constituted in the very inchoate architecture of the gender-category of men. Indeed, the very form, and not simply the judicial conclusion, of the struggle for SM's body continues to constrain feminist empowerment in the aftermath of the Otieno litigation.

The S. M. Otieno case also awakens other lines of critical observation on the ways in which feminist discourse has proceeded in anthropology, cultural studies, history, and sociology. Caroline Walker Bynum, Valie Export, Emily Martin, and Mary Poovey have produced important studies[2] of the ways in which the development of institutions and practices of surveillance of and intervention in the bodies of women constitute a central piece of the cultural, historical, ideological, and political subjection of women, studies revealing, moreover, that—at the very same site of the body—women have constructed practices of resistance. Yet here, amidst the struggles of Wambui and the Umira Kager, it is the male body that is on the table, opened, scrutinized, violated, and it is through this theater of attention that develops around SM's corpse, and around the living bodies of other men party to the conflict—Ong'ang'o, Kwach, Khaminwa, Odera Oruka Bosire—that the subjection of the silenced, opaque body of Wambui Otieno is finally achieved.

The immense public notice of the case throughout Kenya provides another challenge in the comprehension of the dissonance between the courts of Kenya, with their self-confirming authority, and the meaning and reception of the conflict by Kenyans at large. The work of Carlo Ginzburg on the formulations and reformulations produced and articulated by the miller Menocchio[3] invites a close examination of the ground lying between a formal and self-presented legal system and all its apparatus on the one side and its popularly received and reformulated constitution as constructed in public discourse on the other.

Simultaneously, two arenas—One Ojijo Road and the tumult (*mahu*) on the pavement in front of the High Court as a continuous evolving arena of discourse, and the mostly solemn proceedings within the High Court—competed for primacy in the evolution of the struggle. Quickly, the contest extended beyond the fundamental appeal to formal jurisprudence for rights to SM's corpse. The proceedings of the High Court were constructed to insulate the essential legal contest from the broader sociology of struggle—but with only partial success. The crowds at One Ojijo Road, those at the gates of the High Court, and the inner circle of

Joash Ochieng' Ougo, Omolo Siranga, and others celebrating the Court of Appeal decision at One Ojijo Road

Umira Kager leadership sought to relate these broader interests and concerns to what they saw, or predicted, as the interest of the court. And, in so doing, they — as audience and as agent — reformulated the court proceedings in important ways.

The worth of the ordinary person, *raia*, represented outside the courts by the Nairobi crowd and inside it by key witnesses such as Mama Koko and Albert Ong'ang'o, served to bridge the gap between the remote authority of the court system and the intelligence and logic of local discourses. At once, the case reminded the mighty of their humble origins as sons of *raia* — even as Richard Kwach sought to mount an exclusive and exalted category of "prominent Luo" and John Khaminwa invoked the existence of a category of "prominent Kenyans" — and reminded the same mighty of their dependence on *raia* for their daily comforts in their residences and for their rich knowledge of the wider society beyond SM's suburban fences and Timan Njugi's downtown offices.

It is also important to find tools with which to pry open such a case, or event, as we come to understand that such struggles for culture and history are present and significant in the recent past of many new nations. They are in fact struggles to constitute control over others by claiming authority over the power to inscribe the record of the past, the transcript of the person, and the description of culture. Here, in a tumultuous battle, the state — through the practices of lawyers and through the operations and decisions of the judiciary and perhaps also through backstage intervention — draws itself and its hegemonies into the intimate spaces and moments in which brother and brother, husband and wife, father and children, organize their material interests and their moral and emotional lives.[4]

Not least, the Otieno case provides many points of access to the production of history, which project has provided the logic of our own entry into the SM story as observers and authors. We began as observers on the sidelines, intrigued by the multivocality of the narrative as well as by the immediacy and power of the various formulations of knowledge it produced. We were taken by the ways in which the struggle for SM's corpse over some several months seemed to condense into dramaturgical form a complex, coauthored work of historical anthropology — *Siaya* — which had developed through a number of projects of research and writing into a complete manuscript on the eve of SM's death. We have grown interested in, and have attempted to find ways of being alert to, critical junctures, fissures, and contradictions located in the interstices of popular and expert representations of culture and history. While this project has clearly gone well beyond its beginnings — and only a certain form of arrogance would allow us to believe that our "sidelines" remain positioned as they were when we began this project in early 1987 (while the case was still in court) — we have in important respects not gone far at all into the project of achieving a comprehension of the modes of production of history and culture that mark, define, give meaning to this struggle for a corpse. We remain committed to the development of productive questions as opposed to the anticipation of final answers and closures. To these we now turn.

First, the contest for control of the program of inscribing SM's life, in death, connected to older struggles for control of the interpretation of culture and to older struggles for authority over the inscription of the past. The authority of expertise was reworked as the testimony of a gravedigger was presented alongside that of a university professor. Who commands the ground upon which culture is interpreted and past inscribed? And by what means? This is seen most generally as a historical question, for this ground was organized over time through a series of contests over historical interpretation and inscription. But it can, through a detailed reading of the text of the Otieno litigation, be examined still more closely in terms of how specific witnesses—by themselves and through the programs of respective counsel—established power over words and thereby came to constitute authorities on Luo culture. Gabrielle Spiegel has taken this further, suggesting that S. M. Otieno's body is a

> metaphor for history, understood as both the unfolding of event and a rhetorical structure of explanation ... [one can] see in the narrative of this struggle a marvelous allegory of the past, a once material existence now silenced, extant only as a sign and as sign drawing to itself, in figurations patterned by pressures originating outside its own intentions, chains of conflicting ideologies which hover over its absent presence and compete for possession of the relics, seeking to invest traces of significance upon the bodies of the dead.[5]

Second, the dead body of SM in its unburied state for 155 days exposed the collapsing generalizations and contradictions in argument from ethnography and history. The very questions of "what the Luo do" or "what is customary" or "what is tradition" were unveiled, through the case, as extensively contested matters. What are the implications of an open, public—as opposed to academic— problematization of such fundamental constructs? Further, one sees the persistence of "tribalist" explanations of this struggle—as well as of concurrent and recent conflicts in Canada, India, Liberia, Rwanda, Sri Lanka—as an epiphenomenon of not so much the appearances of tumult of One Ojijo Road as the seemingly ceaseless search for the "primitive" in Western thought.[6] What is the fate of worlds in which complex interests and discourses, which themselves problematize and subvert stereotypes are, ultimately, reduced in the texts of historians and journalists to the barren formulae of tribes and tribalism?

Third, one is interested in the underlying sociology of power in which the litigation was, from one perspective, deeply immersed. The practices of the courts, and virtually all the participants in the litigation, constructed a wall between the work of the court and the lattice of power in the Kenya of the 1980s. The comradeship between Odinga and Wambui, so critical to an understanding of the Umira Kager clan's program of mobilization of support, lay outside the litigation but underlay it in important respects. The old lawyer networks of SM, connecting the dead body in the morgue to the living bodies of both counsels and the jurists of the High Court and the Court of Appeal, were suppressed within the litigation. Can one move beyond the observation that the legal author- ities were, in an important sense, presiding over the burial of one of their own to a more inchoate speculation that they were at the same time presiding, unknow- ingly, over the interment of the rule of law and an independent judiciary in Kenya?

Fourth, one is reminded of the fact that the Otieno case was in part about erudition, rhetoric, and representation by laymen and by professionals—about a world at once real and imagined, a world of actions, but also of intentions, a world at once vast in opportunity and constrained in marginality, a world of power and control but also one of unpredictability and death. This tumult of tensions between the secure and the uncontrollable gives the Otieno case such moment and empowers both the rhetorics of participation and the paths of interpretation—along but one of which the present work proceeds. And, we may ask, where are the sites of the critical interpretive practices: within the discussions of the two authors of this work and the operations that they have brought to bear on the issues, separately or in combination ... or within the discussions that developed at One Ojijo Road, at Nyamila, in front of the Law Court, in the law offices of Kwach and Khaminwa? The record of the case constantly works to shift our attention from One Ojijo Road and Khaminwa's chambers to the world that SM inhabited, to subject our practices of reading and interpretation to the "more authoritative" practices within the courts where evidence is scrutinized and witnesses deposed. Is not this the way that power works? Is not this shifting of authority—to read, to interpret, to claim to know truth—from ourselves to those recognized by the state exactly what we mean when we speak of lawyerly practice and lawyers extending in important ways the postcolonial state in Kenya?

Fifth, one is led to ask if, and possibly *why*, such powerful debates as that surrounding the disposition of SM's remains are particularly characteristic of relatively young nations. Perhaps these debates may be seen as moments of popular assertion in which self-presented state hegemony is seen to be thinly veneered and in which space for competing arenas of self-regulating activity can be identified and enlarged, whether they be the search for a woman's rights on the part of Wambui, the widow, or the search for authority by the leadership of the Umira Kager clan.

We must remind ourselves that the Umira Kager's quest for control of SM's corpse is another piece—or a phase, or a moment—of processes of formulation and articulation of interest. It is a process that cannot be understood by reference to explanations of clanism or tribalism, as if there were some deep and immutable structure that gives form, direction, and unity to its political, economic, and cultural exercises. We see within the Umira Kager, not such a deep structure, but rather, specific acts and expressions of interest mediated through meetings, nego-tiations, decision making, contracts, bank accounts, and context-specific rhetorical improvisations. Where the state—Kenya—and the nations—Luo and Kenyan—were porous entities, the Umira Kager emerged as the repository and motor of its own history, of its progress in Africa, but also as the repository of its "neighbors"—other Kenyans, the courts, the legal profession, the *raia*. The case may call our attention to the asymmetries among entities we tag as "clans" and the homologies among entities that are hardly ever viewed under the same light.

And we should also remind ourselves that this grand, conflicted discourse on tradition, culture, philosophy, gender, and law is not simply and only a product of a postmodern context in which all things are thrown up for fresh evaluation and redefinition. Indeed, we have sought to focus not only upon the expansive and creative production of culture and history in the courts of Kenya but also upon the constraints, rigidities, and economies that have informed the construction of these historical and cultural texts.

We must also see the poetics of it all: at 5:00 p.m. on 20 December 1986, as he toured his nephews about his Ngong estate, Silvano Melea Otieno was the epitome of the "developed" African, with his property, his investments, his legal

Mourning SM at Nyalgunga

expertise, his learning, his Christmas plans. SM was, at that moment, proof positive that the ideas of development—the theorized, programmed, funded, and induced transitions from "traditional society to modernity"—held cogency as well as promise. Within seven hours, as Wambui uneasily received SM's relatives from One Ojijo Road, all the contradictions of "development," "traditionalism," and "modernity" were fully revealed. We may ask what lessons are to be derived from the observation that all parties to the struggle for SM's body had mastered and also substantially unveiled the problematics of these constructions? Are we to complete our reading of the case with a view that the several parties were, suddenly, instantly, "postmodern"? Or are we to see this struggle as a very broad and deep inspection of the very means of knowledge by which lawyers, Luo, Kenyans, women, academics, states, ethnicities, come to be comprehended (if not also controlled)?

When read well, such contests provide extraordinary opportunities to observe what Sally Falk Moore has called "change-in-the-making." The contest for Otieno's body is a many-layered experience, from which understandings of the articulation and play of various positions and interests in contemporary Kenya can be wrung. But the challenge here goes beyond producing a text on Kenya from a complex, many-layered, legal conflict full of little texts. The essential challenge is in seeing this struggle for the body of Silvano Melea Otieno as itself constitutive, and not, as Geertz and others might read it, simply reflective or diagnostic of culture and history. In her introduction to *Social Facts and Fabrications: "Customary" Law on Kilimanjaro, 1880–1980*, Moore relates that

> small-scale legal "events" in the rural neighborhoods of Kilimanjaro today bear the imprint of the complex, large-scale transformations.[7]

In regard to the contest for Otieno's body, we might turn that around to consider the ways in which large-scale transformations bear the imprint of complex small-scale events, to see how the living nation, with its specific and notable silences, is constructed out of the dead body, with its particular and powerful orations. *Thu Tinda!*

> —nothing happens, only a blink
> of the sun, nothing, barely a motion,
> there is no redemption, time can never
> turn back, the dead are forever
> fixed in death and cannot die
> another death, they are untouchable,
> frozen in a gesture, and from their solitude
> from their death, they watch us,
> helpless without ever watching,
> their death is now a statue of their life,
> an eternal being eternally nothing,
> a ghostly king rules over your heartbeat
> and your final expression, a hard mask
> is formed over your changing face;
> the monument that we are to a life,
> unlived and alien, barely ours,
>
> —when was life ever truly ours?
> when are we ever what we are?
> we are ill-reputed, nothing more
> than vertigo and emptiness, a frown in the mirror,
> horror and vomit, life is never
> truly ours, it always belongs to the others. . . .
>
> —Octavio Paz, "Sunstone" (1957)

# *AFTERPIECE*

What the case was *really* about!
How the story *should be told*!

As the authors presented pieces of the developing book manuscript at conferences and seminars, readers and discussants—both those familiar with recent
events in Kenya and those with informative experience and interests elsewhere—
seemed inclined to mount arguments, interpretations, and re-presentations around
two particular issues: what the case was *really* about and how the story *should be
told*! Out of a recognition that the present account of the case is but one of a
number of "productions of history," and that commentaries, interpretations, and
histories of the case and its surrounding contexts will continue to be spoken and
inscribed, the authors invited several readers to offer brief commentaries on
either or both of the above two points to be published together as an "afterpiece"
to the book.

## Corinne A. Kratz[1] (Anthropology, Smithsonian Institution)

The questions: What was the case *really* about? How should the story be told?
How do these questions shape our commentaries? Was the Otieno case *really*
about any single topic or concern? Wasn't it a set of interconnected stories
involving multiple concerns, often conflicting but sometimes overlapping? This
book shows how a number of these stories unfolded and intersected, how many
diverse issues were simultaneously debated, silenced, and reformulated over the
course of the cases. "Its" telling, like any telling, is about selection, inclusion, and
omission, as well as about burying SM. Our commentaries are a welcome and
opening gesture, but they do not erase the closures intrinsic to any text. Which
stories were included, how are they constructed, and where do the stories stop?
  Assertions about the *real* subject of the case are political and rhetorical
arguments of emphasis, of relative importance, and of effects experienced or

imagined from a particular perspective. They depend on who is naming the *real* subject and in what context. How do they deploy their closures and silences? Such assertions also illustrate the difficulties of narrative simultaneities. If you present legal questions raised by the case, issues of gender pop up; discuss ethnicity and questions of modernity, and tradition emerge.

To lay out the many stories, topics, and agendas contained in the Otieno case—how the case was about so many things—is the critical first step in academic analysis (not without its own rhetorics, claims to authority, and interests). It raises the question of other stories not yet mentioned (and I will tell yet another one below). Perhaps more importantly, it lays the groundwork for other questions, for close analyses of some parts of the case. Some analyses might combine Okoth-Okombo's linguistic techniques[2] for discussing notions of kinship and home with the emphasis on the political implications of intersecting vocabularies and stories that is shared by Joan Scott and bell hooks. Scott shows how the nineteenth-century story of class was articulated through images of gender difference,[3] while hooks shows the way racial discourse relies on a vocabulary of gender.[4]

There are further questions to ask of the Otieno case: how did different stories not only intersect but absorb and incarnate each other? How did testimonies consume and respond to each other? How is the story of ethnicity told with the vocabulary of modernity? How does a rhetoric of gender articulate understandings of personhood and death? Are silences linked? Could the silencing of Virginia Wambui's personal history and political involvements be related to the gagged (but present) story of class divisions within the Luo community? Wambui's social and political capital was not nil, as Cohen and Odhiambo claim here[5], but it *was* publicly disarmed. Her class and social standing informed and empowered her public battle, even if it was rendered mute and legally irrelevant.

Simultaneous stories combine the questions of what the case was really about and how the story should be told. There is another such combining question to raise about the case of Virginia Edith Wambui Otieno *v.* Joash Ochieng' Ougo and Omolo Siranga, one that produces a story of ambiguity in the very definition of parties to the legal contest. What was the legal standing of the Umira Kager clan in the case?

The clan's adversarial role was accepted and assumed by virtually everyone:

Wambui (files for a restraining order against the Umira Kager clan);
the lawyers (Kwach: "my clients are not a *group* of cannibals"; Khaminwa: "The fact that Umira Kager clan believes in ghosts . . . .");
the newspaper accounts (reporting the case as a struggle between the "Kikuyu lady" and the clans);
the public (phrasing things as the newspapers did in their constant discussions of the case, and in clan meetings and demonstrations);
and the authors of this book (references *passim* to the dispute between Wambui and the clan, to Kwach as the clan's counsel).[6]

It seems clear that Siranga represented the clan as Joash's codefendant, and that he participated actively in the dispute as elected head of the burial committee formed by members of the Umira Kager Welfare Association and Ger Union. Perhaps the decision to file suit jointly broadened and strengthened the brother's case, cloaking both in the shadow of the clan to evoke the jurisdiction of customary law. Nonetheless, officially the contest was between individuals; legally, the clan was not party to the case.

This official reading emerges in Justice Shields's initial decisions and in Justice Bosire's questions during testimony in the full High Court trial. Interpreting the case as a contest of individuals, Shields ruled for the wife rather than for the brother, in accordance with common law.[7] Seeking to clarify the vagueness of "collective clan decisions," Bosire called this notion "idle. . . . A line must be drawn somewhere to show who are involved in making the crucial decisions." Shields did not question the role of the clan in a legal case between individuals; the interpretation of Joash and Omolo's involvement in the case (as individuals or as clan representatives) was part of the debate over the jurisdiction of common law, customary law, and Kenyan statutory law.

Joash and Omolo's joint position as codefendants was critical to the way the case proceeded. Consider the alternatives:

(1) Joash files alone, leaving the case far more open to common-law interpretation as a contest of individuals.

(2) The Umira Kager Welfare Association and Ger Union contests Wambui's claim alone or with Joash. As a registered society, the Association's involvement evokes statutory law. The initial question would be whether an association under statutory law has any right to claim a contested body; recourse to customary law would be difficult.

(3) The Umira Kager clan files alone or with Joash. Does a clan have legal status as a juristic person to assume such a role?

(4) Joash files jointly with another individual who is clearly involved as a clan member. This draws the clan shadow over their official involvement as individuals and raises the question of legal jurisdiction: customary, common, or statutory?

Questions could thus be raised about the juristic personhood(s) of the clan. What is the relation between the Umira Kager Welfare Association and Ger Union and the Umira Kager clan? James Clifford describes a legal case in which the Mashpee Wampanoag Tribal Council, Inc. sued for possession of a large tract of land. The Mashpee Wampanoag Tribal Council, Inc. is "the business arm of the tribe." Incorporation created personhood, but "no self-respecting tribe would become incorporated."[8] Would a self-respecting clan incorporate?

The angle of the sociolegal story came into focus for me retrospectively, in conjunction with another dead Luo whose tragic death, rather than burial, has been and is the object of investigation and dispute: former Minister for Foreign Affairs, Dr. Robert Ouko. Shortly after a judicial commission of inquiry into Ouko's death opened in October 1990, the question of the *locus standi* of Ouko's Ominde clan was raised.[9] Were they entitled to their own legal representation? After "lengthy explanations" but little debate, the commission found Oki Ooko Ombaka's argument that the clan should be represented under the Inquiries Act as a "person whose conduct is the subject of inquiry under this Act, or who is in any way implicated or concerned in any matter" to be sound. The clan's own debate was over who should represent them. Could not their interests be served simultaneously by the counsel representing the Ouko family?

The case is quite different, but it raises pertinent questions. Why was a shadow representation for the clan, one that merged clan interests with those of its individual members, unacceptable to the Ominde clan? Why were individual and clan legally separated in this new case (note that customary law had little relevance), and could they have been in the Otieno case? Could Joash Ochieng' Ougo and the Umira Kager clan have been joined as codefendants in the Otieno case, or could the case simply have pitted Wambui Otieno against the Umira Kager clan? Has the Otieno decision given the clan a stronger, more assertive legal position? Has the clan now become a juristic person by precedent rather than by legislation or registration? Repercussions from the Otieno case certainly echo in the way the Ouko inquiry is unfolding. The Ouko inquiry also has implications for our retrospective understanding of the Otieno case.

## Peter Amuka (Folklore, Moi University)

Perhaps the greatest strength of this book lies in its tacit admission and argument that the S. M. Otieno trial, while invoking contested oral and written authorities on burial, was in fact an opportune moment to create appropriate and alternative texts to determine the location of Otieno's burial. A related and vital strength is also to be found in the implied statement that this creative process was open-ended and not foreclosed by the final judicial opinion. Ultimately, only the most powerful text triumphed not on the basis of any intrinsic quality, but because legal convention had established, over the years, that in a power game like this one there had to be a loser and a winner. There might have been other powers behind legality, but then the court's voice was the synthesizer and such powers are only made visible by the book's attempts to highlight the role of the extralegal forces.

As a reader, I find myself in a dilemma: neither the texts excluded from, nor those used in, the judicial ruling help me decide the best way Otieno ought to have been buried. In a way, the book has many texts, many possibilities. Thus, apart from the Nyalgunga burial and what led to it, the references to theater interest me because drama normally seeks and finds convincing resolutions. A reader is necessarily outside the law courts and may witness, imagine, or create other texts—other dramas—to fit his context. This book is about what the elders did and decided in the courts; drama is (was) about what the youth contributed outside.

It was the youth of Kenya who resolved the deadlock regarding how and where the corpse should be interred. The answer was theatrically conveyed, but the press said little or nothing about it. After all, the mass media—like other institutions that the young will grow into—belong to the elders. Thus the SM court drama dominated major newspapers and overshadowed other and related dramas that did not coincide with it. These dramas were enacted by the youth in schools all over the country.

The S. M. Otieno saga may be viewed as a signifier of the failure of Kenyan elders to bequeath to the youth a cultural direction for the 1990s. Elders, the young are often reminded, carry illuminating wisdom and knowledge. Yet for 155 days, those same elders strained helplessly to determine Otieno's burial site. That Otieno himself reportedly knew of his failing health in good time and yet passed away without writing a will implies one thing: he died with an abiding faith in his peers' mastery of established and clear cultural procedures for the disposal of a corpse. Only the youth knew the way out; a recapitulation of relevant events will clarify how and why.

Popular demonstrations in Nairobi, public statements by politicians, legal proceedings in the law courts, and theatrical performances by secondary-school youth brought into being a state of tension between culture and power. In certain cases, the two collaborated to achieve particular objectives. A good example is the judicial decision to bury Otieno's body in Nyalgunga—the rural countryside. One may argue that in this case a culture reflecting "rural idiocy" won. To this extent, the "enlightened" urbanites lost. But one need not overlook the irony of the whole situation, because the majority of those who fought so hard to bury Otieno in his birthplace were literally lifelong urbanites; after the burial they returned to the cities without fulfilling most of the funeral rites mentioned in court. Otieno's mourners carried a double consciousness, one rural, the other urban. The former was successfully used in court but largely ignored at a practical level. In the final analysis, urban consciousness triumphed because the mourners hurried back as if they had been to Langata, Nairobi, for a weekend burial. The same Luo community that had fomented so much tension and anxiety in Nairobi and beyond was unable to accord Otieno a climactic burial in accordance with what was said to be his authentic cultural heritage. The elder's climax to the Otieno story was, therefore, no more than a burial site.

Without saying it, the youth sought to push Otieno's corpse into artistic life, beyond the limitations of cultural confusion. They created dance drama based on some of the funeral rites to which Otieno was entitled. They choreographed and produced scripts to include the major rite of *tero buru*: Otieno's body was treated with the fanfare and intensity that music and dance contribute to the process of metaphysical transition from life to death. In many respects, the texts this book describes and discusses represent rituals of burial verbally created in the charged court proceedings. Otieno was literally buried in court with conflicting words before he reached his final resting place. The actors relived scenes of battle, jesting, and feasting, and emphasized the aura and sense of joy with which the dead must be escorted back to the spiritual world of a "new life." Outside the courts, they had theatrically made the point that the elders erred in shrouding Otieno's life-after-death in acrimony and chicanery. The scenes of mock battle seemed to represent what had transpired in the law courts between the contending parties, while the resolution of the conflicts through ecstatic joy and dance demonstrated what the youth thought ought to have been enacted at the end of the court war.

The youth appeased Otieno's spirit in other ways. Whereas elders kept committing the abomination of repeatedly addressing Otieno's body by name, the young *artistes* sang and danced in Otieno's honor without mentioning his name. It is polite to address a dead body as *dhano*—person—and not by name before burial. A praise-name maybe ... But only very rarely should a spirit be addressed by name. As it was, the sacrilege continued in the law courts and newspapers for a little over five months. Only an angry spirit went into the Nyalgunga grave and only the youth symbolically assuaged it through drama.

One more implication of the theatrical response: the young artists seemed to be saying that Otieno's descent into the world of the ancestors ought to have been celebrated. If we go by the belief that the dead are spirits or *yamo*—wind—

then the message is that nobody should lay claim to that which is supernatural and abstract. Fear of being haunted was cited in court to win a legal battle rather than prove a religious point. Put another way, Otieno was lent to Wambui by their society and not given in perpetuity (Wambui was also on loan). Marriage, one may argue, is a rite of passage during which one body is lent to the other "till death do them part." In death, the body changes in spirit, outgrows marital boundaries, and, like the *yamo* that it is, blows itself into social property. No one can pocket the wind. Nor can it be appeased by quarrelsome mourners. Neither the Nyalgunga community nor Wambui had a right to haggle over a spirit (which their court wrangle reduced to a mere body!). The mock battles of *tero buru* ought to have been fought over this spirit after a peaceful burial somewhere. The legal exchanges in court were real battles and unbecoming before the superhuman. It was as if the litigants were engaged in *tero buru* before burial and not vice versa as tradition demands. Were elders acting the wrong script, one may ask? The answer is "yes," going by the interpretation already derived from the *tero buru* drama.

The message from the youth is that the elders misinterpreted Otieno's corpse and produced something akin to farce. Two graves for one body in a nation-state moves the drama close to tragicomedy. Nobody seemed to know how and where to put Otieno's remains to rest; there was no cultural charter and direction, hence the protracted war in court.

The cultural metaphor of the coexistence of the living and the dead, the natural and the supernatural, eluded the elders, but caught the potent and creative imagination of the school-going youth and resulted in dance-drama and a "fitting burial" in theaters all over the country.

## Martin Chanock (Law, La Trobe University)

My comment addresses itself only obliquely to the two points specified. But as the reader's knowledge of the "case" and the "story" will in most cases come only from the text, it must be legitimate to comment on the nature of the text itself.

I read this without any prior knowledge of Otieno's case other than a handful of news clippings, but conscious of the development of the different ways of "knowing" Africa. From this viewpoint I offer impressions, not analysis. This text is a significant example of the change in the way in which Africa will be known, but it is not a change in the domination of that knowing by Western knowers. How different it is from the sort of classical anthropology that was the science of colonialism. How different too from the inspirational African history of the first two postindependence decades. The confident science of the European observer is absent; so too is the unproblematized "African voice." Exploitation; dependence; nationalism and nation building; development: the dominant story lines of the past are missing. This is not just because the subject matter is different, it is because confidence that there is either science, or a "true" story, or an expected future, has apparently gone. But what has brought about the changed mode of understanding? Clearly it is not the subjects who have changed, but the observers. Knowing Africa has been changed by changes in consciousness and ways of knowing in the postmodern West. The result is another authentically foreign way of knowing. A central theme is the struggles that "evoke and produce" histories, but, as before, these struggles will be won by the foreign referees.

"How should the story be told?" But what is "the story"? Is it simply that presented by the authors—the Otieno case and the processes of Kenya in the making that it illustrates? Or is it inextricably connected with other stories? I think that there are two stories. One is the story of the political context of the Kenya in which the Otieno case happens as a legal and cultural event. The other is the story of the growth of the discursive framework used by the authors. The story of Cohen and Odhiambo as the carriers of this discourse is now a part of the Otieno story, as the text is a meeting place between events in Kenya and postmodernist developments in Western thought. It is significant that the authors list at the end of their text, a list of texts quoted in the court and consider explicitly the kinds of knowledge accepted and rejected in court because this is a part of the story. Similarly, the wide range of postmodernist texts that feature in the footnotes are a part of the story, not in Kenya, but as it enters the Western intellectual world. So the story consists of three stories of which one is told and two are peripherally present. It is clear that the authors know that without the political crisis in Kenya and the climate of oppression present there, the strategy, tactics, discourse, meaning, and popularity of the case may not be so explicable. The importance of the public discussion exists in a context in which many terrible and dangerous things may not be discussed and a range of possibilities from vacuum filling to symbolic interchange affected the way in which both case and story developed. The most obvious version of the story would be that of an embattled authoritarian regime taking refuge in the most conservative and controlling version of the country's common law, which is not a unique response to crises of authority. Secondly, the way the story is told (and perhaps the decision to tell it) can be related to disciplinary developments outside of Kenya, quite unrelated to the production of Kenyan cultural history. In particular the determination not to prioritize a political narrative reflects the current state of Western social science and constitutes the story in a particular way. In the end, the story may have as much to tell us about Western cultural history in the making as about Kenyan.

In the dramatic encounter described, all the parties are locked in conflict about the "truth," about real intentions, and the real state of law. The institution in which the drama is played out is a court that sees itself as establishing facts, and finding law. Only the authors deny "truth." Apparently open to multivocality and many authentic meanings, the story as told gives them no real recognition. Indeed, it finds truth in an area not part of the contestants' avowed contests. In the end, to Cohen and Odhiambo, the story really is about something: the suppression of the women's voice. There are traces of earlier ways of writing here—false consciousness and the revelation of economic interests; or the invalidation of local knowledges by the privileging of structure and function. Internal versions of the truth in the end have less validity than outside ones.

Legal processes shape the "facts" that are heard. Behind the self-presentation of mechanistic logic are many choices. Litigants choose which facts to raise; rules of evidence exclude and include; and judgment finally sorts out what is more believable from what is less so. When this is done, "law" must be "applied." Again, the process is full of contingencies, and the application of common law can yield a wide variety of results. The processes of choices and exclusions apply also to historical writing. The difference is that a *result* is not the necessary end of this process. In considering legal processes, perhaps the focus needs to be on the court's preferred outcome. With this focus, the story of Otieno, in the context of contemporary Kenya, becomes less and less mysterious.

## Sally Falk Moore (Anthropology, Harvard University)

The Otieno case is presented here as a momentary point of intersection of many contested ideas and values that are being fought over in Kenya today. The analysis emphasizes concepts and opinions rather more than the structure of the social arenas within which contentions are taking place. The dissection of the case admirably shows that the quarrel over "symbols" and the making of "reality" are inseparable parts of the same process of social construction. But the focus on the content of the case, its protagonists, and its "text" backgrounds the mounting political pressures and social and economic strains that threaten in Kenya.

By quoting from the talk of many persons, this volume uses the voices of contemporary Kenyans to raise the issues on which the editor-writers of this book wish to comment. Opinions expressed in the quotations are illuminated by informed and insightful editorial discussion. But Professors Cohen and Odhiambo seldom address directly the matter of how the partisan positions of these many individuals are causally tied to the present and future of the country. They declare in the conclusions that they are "committed to the development of productive questions as opposed to the anticipation of final answers and closure."[10] This self-denying proposition explains some of the style of the account, and the fact that it makes no assertions about which conflicts are already or are likely to become the most important. But, between the lines and in the notes and in background comments, Cohen and Odhiambo have sprinkled strong statements about President Moi's well-known, systematic interest in blocking whatever activities he perceives to constitute a challenge to his absolute authority. Thus, while Cohen and Odhiambo declare that they are practicing a self-imposed avoidance of conclusions, this is plainly not altogether the case about all topics. It is not so with respect to President Moi, and it is not so with respect to their analysis of many peculiarities of logic in the testimony before the court, nor is such tentativeness evident in their statements about the gender attitudes of African men, nor is it apparent in their discussion of such political mobilization of Luo as was involved in connection with the dispute.

Thus, Cohen and Odhiambo do more political analysis than they say they are doing. They are not just raising questions. They do come to some strong conclusions about the recent past. But these are presented as background to a postmodern analysis of culture and text, rather than as having a central analytic place. In this posture the authors are clearly addressing themselves to an academic discussion about the nature of writing, knowledge, and contemporary historical interpretation that is going on in anthropology and in other quarters. They persuasively capture a sense of the great multiplicity of perspectives that can be adduced in addressing an event and the dynamism of contests over meaning within events. That is an important contribution.

It is surely the point of this volume that there can be no single answer to the question of what the case was really about. There are as many answers as there are stakes in the myriad contests about "reality" that are obviously going on. Often, the effort of the quoted individuals to present their particular versions of reality is best understood as an active attempt to make reality conform to those versions. The statements are not simply descriptions. That dimension of the historical dynamic is made very clear. And, of course, the legal case shows that certain versions do become officialized, at least temporarily. There are reasons why particular versions succeed at particular moments, and the reasons are sometimes knowable. In much of this book, Cohen and Odhiambo seem less interested in tracing those causal sequences, and more interested in analyzing the place of rhetorical production in the struggle over "history."

No book can do everything. This one has attempted a great deal, so it is probably too much to ask that a dissection of this event also deal frontally with the political confluence of some of the ideas and activities being pressed forward within it. The account presented here has admirably disassembled many of the competing positions and conflicting conceptions of reality evoked by the struggle over S. M. Otieno's body. What is not done is to reassemble them again, to reconsider the potential significance of the temporal and political intersections of these contests in a variety of arenas at the collective level. (For example: What are the probable connections between ideas about gender, the "place" of women, and the maintenance of ethnic boundaries? Were there submerged property issues in the S. M. Otieno case and how are these connected with economic processes under way in Kenya today? What is the relation between politics, local and national, and social boundaries defined by gender, education, ethnicity, occupation, and the like?) The analysis of the historical process invites a consideration of the societal consequence of the intersection of so many interests. It invites addressing the confluence of some of these mini-scale individual activities and attitudes as they are played out in the collective arenas of competition. That would be another book. This one has achieved a great deal within its own self-imposed limits.

### John Lonsdale (History, Cambridge University)

E. S. Atieno Odhiambo and David William Cohen question the propriety of reconstituting the life and marriage of the recently deceased in an academic text; we must be thankful that they overcame their scruples in so scrupulous a way. It is difficult to think how there could be a more luminous enquiry than they have given us here into the sort of daily, plebiscitary, making of a national culture that Ernest Renan a century ago would have thought exemplary.[11] The people in this book really live, Kenyans both alive and dead, making themselves a social and political culture, divided in many different ways, but over issues of common concern. But I would not be allowed to get away with merely giving the advice that, "This is terrific stuff, read it if you want to feel what it is like to be on the way to becoming a Kenyan." And there are in fact some silences or absences in the account that are worth further brief rumination. I think particularly of death, nationality, gender, and scripture.

Atieno and David do not really confront the question of death and nationality in the way in which, for instance, Ben Anderson invites us to.[12] They talk about the lineages of long-dead Luo corpses, but not enough, or not directly enough, about the recent Luo dead. Luo obviously argue about the disposal of the dead not so much because they want to reclaim the past but because in so doing they wish to claim the future. But which future? In the distant days when Oginga Odinga was *Ker* of the Luo Union (East Africa) — and how buoyant that parenthetical geography of intention now seems! — Luo, as the Langata cemetery records show, buried their urban dead in town. This was not merely because the roads back "home" were then slow and motor transport a luxury. Rather, Luo were colonizing urban opportunities. Nairobi, Dar es Salaam, and Kampala were outposts of *Piny Luo*; the migrations of the JoRamogi were continuing.[13] The future was opportunity, the place of one's buried placenta too often a place without a future, not a promising site in which to invest a reputation or to which to transport a corpse. The argument about SM's burial does more than reveal one of Kenya's, and Luoland's, "little republics" of self-regulation in face of the state. Does it not also say much about the felt narrowing of Luo futures? It is only recently, to take another example, that British military dead have begun to come home in coffins rather than being buried in some corner of a foreign field.

I would also have liked to benefit from more discussion of what is hinted at in the Kenyan connections between gender and nationality. In the SM story, Luo are mostly men and tribal, Kikuyu are scarcely present at all but are, by implication, mostly women (of doubtful reputation) and Kenyan. Why did Wambui Otieno not apparently try to mobilize her own resources of connection in and out of court? What did she mean when she said, after losing control of her husband's body, that she had "gone back to Kikuyuland"? Had "Kenya" failed her — that female realm of kiosk owners and bar attendants — so that she felt obliged to retire to an ethnic domain of male kin? If, for instance, this drama had been transposed sixty years back in time, to the late 1920s, then one would find that the Kikuyu world of Kenya that was constructed by Kenyatta, the young editor of *Muigwithania* and his correspondents, was not at all unlike that of the Umira Kager of the late 1980s. Male Kikuyu in Nairobi were thinking of clubbing together in order to bury their dead back home in *bururi ya Gikuyu*; they were also calling for a ban on women traders and for a lowering of their scandalously high hemlines; yet at the same time Kenyatta pointed out the wonderful symbolism of the (male) hutments built for the chiefs from every tribe of Kenya who gathered in Nairobi to do homage to the Prince of Wales. He thought the huts comparable to the *thingira* that used to be built for the celebrants of the *ituika* ceremony in which Kikuyu had previously enacted their domestic handing over of generational power. In 1929, then, Kikuyu men apparently saw one threateningly female Kenya that dissolved authority and another one that promoted male power. The tension between male ethnicity and female state-nationality has a long history.[14]

So do Kikuyu corpses. A particular silence in the court proceedings emanated from the corpse of Wambui's paternal great-grandfather, Waiyaki wa Hinga, who died in British custody in 1892. Until SM's burial, Waiyaki's were perhaps the most potent remains in modern Kenyan history, closely followed by those of chief Koinange wa Mbiyu's grandfather. Waiyaki's burial, allegedly upside-down, in distant Kibwezi symbolized for Kikuyu the treachery of British conquest and was thus remembered by the Mau Mau *itungati* in the forests of Mount Kenya sixty years later.[15] Koinange's grandfather's bones had been exhumed in February 1933, to prove the extent of his *mbari's* land lost to white settlement.[16] Past Kikuyu corpses have been every bit as eloquent as Luo remains. There was no call to bring them into the courtroom arena; it was not the control of a Kikuyu body that was being disputed. But was there not Kikuyu gossip in the streets, parallel to that at One Ojijo Road? Did not Kikuyu corpses also sprout their admonitions of propriety? It is something that one cannot tell from this Luo-centric book. One cannot therefore know from these pages how far, if they are, Luo and Kikuyu, men and women, are constructing different Kenyas.

This observation raises another doubt. The authors rightly dismiss the journalist's shorthand offering of "tribalism" as the cause of the struggle over SM. It is, nonetheless, a politically explanatory term in common Kenyan usage. It was one of the many layers of meaning in discussions in which Kenyans talked about being modern, about movement, but also about the relation between hallowed land and whole identities. And it is a layer of meaning that academics find difficult to discuss; it is easier to dismiss it with a remark to the effect that life is more complicated than that. It is, but life can also have, at times, its simplicities or, rather, its constructs of simplicity in the midst of flux. There were crude imaginations of Luo tribal backwardness in court; yes, they served the polemical interests of the litigants, but they, and imaginations like them, are, if only by their silence, present in all the chatter of polite Nairobi. Academic discourse has not yet, to my mind, solved the problem of how one analyses the joint, concurrent constructions of layered ethnic and "state-national" cultures, both of which are equally new and both of which to a large extent construct each other in their deliberate contrasts. We rightly condemn the stark dichotomy between tradition and modernity to which lawyers or journalists appeal, but I do not think that we have yet developed a widely intelligible alternative form of speech. Our evasion perhaps reflects, but does nothing to resolve, the ambiguities lived by Africans in the discursive contest between state hegemony and multicultural association.

Which brings me, finally, to the Bible. In early 1987, Kenyans were eagerly discussing the relationship between a knowledge of Shakespeare as shown by SM and his modern elite status. Three or four months later they were debating in the press the precise nature of King Darius's tyranny over the Medes and Persians, whose satraps had thrown Daniel into the lion's den. Darius, Bishop Gitari had suggested in a sermon that instigated the press correspondence, made a "blunder which he greatly regretted" because he "did not allow a public debate,"[17] an oblique comment on their present governance the meaning of which no Kenyan would have missed. This was as authentically a Kenyan debate as the issue of SM; indeed, there were more references to biblical authority in the court proceedings than Atieno and David seem to have noticed. The Bible contains even more disputed political theory in the guise of bloody historical narrative than Shakespeare, and still more pointed accounts of death, gender, and national futures. Moreover, unlike Shakespeare, it is available to the *raia* in their common vernaculars. The Bible is demotic in a way in which the "man from England" can never be, quoted in rural bars as well as in the smart Bomas of Kenya. And in popular hymns about Exodus or other Bible stories, there is much biting criticism of the elite, which, if still coded, is nonetheless more direct than that which the common people allowed themselves in the court of appeal.[18] There is even more to explore in the making of the modern Kenyan political consciousness than we so richly provided with here.

### Michael M. J. Fischer (Anthropology, Rice University)

> . . . while the British were busy creating "tribes," the leading proto-elites were creating the Luo nation. . . . [Jomo] Kenyatta and [B. A.] Ogot . . . participated in the invention of these ethnic communities — if they were not actually responsible as their foremost inventors . . . Ogot's *History* appeals most readily to the lawyers and advocates . . . for the purposes of establishing the claims of their clients. Jomo Kenyatta wrote *Facing Mount Kenya* as a charter for Gikuyu nationhood. But its most ready function in Gikuyu society has been in the courts: as an authority on family law, particularly relating to dowry and divorce.
> —David William Cohen & E. S. Atieno Odhiambo[19]

Three virtues of a "deconstructive" account such as the present one — that is, an account that plays off against one another a number of contesting voices, interests and perspectives so as to expose the complexity of social issues involved, but that itself refuses to choose a "correct" interpretation — are (i) to demonstrate the ways in which both "custom" and "modernity" are interpretive, political constructions; (ii) to illustrate the ways in which the courts become a primary setting for choosing and enforcing interpretations; and (iii) to provide a powerful means for postcolonial writing, that is, for avoiding many of the dangers of constructing the subjects of the text as distanced, exotic, stereotypic, temporally displaced, ahistorical, or essentialized "Others."

The first of these virtues acts to counter interpretations that claim to represent transparent truth, and provides the grounds for cultural critique: it works effectively, for instance, in the cautionary tale about feminist positions (in chapter 3) where it is shown how mobilizations of "feminist" opinion are crosscut and undercut by countervailing pressures; but it seems to work less effectively in evaluating changes in funerary custom: it is not only I who feel this, for the authors themselves finally (in chapter 5) provide a "correct" account of the historical provenance of customs that once existed but not recently, or those that are figments of the imagination and/or rhetorical semiotics of the litigants.

The second virtue provides the cautious beginnings of a new sociology of the state, but the authors' politics of representation becomes submerged here, only suggesting in a single throwaway sentence, albeit powerfully, that this case may well represent the death of an independent judiciary in Kenya (discussions of the case by Kenyans I've talked to often contain among other factors a series of speculations about the role and motivations of the president of Kenya in nudging the courts to the final judgment, none of which is represented in this text). In similar fashion, there seems to be a lapse of cultural-critique potential in presenting the position of Wambui Otieno and the role of women's networks: there is a potent image that Wambui "in presenting her claims for [her husband's] remains became socially dead. Her social and political capital nil . . . ," but little explanatory or descriptive substance that could serve to unpack this process of marginalization. That is, not only is there a lack of information, for example, about Wambui's previous marriages, Kikuyu connections, political history, intermarriage networks among the new elites, the social connections that those pasts and sociologies provide (these are mentioned only in passing, as if one only needed to focus on and unpack the patrilineal, and the Luo sides of Kenyan society) — but more importantly, there is therefore a (perhaps unintentional) politics of representation that sides with what is presented, and militates against what is left out. Despite the authors' evenhanded sympathies for Wambui's case as well as that of the clan, in the end, the text, like the court, drops the elements of accounts that would support Wambui, and the postcolonial reaction for patriarchal controls and against individualism and feminism is allowed to prevail. But most importantly, there seems to be an absence of material (i) about the shifts in political and social alliances of the Luo and Kikuyu that are but hinted at in the references to Oginga Odinga; (ii) about the semiotic structures of the funerary rites among Luo, Kikuyu, and Christians; and perhaps (iii) about the "social drama" of the entire S. M. Otieno affair itself. Obvious questions remained unformulated (much less answered): why was the solution of "one body, two funerals" not an acceptable compromise, when it is not unusual procedure for the Luo? Formulating such questions in terms of, say, the idea of social dramas, might facilitate formulating explicit models of "structural change" underlying the play of voices and interests, and these might be complementary rather than preemptive to the play of voices and interests, giving added power to the array of deconstructive possibilities and sharpening the understanding of constraints against, and obstacles to, the mobilization of certain possibilities, voices, interests, or perspectives.

I would like to elaborate very briefly on several of these points: (i) the semiotics of funeral symbolism and their role in constructing a contemporary national imaginary that is a tapestry of contested and changing ethnic contrasts, relationships, and alliances; (ii) social dramas and structural change; and (iii) cultural critique and the questions of institutionalizing (post) modernity and the traditionalizing strategies of political mobilization and dividing opponents.

> The elders . . . the intelligentsia . . . the church and other organizations owe it to themselves and to their communities to ensure that customary laws keep abreast of positive modern trends so as to make it possible for courts to be guided by customary laws.[20]

Feeling I needed more information than the authors supplied, I started talking to Kenyans about the S. M. Otieno case whenever I happened to run into them. I also asked friends who were scholars of Kenya for accounts of funerary rites among the Luo and Kikuyu, since in anthropological studies, funerals often serve as rich vehicles for unpacking and displaying social dynamics; thus I was lent, by Ivan Karp, the Nairobi University conference volume on the S. M. Otieno case edited by J. B. Ojwang and J. N. K. Mugambi, which contains a very useful preliminary anthropological survey, a useful linguistic analysis of the different nuances that English and Dholuo terms convey and how these are manipulated by various Dholuo-speaking and non-Dholuo-speakers in the court, and a series of essays on the role this case plays in the development of the respective roles of customary, British common, and Kenyan legislative law in the legal system of Kenya, with a particularly sharp rebuke by E. Cotran who wrote the case book on which the court relied for precedents and previous legal rulings.

## A Kikuyu Male Professional

TWA Flight 744, from Washington D. C.'s National Airport to New York's J. F. K. International Airport, 18 November 1990. My seatmate is a Kikuyu economist returning from a three-week seminar at the World Bank on supervising banking systems. Does he know about the S. M. Otieno case? Of course. Can he tell me about Kikuyu and Luo funerary customs? He provides a neat oppositional account: Among the Luo, the wife is not considered next of kin, and a man's brother inherits his property, including the wife; among the Kikuyu a wife is considered next of kin and she inherits from her husband. Luo bury in their ancestral sites; Kikuyu were migrating folk, each was supposed to set up a new residence and you were buried where you died. Luo spend lavishly on funerals; Kikuyu spend little on funerals, and once upon a time disposed of the dead by simple surface exposure. (Indeed, he mused, how old could burial among the Luo be, how long would they have had metal shovels? Moreover he said the government had to intervene via educational campaigns against the pauperization of Luo through excessive spending at funerals feeding huge numbers of relatives until all resources are exhausted.) Luo are family and clan oriented: there are always many kinfolk around; Kikuyu are more individualistic, have small families with few relatives about. Kikuyu were Christianized first. S. M. Otieno was wealthy; but Wambui was domineering (was there a hint of pride here?), and probably not much liked by SM's brothers and clan, and probably made even SM himself uncomfortable.

## A Luo Woman Entrepreneur and Social Worker

Bombay, International AIDS Conference, 9 December 1990. Three representatives from Kenya are present: I ask one if she knows about the S. M. Otieno case. Of course, and she will be delighted to tell me about it. We have a very long discussion. At first she says that since her father had been an orphan raised in a Christian mission school, then attending Makerere University, and since she had been raised in the city, her family knew little of traditional customs. But as she speaks she supplies more and more details: it is one of the richest accounts of Luo funerary customs I've run across, but also a rich set of perspectives from women's positionings in Kenyan society.

As a social worker, and one struggling against the AIDS epidemic, she spoke of the new implications and the exploitative aspects of traditional customs like the Luo levirate. Before AIDS was understood, and even now, when a man died of unknown causes and his widow was quickly remarried by levirate, she could spread the disease not only to her new husband and his other sexual partners, but also to children she might bear. A widow taken by the husband's brother could bear children in her husband's name, but the woman could also be abused as a kind of servant. The social worker also had a very rich sense of gender politics both regarding Wambui and S. M. Otieno's marital affairs and regarding the presidential politics affecting the case.

About the Kikuyu she was less fulsome, but the relation between Kikuyu and Luo proves again significant: for one thing, when she separated from her husband and took the children with her, she was called "a Kikuyu woman." Kikuyu women, she explained, tend not to stay with one husband, and when they leave, they take their children with them, in sharp contrast to Luo, where children belong to the husband, and a wife is always considered to be the wife of her first husband to the extent that when she dies, her son must bury her in her first husband's homestead. Kikuyu in general do not have many customs and traditions from the past, partly because they have "lived with the white man so long" (seconding the economist about being Christianized earlier), but also because they intermarry more frequently with all other groups. Regarding funerary customs, Kikuyu were traditionally afraid of the dead body and did not merely abandon corpses in the forest; but when someone was terminally ill, they would tie him to a tree with a noisemaker on a string; at meal times they would pull the string from a distance, and when there was no answer, they assumed death had occurred. Nowadays, Kikuyu use the Langata cemetery in Nairobi, or, more generally, bury wherever death occurs; but they do not bury on farms they have in recent years been acquiring. They might have a Christian ceremony, but have no traditional funerary customs.

Luo, by contrast, have fairly elaborate funerary customs, spread over six or seven days, depending on whether the deceased is male or female. People gather from long distances while the body lies in state: four days if a woman, three if a man (Ocholla-Ayayo in Ojwang and Mugambi, eds., has it inversely: three for a woman, four for a man); that is, the same time as the seclusion period at birth (boys are said to be stronger and so are secluded with their mothers for only three days). A six-foot-deep grave is dug at night, usually beginning at midnight. For prominent persons, a *tero buru* may be performed: people put on masks of cattle heads and leaves, hold spears, going out into the wilderness and running back singing and acting like wild beasts, so as perhaps to chase away demons so that the deceased may rest peacefully (another explanation, which Cohen and Atieno Odhiambo think older and more correct, is that it was once a mock fight against an enemy clan; Ocholla-Ayayo provides a third explanation: that it is a fight against the spirits of death, and that it is conducted by an age group). While this rite is less likely to be performed in Upper Matasia, in the S. M. Otieno case it was performed, with people running from the mortuary to the center of town. The social worker remembers it being lunch time, and it frightening her; she remembers a passerby exclaiming in astonishment, "Are these human beings?" Usually a *tero buru* is performed in the morning before the burial, which should occur at noon. It can be quite wild and destructive of property. In the S. M. Otieno case, it was separated from the burial: the government flew the body back to Luoland, lest there be trouble on the road from people who might lie in wait to mob it or even kidnap it. On the third day after the burial, the owner of the homestead performs the sweeping of the grave and house that marks the end of the funeral period, and guests and relatives leave in order of seniority. Throughout the six- or seven-day funerary period, a fire is kept burning (*magenga*) and there is feasting: a feeding of the gathered mourners. Traditionally, people would have gathered bringing with them their property in cattle, some of which would have been available to slaughter for the funerary feasting.

But while the semiotics of these funerary rites can be elaborated (see Ocholla-Ayayo for additional materials), the social worker went on to speculate about the complicated life and psychological reactions of Wambui ("a complicated life, a complicated woman"), ranging from her background as daughter of a powerful family, and as a fighter—in the Emergency, Uhuru, Mau Mau; to her children by white men; to her marriage to S. M. Otieno, initially as a marriage of convenience, with the two spouses later deciding to have children; to the rumors that she killed S. M. Otieno because he wanted another woman or wanted out of the marriage; to the rumors of oddities in the case, such as the disappearance of the will of S. M. Otieno, allegations of money spent to cover up the alleged murder and the disappearance of the will, and the original television announcement of S. M. Otieno's death that quoted another dead lawyer as if he were alive; and above all, to the rich yellow journalistic magazine accounts of the aftermath of the funeral, according to which Wambui swore to get the body back and rebury it, even if it were to take a hundred years and if she were to have to wait until the president were gone; of her turning to healers to help cleanse her of what she'd done (the murder); and of the visions or dreams that she has had in which S. M. Otieno told her that he was not happy where he was buried.

The rumors of murder need not be taken literally, nor need they be dismissed as mere rumor; perhaps, rather, they are a variant form of the tendency of Luo traditional thought according to which natural causes are never sufficient to explain a death: social causes must also be present. Ocholla-Ayayo, in outlining the different varieties of social causes for deaths (witchcraft, sinful conduct in breaking taboos or oaths, revenge-seeking spirits, and so forth), notes that "the sudden death of Otieno could not be believed by the Umira Kager clan members to be natural, because in that community, death is traditionally not seen as natural," and also notes that the Umira Kager clan demanded a second postmortem on Otieno's corpse in their presence to determine the true cause of death, because this can determine the form of the burial.

Certainly at least this form of speculation on the part of my informant and on the part of the magazines that reported such things can be read as a recognition of the trauma of the widow that was repressed by the final judgment of the court. My informant, after listing all these allegations and rumors of nefarious doings on all sides, concluded: "Perhaps as a man, the president was concerned that precedent not be set of women lording it over patriarchal custom." It certainly seems to be the case that the state wanted to emphasize respect for Luo custom over the notions of freedom from custom as a mark of the modern Kenyan. It has been suggested that in part this had to do with the politics of breaking apart opposition to the current government that was spearheaded by Kikuyu-Luo alliances: the government attempted to use the Otieno case to split such horizontal alliances through appeals to ethnic chauvinisms in the disguise of "respect for African culture." Wambui's lawyer was a Luyia Quaker married to a Kikuyu and, as Cohen and Atieno Odhiambo report, the president was disturbed that he was given an honorary Ph.D. in the U.S., and so in response elevated the lawyer for the Umira Kager clan, for contributions to preserving African culture. My informant

noted that the day S. M. Otieno was finally to be buried, secondary-school
students were turned out in great numbers by the government to meet the
winning lawyer and ask him about, and celebrate, the "African customs" that had
been vindicated and preserved by the case.

What is especially interesting about my informant's and Ocholla-Ayayo's
accounts emerges despite the fact that both allowed their Luo identifications to
emerge, painting Wambui in less than positive terms — Ocholla-Ayayo ends
with a catalogue of rites that Wambui would not have been able to perform, and
metaphysical justifications for these rites in Luo thought; my informant stressed
Wambui's arrogance: that as a woman backed by a powerful family, she would
have the resources to act against an infidelity if she so chose; that instead of
burying the body when the first judgment gave it to her, she took her time,
boasted to the press, and thereby provoked the Umira Kager clan; and that had
she buried the body immediately, the clan would have simply followed the
procedure for those who die abroad, to take a leaf (Ocholla-Ayayo says a fruit)
and bury it symbolically in place of the body. But despite these shadings — or
rather, as a function of what these shadings expose in terms of alternative
possibilities — my informant's elaboration of women's perspectives and Ocholla-
Ayayo's elaboration of the semiotics is coded in the variable features of funerary
rites. There is, clearly, a semiotics of social status, of the social implications of
mode of death, of redistribution of the social relations of a deceased person, of
linkages to other rites and the social units that perform them, of cosmological
notions of transitions of the deceased into an ancestor. These elements expose
and map out a social, cultural, and psychological terrain, one that is neither
simple, nor traditional, nor confined to the Luo conceived apart from other
Kenyans.

> One newspaper writer observed that there was that crushing moment
> when Wambui burst into uncontrollable tears as she pointed to the
> grave and the cross she had prepared for his body at Upper Matasia. . . .
> beneath the veneer of solemnity at the burial ceremony was an underlying
> but powerful atmosphere of joy, of victory, like the entire community
> had successfully vanquished an enemy who was out to destroy everything
> they stood for.[21]

In anthropology there is a now-classic device for analyzing culturally rich
and socially complex affairs such as the S. M. Otieno case. Stemming from the
case-study methods that Max Gluckman and his Manchester School imported
from the law, expanding their focus from lawyers' questions of rights, customs,
enforceable obligations, and precedents into the underlying sociological functions
and dynamics, these methods were further elaborated by Victor Turner into a
way of probing not only social structure, but psychological dynamics and cultural
hermeneutics. The S. M. Otieno case is a "social drama" of the sort that would
have delighted Turner. In the simplest, most schematic formulation of Turner's
social dramas, two of the four critical features or stages are the expanding nature
of the conflict to encompass ever-wider parts of society, and in the end either a
successful reassertion of a normative structure on all parties or alternatively a
fission into new social units. In the S. M. Otieno case, the social drama expanded
to include the entire nation. Not only does one find the conflict resolved at the
highest levels of the state judicial and political system, but one finds it addressed

both locally, in everyday life, and globally. I found it possible to interview any Kenyan I ran into from Washington, D. C., to Bombay, and to receive detailed information, facts, and interpretations on the case. (There are, of course, social dramas, the recent Salman Rushdie affair, for example, that reach across national boundaries and expose global cultural competitions and stratifications that cannot be resolved by any single state structure.) The immediate resolution of the S. M. Otieno case operated on two levels: there was both an enforcement of normative order by subordination of the court to the political will of the office of the president of the state; but at the same time, the social drama itself and the vehemence of the assertion of the Umira Kager's clan solidarity signal a new fission of social units away from earlier Kikuyu-Luo alliances and away from urban-rural dichotomies and tensions.

The lively presentation of the S. M. Otieno case in this volume utilizes a self-described "deconstructive" technique of playing the huge variety of voices and interests in the case against each other so as to explore the richness of the social and cultural (and to a lesser extent psychological) dilemmas that the case brought to the surface. I want to applaud the technique of presentation, before returning to some more traditional anthropological tools of inquiry as ways of supplementing, and perhaps helping readers such as myself find ways to interrogate, what the authors present.

First of all, let me suggest that Cohen and Atieno Odhiambo have made a major breakthrough in providing a model of postcolonial writing. They plunge us into the lives of contemporary individuals whose lives are continuous with those of the authors as well as with our own: this is the world in which one of the authors grew up and in which both operate as professionals; these are people with degrees and honorary doctorates from universities in the United States, Britain, and India, with sons and daughters going to school with our sons and daughters. It is a text that treats its subjects as people rather than as sociological roles, as named individuals with real-life connections that are intertextually available in documents of all sorts and who can be found easily in reality; that treats people as contemporaries — professors and gravediggers, police sergeants and kiosk owners, women activists and ordinary, assertive women, lawyers and politicians, old men and college boys, in-laws and kinfolk — rather than as "Third World Others"; that treats status differences forthrightly — the Nairobi lawyer who drives in his Mercedes to the next town to sleep in a comfortable motel rather than stay in his country kin's houses (and carries his own water); that treats of people in all stations of life; and that indexes how the contemporary is connected to profound historical changes, some of which are universal modern dilemmas (conflicts over local community and ethnic solidarities in modern cosmopolitan societies), and others of which are culturally, historically, and geo-graphically specific (the psychology of a modern man who remembers the colonial pass system and its ethnic segregatory discriminations, the urban women who are sophisticated, multilingual suppliers of service to both new migrants into the city and upper-class folk, the use of Shakespeare as a marker of a segment of the mandarin class). As a general mode of writing, the open identification of names, of course, can present serious ethical problems (ones however that journalists have long known how to manage), but since the S. M. Otieno case was a public drama, with available court transcripts, newspaper articles, books about the case, and a variety of other media, some of these issues are simplified. Still, it is both admirable and worthy of emulation that the authors avoid being drawn into the passions of the different interests to the case and maintain an interpretive style that supplies the contexts and background to the positions staked out, both by allowing voice to those interests, and by critiquing them, showing how they are constructed, their limitations and their politics of representation, the exclusions of information that they attempt to impose or the shadings of interpretations they supply.

Had I more space, it might be worth exploring some of the stylistic devices that give this text its vividness and immediacy: the short sentences, rounded characterizations (which make me want to meet Mama Koko), citations of testimony and direct speech, vignettes of confrontations and social-micro dramas (I like particularly the Monday-morning quarterbacking commentaries on the court case by retired police sergeant Christopher Ochieng' Oganga in Mama Rosbella's cattle shed while veterinarian Albert Ongwama sprays for ticks). It reads, I thought, like a cross between Hemingway (the terse, matter-of-fact sentences) and Faulkner (the rich depiction of an ethnographic milieu) with a dash of *New Yorker* sophistication: journalistic immediacy and simplicity honed into a stylish vehicle of both loving portraiture and scalpel-sharp commentary.

I do wonder about the mildness of the discourse of critique in the text: the cases of gender sociology and leftism are symptomatic, the cases of reviewing the historical record ethnographically in terms of customs, previous cases, and socio-logical underpinnings of politics are even more basic. Let me use the former two cases very briefly to raise issues of how texts such as this one can operate as cultural critique, and then also briefly use the latter two cases to reflect on traditional anthropological tools that may still be useful in thinking through this text.

The issue of gender is one that Cohen and Atieno Odhiambo are acutely aware of and they have performed superb groundwork in the analysis of the construction of public maleness and in the delineation of the marginalization of women's voices, especially through the portrait of Mama Koko (and the associated literature produced by such writers as Luise White and Janet Bujra). There is something tautological, incomplete, and unsatisfactory in saying "it was in the last analysis the web of associations of men — counsels, jurists, statesmen — which constrained and silenced Wambui's voice."[22] After all, Cohen and Atieno Odhiambo also say:

> These are the women who made the politician Tom Mboya, who captured the votes for him in slumland Gikomba and Muoroto in Starehe constitu-ency, and who first made Wambui into a leader of the Nairobi People's Convention Party Women's Wing in 1959.[23]

As a descriptive matter, but more importantly as a matter of cultural critique, one wants to have descriptions of the backstage where my Luo informant, Mama Koko, *pims*, and many others operate, manipulate, and exert influence through networks involving women and also men. By the simple virtue of making available such information, one would redraw the sensibilities, or at least the possible sensibilities of readers, performing what Walter Benjamin might have called the redemptive function of ethnography and cultural critique.

A similar lack operates with regard to the sociology of Luo-Kikuyu alliances in the context of urban-rural politics and incumbent-oppositional state politics. The primary hint here is the discussion of the silencing of Oginga Odinga, who in the two books by Cohen and Atieno Odhiambo is variously portrayed as a Luo cultural conservative (in opposition to Tom Mboya), a leader of urban radicalism in alliance with Kikuyu socialists, and a supporter of Wambui in the S. M. Otieno affair. His support for Wambui might simply have had to do with personal relationships: it was he who helped send both her brothers and S. M. Otieno to India for education, and thus it is he who is one of the oldest links between her family and S. M. Otieno. But first, this kind of cross-ethnic, cross-generational, and cross-class network is interesting in itself, and second, it would seem that these shifts in his position vis-a-vis "Luo custom" and Kenyan cosmopolitanism have to do with larger issues of political sociology and the state. Again, were these fleshed out, the S. M. Otieno case might look quite different, providing a possible example of where descriptive ethnography (and history) might perform the redemptive function of cultural critique.

Finally, the issues of the review of the ethnographic and historical record of customs and their sociological underpinnings are similarly matters that are named and dealt with in this book, but primarily by showing the constructedness of positive accounts, how the dead are made to speak in different ways by different interests, how living persons or dimensions of life are silenced or excluded, how social relations are theatricalized and placed on view for society's members to see, how histories and ethnographies of customs are produced differently by different elements, and by suggesting that the processes of traditionalizing and valorizing Luo customs fit within the changing political sociology of Kenya. What still needs to be fleshed out is this political sociology, so that the vignettes and the play of constructions can be evaluated for their social depth and power.

In conclusion, note that the elaborations, supplements, and calls for "more" that I have raised are themselves markers of the success of the present text. The beauty of this wonderful book lies not only in the richness of the individual chapters focusing attention on different ways in which the S. M. Otieno affair was and is culturally constructed, those differences being sites of critical interpretive practices either in use or available for use, but it also lies in the ways in which the book generates further commentaries and engagements such as my own.

# NOTES

## Introduction

1. Isak Dinesen (Karen Blixen), *Out of Africa* (New York: Random House, 1937), 3–4.
2. From an interview of Marieni Ole Kertella conducted in 1962 by Gerald Hanley. Ole Kertella was an Oloiboni of the Maasai and had lived for a very long time in the very Upper Matasia area near Nairobi, where Silvano Melea Otieno and Virginia Wambui Otieno had established a residence. Hanley described his meeting with the Laibon: "I got up to greet him and he shook hands with us. He was a fine looking and dignified old man, over ninety, yet he looked sixty, his healthy red brown skin shining in the electric light as he smiled at us and waited to be asked to sit down. He sat down and looked round at the machinery and then at the microphone on the table before him. ... He said, 'That's the thing I'll talk into. ...'" Gerald Hanley, *Warriors and Strangers* (London: Hamish Hamilton, 1971), 284–90.
3. The attorney Timan Njugi, testifying before the High Court of Kenya, 27 January 1987. The court transcripts relating to the burial of the lawyer Silvano Melea Otieno, the subject of this book, are provided in Sean Egan, ed., *S. M. Otieno: Kenya's Unique Burial Saga* (Nairobi: Nation Newspapers, c. 1987). The quote from Timan Njugi is found on page 40. The Egan volume presents the case record with a number of additional reports from the *Daily Nation*, Nairobi. Catherine Gicheru and Paul Muhoho are credited as reporters for the entire publication. The case was discussed at a special seminar organized by the Faculty of Law of the University of Nairobi, 18 July 1987. A number of papers were presented to this seminar, and these were published together in J. B. Ojwang and J. N. K. Mugambi, eds., *The S. M. Otieno Case: Death and Burial in Modern Kenya* (Nairobi: Nairobi University Press, 1989). The daily and weekly Kenya press contains an extraordinary reservoir of correspondence and commentary on the case. The present authors also have in hand a good deal of private correspondence with Kenyans concerning the case.
4. From testimony of Harry Mugo in the High Court, 28 January 1987, as quoted in Egan, 43. Mugo identified himself by occupation as a professional land valuer.
5. This account of the last hours of SM's life and the first hours after his death is reconstructed, in part, from testimony of various witnesses before the High Court. See Egan.
6. Named "Khama" after the defiant marriage of Seretse Khama—of then Bechuanaland in southern Africa—to Ruth, a *muzungu* (European) "lady."
7. Omolo Siranga, under cross-examination in the High Court of Kenya, as reported in Egan, 49.
8. See David William Cohen and E. S. Atieno Odhiambo, *Siaya: The Historical Anthropology of an African Landscape* (London: James Currey, 1989), 43–59, for a discussion of these extensions to the meaning of Siaya.

9. The *Daily Nation* carried reports on 3 January both of the counterinjunction and of the funeral plans, still in effect on that day, with the body to be collected from the City Mortuary at 10:30 a.m., followed by a funeral service at All Saints' Cathedral, with burial following at Upper Matasia.

10. See M. Tamarkin, "Social and Political Change in a Twentieth Century African Urban Community in Kenya" (Ph.D. diss., University of London, 1973).

11. Egan, 6.

12. He cited the Public Health Act (Cap. 242, Laws of Kenya, Section 146, Sub-section 2).

13. Kenya Court of Appeal ruling, 7 January 1987, reported in Egan, 9.

14. Egan, 15. Five other, though closely related, grounds were noted by Kwach in his memorandum to the Court of Appeal.

15. Egan, 12.

16. Egan, 12–13.

17. Egan, 16.

18. Egan, 15.

19. Egan, 16.

20. Egan, 16.

21. Egan, 16.

## Chapter 1
## One Body, Two Funerals

1. Thomas A. Bass, *Camping with the Prince and Other Tales of Science in Africa* (Boston: Houghton Mifflin, 1990), 53.

2. The authors present as striking, unusual, this construction of SM as a figure obsessed with death. But is it so extraordinary? Brahm's *German Requiem* of 1868 has as its central theme that "in the middle of life we are surrounded by death." See, in retrospect, ironically, the late Bruno Bettelheim, "Freud's Vienna," *The Wilson Quarterly*, xiv, 2 (Spring 1990): 76. In a recent and provocative treatment of the biography, arguing that its narrative structure is rooted in the body's very materiality, Michael Holquist draws attention to Salman Rushdie's declaration in *Satanic Verses*: "The world is the place we prove real by dying in it," a proposition that SM, in his reconstituted person in the courtroom, would have probably endorsed. M. Holquist, "From Body-Talk to Biography: The Chronological Bases of Narrative," *The Yale Journal of Criticism*, 3, 1 (1989), 1–33.

3. Sean Egan, ed., *S. M. Otieno: Kenya's Unique Burial Saga* (Nairobi: Nation Newspapers, c. 1987), 40.

4. Egan, 45.

5. Egan, 42. In his final opinion, Justice Bosire of the High Court constructed his own tests of veracity in judging the relative value of various purported statements from SM.

6. Egan, 42.

7. Egan, 42.

8. One that has continued in Kenya for several years since the burial of S. M. Otieno.

9. And the oration has been carried forward in both space and time, and it has reached beyond the middle class to rural village elders, as exemplified by the compelling message from an uncle of one of the authors, Nehemiah Okoth Oganga, conveyed orally from Siaya to Houston in August 1990: "Come home and build your *dala*, now that you are a professor and a prominent person."

10. For example, see the *New York Times*, 25 February 1987, and the *Washington Post*, 14 February 1987. In "Death and Burial in Modern Kenya: An Introduction," in J. B. Ojwang and J. N. K. Mugambi, eds., *The S. M. Otieno Case: Death and Burial in Modern Kenya* (Nairobi: Nairobi University Press, 1989), 3–4, the Nairobi professor of Law J. B. Ojwang drew attention to the coverage in the *Washington Post*, noting that the Western press's . . . naked simplicity of language clearly and violently distorted the true picture

of the norms, values and social change in an African society" (4). Blaine Harden, the *Post* correspondent in Nairobi at the time of the trial, has revisited it within a long memoir of his experiences as a correspondent in Africa. See his *Africa: Dispatches from a Fragile Continent* (New York: Norton, 1990), 95–129. While the memoir is one of the longest yet published about the struggle for SM's corpse, it is both shallow and naive in its handling of the materials, which include the author's eyewitness accounts of events outside the courtroom. Harden seems to have been unable to comprehend the case as both more and less than a "tribal" dispute. As one reads the Harden treatment, one notes the journalist giving his own final judgment on the litigation, that "[t]he verdict was almost certainly fixed by Kenya's president. There is no other reasonable explanation why the judge would insist on believing the word of one aging gravedigger who loathed Wambui over that of a dozen more credible and disinterested witnesses who said Otieno wanted to be buried in Nairobi" (124). One is only left to grieve about the quality of American reporting of events in Africa.

11. For an important study of a long and complex legal proceeding involving the adjudication of ethnographic facts, see James Clifford, "Identity in Mashpee," in his *The Predicament of Culture: Twentieth-Century Ethnography, Literature, and Art* (Cambridge, Mass.: Harvard University Press, 1988), 277–346.

12. One looks forward to the research on "the politics of mourning ritual in South Africa" being undertaken by Garrey Dennie of the Johns Hopkins University. Tomas Hofer of the Institute for Ethnography, Budapest, and Susan Gal, of the Department of Anthropology, Rutgers, are examining the reburials of the fallen heroes of the 1956 Hungarian uprising. Rosana Guber, Johns Hopkins, has been doing research on the larceny of Perón's hands.

13. On 17 March 1991, the *Sunday Express-News*, San Antonio, Texas, reported that "[t]he body of a Houston teacher has been released to his mother after a squabble erupted between two of his three current 'wives' about where the slain man would be buried. . . . Lawrence Toliver Richardson, 35, was shot to death March 5 in a Houston Community College parking lot as he finished teaching his air-conditioning maintenance class . . . but his body had been held at a Houston funeral home for more than a week while a probate court considered who had the right to bury Richardson." Corinne Kratz kindly brought the story to our attention.

14. 2 April 1987. Chief Justice Miller was ruling on an application from Wambui Otieno to disqualify Justices Nyarangi, Platt, and Gachuhi from hearing Wambui Otieno's appeal of the High Court ruling by Justice Bosire, on the grounds that they had earlier set aside the ruling of Justice Shields and were therefore biased against Wambui.

15. Egan, 183.

16. While writing the present book, the authors have come upon an extraordinary number of individuals who happened to be in Nairobi for business and pleasure during some portion of the litigation who had themselves become arrested by reports of the proceedings in the Kenya press or activities relating to it in the streets. At one panel of the African Studies Association Annual Meeting in Baltimore, in October 1990, seven members of the audience rose and offered extended remembrances and reflections of their own experience of the Otieno case. Many individuals retain precise details of what they experienced and express clear and developed opinions concerning the litigation. Of course, see correspondents such as Blaine Harden who reported for the *Washington Post* and has published a long account of the struggle (in *Africa: Dispatches from a Fragile Continent*, 95–129), and the more interesting though shorter report of Thomas A. Bass, *Camping with the Prince and Other Tales of Science in Africa* (Boston: Houghton Mifflin, 1990), 53–55, opening a chapter entitled "The Dudu World," a visit with, interview of, and report on Prof. Tom Odhiambo, the Kenyan entomologist. Note, as well, the reports contained within Michael M. J. Fischer's commentary at the close of this volume.

17. One is drawn, as in a walk through Karen—through the worlds of SM and Wambui and also Karen Blixen (Isak Dinesen)—to the debates in Kenya and North America concerning such books as James Fox's *White Mischief* and Beryl Markham's *West With the Night* and films such as Sydney Pollack's *Out of Africa*. "Speaking of Karen" demonstrates the complexity of this terrain, so recently the Otienos' neighborhood. While in 1986 the Academy of Motion Picture Arts and Sciences awarded seven Oscars to *Out of Africa* in its Academy Awards competition, Steven Spielberg's *Color Purple*, the other major nominee that also contained important "memoirs of Africa," failed to win a single award. The results were denounced by many Americans as well as by organizations representing African Americans, but also by President Daniel Arap Moi, who declared: "This is not entertainment and we are not amused. The days when Africa was regarded as a dark continent are long gone" (*Washington Post*, Thursday 3 April 1986, B2). *White Mischief*, in its book form, its film version, and in a more recent television account, explores the mysteries and sensationalism surrounding the murder of Lord Erroll on a road that, some five decades later, the Otienos called their own.

18. Y. K. Lubogo, *A History of Busoga* (Jinja, Uganda: East African Literature Bureau, 1960 and 1962), 58.

19. See David William Cohen, "Luo Camps in Seventeenth Century Eastern Uganda: The Use of Migration Tradition in the Reconstruction of Culture," *Sprache und Geschichte in Afrika* (SUGIA) 5 (1983): 145−75 (a paper originally prepared for and presented to the International Congress of Africanists, Addis Ababa, December 1973). See also, H. O. Nundu, *Nyuolruok Dhoud Ugenya* [*Ugenya Genealogies*] (Nairobi: Kenya Literature Bureau, 1987).

20. A number of witnesses in the High Court noted that when SM's brother was taken to Nyamila to be buried, SM slept in his car during the four days of attendance while the body awaited burial.

21. J. B. Ojwang and J. N. K. Mugambi, eds., *The S. M. Otieno Case: Death and Burial in Modern Kenya* (Nairobi: Nairobi University Press, 1989), 181−88.

22. See David William Cohen and E. S. Atieno Odhiambo, *Siaya: The Historical Anthropology of an African Landscape* (London: James Currey, 1989), 133−39.

23. This has been the concern of the Fifth and Sixth International Roundtables in Anthropology and History, the first in Paris in July 1986, convened by the Maison des Sciences de l'Homme, and the second held at Bellagio, Italy, in August and September 1989, at which a much briefer treatment of the Otieno case was presented. An associated interest (also on the conjuncture between guild and popular production of history and anthropology) includes the relationship between the early writings on the Gisu of Uganda by the anthropologist Jean La Fontaine and the historical writing of G. W. Wamimbi, a Gisu school teacher, which appear to have been composed out of La Fontaine's substantially ahistorical writings. See David William Cohen, "La Fontaine and Wamimbi: The Anthropology of 'Time-Present' as the Substructure of Historical Oration," in *Chronotypes*: The Construction of Time, edited by John Bender and David Wellbery (Stanford University Press: 1991) 205−25, 247−53; and the contrast in the production of Luo history early in the twentieth century and its guild version by mid-century as discussed in E. S. Atieno Odhiambo, "Gor Mahia Deconstructed," a paper presented at the Conference on Prophesy and Leadership in East Africa, Birkbeck College, London, 10−12 December 1989.

24. See David William Cohen and E. S. Atieno Odhiambo *Siaya: The Historical Anthropology of an African Landscape*, 7. The challenge here is not to claim that it is a "stifled" cultural debate or a rich one, but to examine the ways in which such a debate over the nature, authority, and meaning of culture proceeds as a complex event, still at one moment and in one arena, explosive and tumultuous in the next.

25. See, for example, James Clifford and George E. Marcus, eds., *Writing Culture: The Poetics and Politics of Ethnography* (Berkeley: University of California Press, 1986); James

Clifford, *The Predicament of Culture: Twentieth-Century Ethnography, Literature, and Art* (Cambridge, Mass.: Harvard University Press, 1988); Dominick LaCapra, "Rethinking Intellectual History and Reading Texts," in Dominick LaCapra and Steven L. Kaplan, eds., *Modern European Intellectual History: Reappraisals and New Perspectives* (Ithaca, N. Y.: Cornell University Press, 1982), 47–85; and George Lipsitz, *Time Passages: Collective Memory and American Popular Culture* (Minneapolis, University of Minnesota Press, 1990).

26. Sally Falk Moore, "Explaining the Present: Theoretical Dilemmas in Processual Ethnography," *American Ethnologist*, 14, 1 (1987, 727–36. In this call for attention to "current history," "process." and "change-in-the-making," Moore argues for a recognition of the important distinction between the practice, now quite developed in anthropology, of reading system out of a closely observed and described event and a more recently emergent practice of seeing within events the "struggles to construct orders and the actions that undo them. ..." (735).

## Chapter 2
## Orations of the Dead

1. Sean Egan ed., *S. M. Otieno: Kenya's Unique Burial Saga* (Nairobi: Nation Newspapers, c. 1987), 22.

2. In May 1983, President Moi announced at a public rally in Kisii, western Kenya, that "a certain powerful Minister" had been engaged in treasonable activities aimed at the overthrow of the constitutional government of Kenya. The call was taken up by the president's acolytes, and it reached a crescendo in Parliament when Cabinet Minister Elijah Mwangale named Charles Njonjo, Minister for Constitutional Affairs, as the *Msaliti* (traitor). Subsequently, a judicial commission was set up; it heard evidence and produced the *Report of the Judicial Commission Appointed to Inquire into Allegations Involving Charles Mugane Njonjo (former Minister for Constitutional Affairs and Member of Parliament for Kikuyu Constituency)* (Nairobi: Government Printer, 1984). The legal aspects of this Commission are discussed in J. B. Ojwang, *Constitutional Development in Kenya: Institutional Adaptation and Social Change* (Nairobi: ACTS Press, African Centre for Technological Studies, 1990) 1, 58–59.

3. Egan, 40.

4. The court removed itself to Westlands Cottage Hospital, Nairobi, for the purpose of taking testimony from Mr. Ong'ang'o, who lay in hospital following surgery.

5. Egan, 83. Mr. Ong'ang'o reported that the grave in Nyamila was being dug for the remains of Mr. Simon (Simeon) Odhiambo, who had died in Nairobi Hospital. Simon was a brother of SM.

6. Egan, 18.

7. Egan, 43.

8. Egan, 43.

9. Egan, 43. Wambui Otieno and other witnesses also remarked on SM's reaction to the death of his friend and clansman Hilary Ochola. Wambui: "In 1980, Mr. Hilary Ochola, manager of Bomas of Kenya died. But although he was a very close friend, Mr. Otieno never attended his funeral. ... The place of burial was changed. His wishes were that he be buried at his farm at Koru in Nyanza. But the Kager clan disputed it and buried him at his ancestral land at Simerro in Ugenya. All the Luo rituals were to be performed. My husband said he would not attend and would not allow me or the children to attend the burial" (Egan, 22).

10. Egan, 43.

11. Egan, 22. "Consent" here refers to the consent of the President of Kenya to permit burial at the Langata residence.

12. Egan, 22.

13. Egan, 22. See above for full quote.

14. On 22 January 1987, Wambui introduced into court a handwritten letter which she said SM had written in 1956 from India, which revealed, she claimed, tensions between SM and his relatives in western Kenya even then.

15. For a discussion of the significance of the burial of the placenta, see David William Cohen and E. S. Atieno Odhiambo, "Ayany, Malo and Ogot: Historians in Search of a Luo Nation," *Cahiers d'Etudes Africaines* 27 (1987): 3–4, 107–8, 269–86; see also our *Siaya*, Chapter 2.

16. Egan, 48.

17. Egan, 49.

18. Egan, 55. Joash also related to the court efforts to negotiate with Wambui immediately following SM's death, saying that he had visited her at Mr. Otieno's house at Langata five times. Joash: "She said she wanted us to make an understanding that Mr. Otieno be buried in Nairobi according to his wishes. I told her straight away that that was impossible because Luo-customs and traditions and Mr. Otieno's wishes, it couldn't happen. She became very wild and told me that I should leave if that was the case" (Egan, 55). It was reported, as well, that Wambui called the police to remove Joash from her property.

19. Egan, 34.

20. This notion of a distinctive category of "prominent" persons in the Kenya of the 1980s was raised into debate at different points in the S. M. Otieno litigation. See the *Daily Nation*, 17 April 1989, for a further refinement and elaboration of a category of prominent persons from Siaya.

21. Indeed, a number of witnesses beyond Wambui comment extensively on various financial and property dealings in which SM was involved. The discussion of the Otienos' wealth within the High Court proceeding reached its most poignant level when John Khaminwa, examining Wambui, asked "Did he [SM] at any one time say that the union [the Ger Union of Kenya, SM's clan association of which he was member [Number 18] should be responsible for [the costs of] his burial?" Wambui replied, "No. He had no need to. He was not a poor man for his family not to afford the burial!" The court transcript then noted: "This remark elicited a murmur in the audience" (Egan, 24).

22. The farm at Upper Matasia was registered in S. M. Otieno's sole name.

23. Identified in Land Registry as LR Alego Central/Nyalgunga/1983.

24. Egan, 24.

25. Egan, 33.

26. Egan, 5.

## Chapter 3
## Silences of the Living

1. Sean Egan, ed., *S. M. Otieno: Kenya's Unique Burial Saga* (Nairobi: Nation Newspapers, c. 1987), 94.

2. Reported in the *Weekly Review*, 20 February 1987, 7–8.

3. *Weekly Review*, 20 February 1987, 7–8.

4. *Weekly Review*, 20 February 1987, 8. Omolo Siranga's reaction to Wambui's declarations was also reported in the press. Siranga was said to take great exception to Wambui's announcements about the Umira Kager clan. He said that "[w]e have married *even white women*, but we have never seen anything like this before" [emphasis added].

5. See Timothy M. Njoya, *Human Dignity and National Identity* (Nairobi: Jemisik Cultural Books, 1987).

6. The "genealogy" of church-state relations is immensely complex and extremely important. There is also a valuable literature developing on the subject. See John Lonsdale, with Stanley Booth-Clibborn and Andrew Hake, "The Emerging Pattern of Church and State Co-operation in Kenya," in E. Fashole-Luke et al, eds., *Christianity in Independent Africa* (Bloomington and London: Indiana University Press, 1978), 267–84, for the 1960s; H.

Okullu, *Church and State in Nation-Building and Development* (Nairobi: Uzima Press, 1984) for the 1970s; and the numerous writings and interviews in the Kenyan press of the Rev. Timothy M. Njoya, for the 1980s. The tone of the dialogue for the 1990s has already been set, with the various church memoranda to the KANU (Kenya African National Union) reorganization committee as pace-setters of critique of party and state. See the *Weekly Review*, 10 August and 17 August 1990.

7. Egan, 181. To the best of our knowledge, she has not actually done so. One might also observe that there is no such court for the arbitration of personal law.

8. Lynn Thomas, of Johns Hopkins, has been working on a study of "women before the law in Kenya, 1964–1980," which reveals many of the risks and difficulties of generating a feminist debate or organizing debates around women's issues in Kenya. From a more polemical feminist position, Patricia Stamp, of York University, has completed a study of the Otieno case, focusing on the embattled nature of Wambui Otieno's situation within the case, before the law, and in Kenyan political life. Stamp's perspective in many ways joins—indeed extends—the view taken here of the structural, political, juridical, and rhetorical constraints on the constitution of a feminist position in Kenya in the 1980s, thus complementing Lynn Thomas's work on the period immediately before. Patricia Stamp has, in "Burying Otieno: The Politics of Gender and Ethnicity in Kenya." *Signs* 16/4, 1991, 808–45 detailed this assault on Wambui Otieno's credit during and after the litigation.

9. Under examination by Khaminwa, Wambui declared: "I joined several political organisations and particularly Mau Mau in 1953. I fought for independence and this judiciary. . . . I was detained for three years . . . I've held several posts in women organisations in Kenya and abroad. In 1969, I was the first woman to run for the Langata parliamentary seat" (Egan, 18).

10. (Chelagat Mutai, "Still Committed to the Struggle" [an interview of Wambui Otieno], April 1979, 10–12. We are grateful to Lynn Thomas for bringing this interview to our attention. Patricia Stamp has produced a more extended treatment of what she views as Wambui's embattled feminist position. The discussion of intermarriage in Kenya is an interesting one. Many observers of the S. M. Otieno litigation fix as its source the conditions and tensions produced by a rare, if not unique, case of intermarriage. The case was used by many to invoke a lesson on the perils of courtship and marriage beyond one's ethnic group. On the other hand, the circumstances of SM and Wambui were constantly compared to an array of well-known examples of intermarriage that appeared less fraught with the tensions of the Otieno situation. And the Kenya press induced experts to comment on the future of intermarriage in Kenya. At least one authority, an historian (and one of the authors of the present text) pointed out that for hundreds of years prior to Wambui marrying SM, the people of Kenya had been actively intermarrying across ethnic and linguistic borders. See the *Sunday Nation*, 26 July 1987.

11. Patricia Stamp, "Burying Otieno: The Politics of Gender and Ethnicity in Kenya." *Signs* 16/4.

12. For the historical origins of the "Nairobi crowd," see Frank Furedi, "The African Crowd in Nairobi: Popular Movements and Elite Politics," *Journal of African History*, 14, 2 (1973), 279–90.

13. "Okola Skoch" is the nickname of Okola ka Yewa, one of the early labor migrants from Siaya to the Kenya coast. He was early celebrated for his fascination with things *"mzungu"* (foreign, European, Western) and still speaks Ki-Swahili with a Scottish accent. See Cohen and Odhiambo, *Siaya* 112–15, for a discussion of the early *jonanga* ("people of clothes"), including Okola Skoch.

14. Indeed, some voices suggested that Dr. Nyamodi, who through much of his life was an intimate friend of SM's, should not be buried until the completion of the rites for SM . . . that they should be "buried in order!" in the words of Mwalimu Charles Obonyo Sira, age-mate to both.

15. These quotes from reporters covering the Nyamodi funeral are taken from the *Weekly Review*, 20 February 1987. Oginga Odinga was, of course, one of the founders of the Luo Union (East Africa).
16. The organization had issued opinions on the circumstances of the case from early in January 1987. So, on the one hand, the petition campaign cannot be viewed as a spur-of-the-moment affair; on the other, the form and moment of the petition campaign seemed to draw heavily on the "progressive" remarks heard at the Nyamodi funeral.
17. Indeed, police were brought out to force members of the organization to take down booths and posters featuring Grace Ogot's photograph. Two women were arrested at this time.
18. According to one petition leader, the campaign posted a page from a newspaper that, coincidentally, included a story on the petition drive and Grace Ogot's picture from another story in adjoining columns. This caused distress to Mrs. Ogot who is said to have gone to the police with a demand to remove the posting.
19. President Moi's expression. One may point out that "feminine" virtues such as being "graceful" are in reality "virtues of subservience." See Jane Braaten, "Towards a Feminist Reassessment of Intellectual Virtue," *Hypatia* 5, 3 (Fall, 1990), 1–14. See also, Mary Daly, *Pure Lust: Elemental Feminist Philosophy*. (Boston: Beacon Press, 1984); and Sarah Lucia Hoagland, *Lesbian Ethics: Toward New Value* (Palo Alto, Ca.: Institute of Lesbian Studies, 1988).
20. Weekly Review, 6 March 1987, 2.
21. To assert a sense of continuity is not to offer, therefore, a critique of the recent work, which is of great value and power and based on quite remarkable research that has brought women substantially out of the shadows cast both by colonial and postcolonial authority and by humanistic and social-science research. At the same time, such research has repositioned and reframed the study of fields of social history and social science such as work, production, consumption, and health, and opened fields of study in the humanities concerned with voice, interpretation, and power.
22. In a recent work, Marianna Torgovnick, *Gone Primitive: Savage Intellects, Modern Lives* (Chicago: University of Chicago Press, 1990), has suggested continuities among women writers of ethnography addressing the "primitive" or exotic (235–38, 292n). She has also proposed a closer and more extended treatment of what she sees as a genre of writing by women about the "other."
23. Patricia Stamp ("Burying Otieno") suggests that such a feminist position was, in part, forced upon Wambui by her Luo adversaries, who sought to use issues of gender as a means for refurbishing their ethnic-group politics. See also Maria Nzomo, "The Impact of the Women's Decade on Policies, Programs, and Empowerment of Women in Kenya," *Issue*, 2 (Summer, 1989); 9–17.
24. For example, in his closing argument in the High Court, Kwach asserted that "Women are very migratory in nature. There are certain things that have acquired permanent status. You do not leave burial matters in charge of women" (Egan, 95).
25. Though the specific case came after their High Court battle had concluded.
26. Khaminwa might equally have conveyed the lesson—sometimes the stuff of joking and jesting among men in Kenya—of "man's *inescapability* from first marriage," a possible rejoinder to Kwach's postulation of women as migratory and thereby unqualified to direct the organization of, and be socially centered within, a husband's funeral.
27. J. B. Ojwang, "The S. M. Otieno Case and the Problems It Raises: An Introductory Note," Nairobi Faculty of Law Seminar, Death, Burial and Society: Social, Cultural and Legal Perspectives, 18 July 1987, 2.
28. Note that Wambui Otieno only spoke to her essential agenda following the announcement by the Court of Appeal that her claim to her husband's body had failed.
29. Work in progress. See also Luc Boltanski, *The Making of a Class: Cadres in French Society*, trans. Arthur Goldhammer (Cambridge: Cambridge University Press, 1987).
30. Egan, 86.

31. Popular song of George Ramogi, 1972.

Nene apari kod Ooko Bwana
Luka Omera,
Janam otera nyaka adonjo Rawila yaye ora, osiepna!
Od Luka ne wabudhe gi funde yaye omera!
Janam otera nyaka achopo ei ode, Bwore malo osiepna!
Be wapar maka Willy Ogada, yaye ora,
Janam orwaka ka wadonjo Kapango Bwore malo.
Janam orwaka ka wadonjo Kapango Bwore malo, osiepna!

32. See Cohen and Odhiambo, *Siaya*, 112.

33. Egan, 48.

34. Egan, 74.

35. These quotes are all from Siranga's testimony on 29 January 1987. Egan, 47.

36. Egan, 47.

37. Duncan Okoth-Okombo, "Semantic Issues," in J. B. Ojwang and J. N. K. Mugambi, eds., *The S. M. Otieno Case: Death and Burial in Modern Kenya* (Nairobi: Nairobi University Press, 1989), 93.

38. Okoth-Okombo, 93–94. For English-speaking Luo steeped in English history and the culture of the British Isles, the word *homestead* is perhaps most reflective of the meanings of *dala*, with its associations with yeomanry, cottages, rural gentry, the center of domestic life, and so forth.

39. E. E. Evans-Pritchard, "Luo tribes and clans," *Rhodes-Livingstone Journal* 7 (1949); 24–40.

## Chapter 4
## Living Bodies and Their Knowledge

1. Donald Anyasi Namireri, Messenger, Faculty of Arts, University of Nairobi, spoken to Professor Gideon S. Were, Dean, Graduation Day, 26 October 1973.

2. See Sean Egan, ed., *S. M. Otieno: Kenya's Unique Burial Saga* (Nairobi: Nation Newspapers, c. 1987), 22.

3. See, for example, Kenneth King and Ahmed I. Salim, eds., *Kenya Historical Biographies* (Nairobi: East African Publishing House for the Department of History, 1971) and B. E. Kipkorir, ed., *Biographical Essays on Imperialism and Collaboration in Colonial Kenya* (Nairobi: East African Literature Bureau, 1980).

4. See, for examples of important work on an emergent Kenyan urban middle class defining itself out of and against the world of ordinary folk, Janet M. Bujra, "Women 'entrepreneurs' of early Nairobi," *Canadian Journal of African Studies* 9 (1975); 213–34; Luise White, "A Colonial State and an African Petty Bourgeoisie: Prostitution, Property, and Class Struggle in Nairobi, 1936–1940," in Frederick Cooper, ed., *Struggle for the City: Migrant Labor, Capital, and the State in Urban Africa* (Beverly Hills, Calif.: Sage, 1983), 167–94; Nikki Nelson, "'Women must help each other': The operation of personal networks among Busaa Brewers in Mathare Valley, Kenya," in Patricia Caplan and Janet Bujra, eds., *Women United, Women Divided* (Bloomington and London: Indiana University Press, 1979), 77–98. See also Gavin Kitching, *Class and Economic Change in Kenya: The Making of an African Petite-Bourgeosie, 1905–1970* (New Haven: Yale University Press, 1980); and Philip Amis, "Commercialized Rental Housing in Nairobi, Kenya," in Carl V. Patton, ed., *Spontaneous Shelter, International Perspectives and Prospects* (Philadelphia: Temple University Press, 1988), 235–57.

5. See the writings of Marjorie Oludhe Macgoye, including *Coming to Birth* (Nairobi and London: Heinemann, 1983), *Present Moment* (London: Heinemann, 1986), and *Street Life* (Nairobi: Heinemann, 1987); also, Eric Onstad, "The History of the Nairobi Street Hawkers" (M. A. Thesis, Department of History, University of Nairobi, 1990). See also

Frank Furedi, "The African Crowd in Nairobi: Popular Movements and Elite Politics," *Journal of African History*, 14, 2 (1973); 275—90. And there are important life histories of the so-called faceless and powerless in South Africa. For example, see Ted Matsetela, "The Life Story of Nkgono Mma-Pooe: Aspects of Sharecropping and Proletarianization in the Northern Orange Free State, 1890—1930," in Shula Marks and Richard Rathbone, eds., *Industrialization and Social Change in South Africa* (Harlow, Essex, U.K.: Longman Group, 1982), 212—37; and Charles van Onselen, "Race and Class in the South African Countryside: Cultural Osmosis and Social Relations in the Sharecropping Economy of the South-Western Transvaal, 1900—1950," *American Historical Review*, 95, 1 (1990); 99—123 (the life of Kas Maine).

6. For a comparable situation of such production of knowledge by the Luo who were resident and working in Uganda, see Cohen and Odhiambo, *Siaya*, 47—49.

7. American audiences have recently witnessed a parallel opening of the lives of servants within the prosecutions of Imelda Marcos and Leona Helmsley in New York.

8. In his summing up before the High Court, Richard Kwach attempted to dispose of a number of Khaminwa's witnesses as ". . . a rug-tag [*sic*] of witnesses — one woman who can't spell her husband's name, a vegetable seller, a labourer, a 16-year old child. . . . Would a man of 55 years, a man of Otieno's standing, condescend to speak to a 16-year old child. . . . My lord, a man is judged by his peers, men and women of one's class. If you would like to know about me, don't ask my gardener" (Egan, 95). Paradoxically, as we shall see below, it was to be Kwach's most plebeian witness who proved to be most credible in Justice Bosire's eyes.

9. Richard F. Shepard draws this observation from an unusual and evocative "reading" of an old *New York Times* crossword puzzle that he found, which was constructed in terms of the events and meanings of its time, 1942. See "About Men," *New York Times Magazine*, 30 September 1990, 46.

10. That it is possible to write their history is demonstrated powerfully in work on South Africa. See footnote 5, above.

11. Egan, 42.

12. Egan, 95. This is reminiscent of Gaby Omolo's elocution of 1970:
"Aa, wod mama
Ndalo ma nene wasomo kodi Rang'ala
To ibeto kuon gi obambo abeta ni,
Sani diluonggi mana in Rubbish?"
"Ah, son of my mother
When we were in boarding school with you at Rang'ala
You used to clear *ugali* and dried fish with a keen appetite
How can you turn around now and call them Rubbish?"

13. With due acknowledgment and respect to the late historian, critic, and statesman, C. L. R. James, *At the Rendezvous with Victory: Selected Writings* (London: Allen and Busby, 1984).

14. In his closing argument, Kwach argued: "It has also been suggested that when Otieno and Wambui visited Siaya, they used to carry their water. I would hate anyone to think that I would do that." Justice Bosire then intervened to ask, "But what if you are not sure that the water you find there is pure and good for drinking?" And Kwach replied, "My lord, I would like to tell this court something. When I stand at my home, I can see Otieno's home across the river which separates us. We have been drinking from this river from time immemorial." Bosire: Do you boil it first or what? You might suffer from bilharzia or other water-borne diseases?" Kwach: "Look at me. I have no problems?" (Egan, 96).

15. Egan, 41. Here one notes the ordinary interrogating the mighty, reminiscent of Christopher Hill's work, *The World Turned Upside Down: Radical Ideas During the English Revolution* (London: Temple Smith, 1972).

16. Mama Koko said that she did not speak Dholuo. Richard Kwach focused on this point to impugn her memory of conversations at the funerals at Nyalgunga in Siaya.

17. Dr. Yusuf Nzibo, personal communication.

18. Egan, 41. One is reminded of the witness in the Njonjo inquiry, K. Wakori, who remarked when asked where individuals sat as they ate the pork and eggs that former Attorney General Charles Njonjo meted out — "from the generosity of his heart" — to his drivers and support staff for breakfast: "Heh! How can you sit at Njonjo's table?!"

19. The Luo broadcasting service of the Voice of Kenya has had, over the years, a "signature tune":

| | |
|---|---|
| "Ng'ato to en ng'ato | A person is a person |
| Ma kata ineno ni ochalo nade | However mean he looks |
| Dhano to en dhano | His Being is Being |
| Ka ma noyikee ni mana tie | He will always have |
| | a place wherein to be buried." |

See Cohen and Odhiambo, *Siaya*, 119–20.

20. Egan, 153.

21. Officially the case is known as Virginia Edith Wambui Otieno *v.* Joash Ochieng' Ougo and Omolo Siranga. The Bosire judgment was an interim one. The case was appealed by Wambui to the Court of Appeal, Kenya's highest judicial authority, which ruled that Otieno shall be buried at Nyamila village, Nyalgunga, Alego, in Siaya.

22. Bosire, in Egan, 111.

23. Bosire, in Egan, 110.

24. One might draw a comparison between Justice Bosire's evaluation of different forms of authority and James Clifford's discussion of the mobilization of argument in the case of Mashpee Tribal Council v. New Seabury *et al.*, in the United States Federal Court, which also involved transformation of personal experience and scholarly expertise into argument. See James Clifford, *The Predicament of Culture* (Cambridge, Mass.: Harvard University Press, 1988).

25. See Egan, 79–82. There were other angles of view into Professor Odera's testimony before the High Court. A letter writer to the *Weekly Review* despaired: "The rare spectacle of a professor in our national university declaring publicly his belief in ghosts and spirits ... is a sad reality ... that we have to face in a society which, though fast changing to the modern, has a history deeply rooted in mysticism and belief in the supernatural" (1 May 1987, 2).

26. And, of course, other parts of Nyanza Province.

27. One recognizes, with Parker J. Palmer, the problematic inherent in trying to "recover the human" — read "sagacity" — through "science." See "A Critic of Academy Wins Applause on Campus," *New York Times*, 12 September 1990, B7.

28. Egan, 111.

29. Odera Oruka, in Egan, 79.

30. Through a comparison of two witnesses for the one side of the litigation, we are better positioned to constitute a close and extended surveillance of the two witnesses, counsel, and the judge (five men!). There are no substantive differences between the positions of Ong'ang'o and Odera Oruka but, in another sense, everything is different.

31. In his argument before the Court of Appeal, Khaminwa raised this very issue — that, given that Justice Bosire wrote his opinion "... of 33 well-typed pages, and with all the problems of secretaries to write a judgement in that short time between 1 p.m. on February 11 and 11 a.m. on February 13 ..." including time for reading 174 pages of transcript plus exhibits, Bosire may have adjudicated as he went along. "Alternatively, and I do not believe that this happened, the learned judge was writing the judgement as we went on with the case. If that is what happened, my lords it is extremely irregular" (Egan, 126).

32. For a description of *kotma*, court messengers in colonial Africa, see Chinua Achebe, *Things Fall Apart* (London: Heinemann Educational Books, 1958).
33. For a scholar's description of the functioning of these courts, see Bruce Berman, *Control and Crisis in Colonial Kenya: The Dialectic of Domination* (London: James Currey, 1990), 214–16.
34. Oral information from Mrs. Aidah Betty Odinga.
35. See further discussion in text, below. For a discussion of the tensions around notions of community and equity in Luo thought and practice, see *Siaya* chapter 6, particularly pp. 119–20: "Some rural people have sought to mediate some of the tension that has emerged because of this differentiation by reiterating the essential humanity of all beings; the sense of this is presented in the Voice of Kenya song [the signature tune from the Luo broadcasting service—'A person is a person, however mean he looks, his being is being, he will always have a place wherein to be buried']. . . . It is a refrain that reaches out for moral equity in circumstances where economic equity is not be dreamt of." For the text of the signature tune, see note 19, Chapter 4 above.
36. Some observers of, and participants in, the litigation saw the struggle as being one over the inheritance of S. M. Otieno's property and have variously interpreted different positions taken as gambits to grasp control of his property. For example, the datum that Wambui locked the gates to their Langata residence immediately upon word of SM's death is read as a ploy to give her time to remove some of his property from the range of access and view of visitors and, in one variant, to give herself time to find and destroy his will so that she could, in the intestate situation, impose her will upon the disposition of his remains and personal property.
37. Cohen and Odhiambo, *Siaya*, 87.
38. Perhaps for many Kenyans it—"prominent Luo"—was very much an unproblematic category. In a long article on Siaya (entitled "The citadel of elitism fails to match early promise"), the *Daily Nation* included a list of "prominent personalities" in a box labeled "Facts and Figures of the Area." The names of twenty-three such individuals are mentioned, including one of the authors of this book and several who played important roles in the struggle for SM's corpse. See *Daily Nation*, 17 April 1989.
39. And as noted above, in his summing up Kwach attempted to categorize and depose in one sweep the testimony of all of Khaminwa's "ordinary" witnesses.
40. Egan, 40.
41. Egan, 157.
42. *Reflections on the Revolution in France*, in E. J. Payne, ed., *Burke: Selected Works* (London: Clarendon Press, 1898) ii, 118.
43. Egan, 34.
44. Egan, 177.
45. See below, at the end of this chapter, a reconstructed "map" of the Jairo Ougo lineage of the Umira Kager from evidence that Wambui Otieno herself presented in court.
46. Egan, 27.
47. See Cohen and Odhiambo, *Siaya*, 92–93.
48. For a comparable role in another Kenya setting, see Peter D. Little, "Woman as Ol Pa'yian [Elder]: The Status of Widows among the Il Chamus (Njemps) of Kenya," *Ethnos*, 52, i–ii (1987); 81–102.
49. Egan, 177.
50. From Wambui Otieno's testimony as reported in the Egan text.
51. Helen is the mother of Mrs. Jane Obuong' Akoth, who with Joash Ochieng' first viewed the body of SM at the mortuary, and of Elijah Oduor Ogutu who was research assistant to one of the authors and, in a letter to the United States, March 1987, noted that "I am having difficulties right now since for several months we have been trying unsuccessfully to bury our uncle, the lawyer S. M. Otieno."

## Chapter 5
## The Productions of Culture

1. Sean Egan, ed., *S. M. Otieno: Kenya's Unique Burial Saga* (Nairobi: Nation Newspapers, c. 1987), 76–7.
2. Egan, 69.
3. Egan, 69. Later, during Khaminwa's cross-examination of Mayamba, Justice Bosire restated his question concerning the "reason for burying a man at his father's home, you don't have an explanation or you don't know?" And Mayamba reiterated, "It is a custom with us" (Egan, 71).
4. Egan, 70. Khaminwa asked, in response to Mayamba's comment about Ofafa's tie, "Has he haunted you personally?" Mayamba replied, "No, I don't belong to that clan." Ambrose Ofafa, a Luo city councillor from Alego, Kalkada, was gunned down by the Mau Mau in Kaloleni early in 1953 for, allegedly, opposing the movement. See Edith Miguda, "The Luo of Nairobi and Mau Mau" (M. A. Thesis, University of Nairobi, 1988).
5. Egan, 97.
6. See the presentation and discussion of the testimony of Charles Machina Ngari, Registrar of Langata Cemetery in Nairobi, in chapter 4 above; and Egan, 40.
7. Egan, 88.
8. Egan, 58.
9. With acknowledgment to Eric J. Hobsbawm and Terence Ranger, eds., *The Invention of Tradition* (Cambridge: Cambridge University Press, 1983).
10. Egan, 63.
11. See Nicola Swainson, *The Development of Corporate Capitalism in Kenya* (London: Heinemann, 1980), 180–81.
12. Paul Mboya, in his 1938 text on Luo culture, notes that "[o]n the morning of *tero buru* young men from all over the *piny* make a run through the wilderness, seeking to engage their enemies if they find them there, and even to kill in revenge if possible." ["Yawuoyi yuoro e kwonde duto mar piny, tero buche e thim mar dhi chulo kwor ka gikedo gi wasikgi e thim, kendo negogi ka nyalore."] See Paul Mboya, *Luo Kitgi gi Timbegi* ["A Handbook of Luo Customs"] (Nairobi: Equatorial Publishers, 1967), 112.
13. Egan, 64.
14. The Bible was also quoted as authority by both sides throughout the court proceedings. See list of texts cited in court p. 141.
15. Egan, 178.
16. Egan, 89. Khaminwa himself may have recognized the irony of this declaration. From 1984, President Moi had been actively promoting the teaching of Anthropology in Kenya's public universities as a "cornerstone of African culture." Nairobi, Egerton, and Moi Universities all have a Department of Anthropology, a remarkable turnabout from the immediate post-Uhuru years when many African intellectuals frowned upon the discipline for its having been a handmaiden of colonialism.
17. Equally, one sees resonance in the discussions of the much contested funeral of an Asante chief in Ghana in 1977. See Michelle Gilbert, "The Sudden Death of a Millionaire: Conversion and Consensus in a Ghanaian Kingdom," *Africa*, 58, 3 (1988) 291–314.
18. Egan, 21.
19. See, for example, Elspeth Huxley, *A New Earth* (Westport, Conn.: Greenwood Press, 1973).
20. See extended discussion on this point, chapter 4 above.
21. See Egan, 35.
22. Egan, 35. Kwach, here, was attempting to undermine Jairus's testimony by letting the young man elaborate a cold, distant, and uninformed perspective on his father's people yet risking the possibility that such a perspective, informed or not, would substantiate Wambui's view that she and SM had raised their family in a world very different from

that of Nyamila. Paradoxically, at other stages of the proceeding, as we have noted at a number of points, Kwach assumed Jairus's distant and cold gaze toward witnesses of Khaminwa who did not share his own class position.

23. Egan, 36.
24. Egan, 35.
25. Magdalene Ougo's husband was Jairo Ougo Oyugi, SM's father.
26. Egan, 28.
27. Egan, 79.
28. Khaminwa, of course, wove a complicated cross-examination of Odera, trying both to draw on the authority of the university professor and to challenge the effect of that expertise on his client Wambui's case. See the section on Odera Oruka's testimony, and Justice Bosire's reading of it, in chapter 4, above.
29. Egan, 81–82.
30. Egan, 88.
31. Egan, 35.
32. See Betty Potash, "Wives of the Grave: Widows in a Rural Luo Community," in Betty Potash, ed., *Widows in African Societies: Choices and Constraints* (Stanford: Stanford University Press, 1986), 45–65.
33. And, according to one authority, *they* chose the levir. See Paul Mboya, *Luo Kitgi*, 123.
34. See E. S. Atieno Odhiambo, "From Warriors to *Jonanga*: The Struggle Over Nakedness in Western Kenya," presented at the African Studies Center, Boston University, Seminar on Popular Culture and the Performing Arts, 11–12 May 1989, to appear in *Matatu* (Institut für Ethnologie und Afrikastudien, University of Mainz) 3, forthcoming; also, the Rev. N. Stam, "The Religious Conceptions of the Kavirondo," *Anthropos* 5 (1910). 359–62; Charles W. Hobley, "Nilotic Tribes of Kavirondo," *Eastern Uganda: An Ethnological Survey*, Occasional Papers, 1 (London: Royal Anthropological Institute, 1902), 26–32; and Paul Mboya, *Luo Kitgi*, 112–24.
35. This has also served as a convenient "exit route" for the modern African state. When one of the alleged coup plotters of 1982, Pancras Oteyo Okumu, was executed at Kamiti Prison, Nairobi, after his court-martial, the officers of the state handed over his clothes, not his body, to the first kin who came to visit him at Kamiti.
36. Recall Kwach's denunciation of ". . . a rug-tag [*sic*] of witnesses—one woman who can't spell her husband's name, a vegetable seller, a labourer, a 16-year old child. . . . Would a man of 55 years, a man of Otieno's standing, condescend to speak to a 16-year old child. . . ." (Egan, 95).
37. This is an example of *tero buru* songs improvised and performed by young Kenyans since the time of the Otieno litigation. This example was inscribed by Caroline and Michael Odhiambo.
38. Refers to the locust invasion of 1931, the year SM was born; his age cohort (*mbas*) was named "Bonyo" or "Obonyo".
39. Sesame.
40. River in Kisumu District. The Nyando floods every rainy season and hits the national news as "a Luo disaster." The phrase in the verse develops from a song sung in colonial classrooms: "River Congo was not navigable," which children hear their parents singing over beer and laughter as they talk about school days several decades back.
41. The hotel in Kisumu where SM was said to have retired during his visits to attend funerals at Nyalgunga.
42. A play on the linguistic difficulties of ordering food in restaurants along the "border" between Luo and English.
43. The Gor Mahia football team.
44. The leading scorer for the Gor Mahia football club during the 1980s.
45. "Toivo" is a Sheng (Nairobi dialect) word for *pombe*, or any local brew, for example, *muratina, kwete, mbare*.

Chapter 6
The Constitution of an African State

1. On his notion of core values for the Luo, see Oginga Odinga, *Not Yet Uhuru: An Autobiography* (New York: Hill and Wang, 1969), 11–14.

2. From a personal communication, May 1982.

3. It is illuminating to compare Odinga's argument from history with the words of Jairo Owino, an interpreter and witness before the Kenya Land Commission some fifty years earlier. "Some say that a house-boy or policeman or any native who is living outside the reserve and has got used to living outside it, and has money, should be allowed to buy land if he wants to. Others of us say that it has never been our custom to allow that sort of thing and it should not be allowed. We prefer that the people who have been living outside should return to the reserve." Great Britain: *Kenya Land Commission: Evidence and Memoranda*, vol. 2. Col. 191, 1933: Native Evidence, Nyanza Province, 2299.

4. Oginga Odinga explained his situation to a friend, Odinge Odera, in these terms: "There is no need for the Luo to be struggling for the body of S. M. Otieno. Otieno was lost a long time ago—*nene olal choon*! So you people are trying to rehabilitate a lost cause." Some guides to the evidently broader resonance of the Otieno case in Kenya are to be drawn from work under way by E. S. Atieno Odhiambo, Bruce Berman, and John Lonsdale on the debates—both popular and expert—concerning the nature and meaning of Mau Mau in Kenya and in the academic guilds more generally; from a most important paper by E. M. Simmonds–Duke, "Was the Peasant Uprising a Revolution? The Meanings of a Struggle over the Past," *Eastern European Politics and Societies*, 1, 2 (1987). 187–224, in which the expositions of several historians are peeled away layer by layer to reveal critical silences and hidden and low-voiced argument along with the broad forces and resonances that surround the productions of history within the alongside the academy. See also Katherine Verdery, *National Ideology Under Socialism: Identity and Cultural Politics in Ceausescu's Romania* (Berkeley, Ca.: University of California Press), 215–55. And, see the important work on the production of history in South Africa—most particularly, the work of Carolyn Hamilton on the struggles for the control and meaning of history, culture, and politics in the production and reception of the Shaka Zulu television series, for which see: "A Positional Gambit: Shaka Zulu and the Conflict in South Africa," *Radical History Review* 41 (Spring 1989), 5–31.

5. According to the reporter, Zachariah Odera claimed to be 120 years old. *Kenya Times*, Saturday, 26 August 1989.

6. *Kenya Times*, 26 August 1989.

7. *Weekly Review*, 29 May 1987, 13.

8. *Kenya Times*, 26 August 1989, 1. Omieri died at Kisumu Museum on 28 January 1989. In a curiosity of connective experience, this note was appended to the text on the day, 15 September 1990, that four living pythons were placed on display at the Piggly Wiggly Store, Norton, Virginia, in the United States, close to the Nyalgunga of one of the authors, and close by one of the sites of coauthoring of this book. A dollar purchased a view of the snakes. *These* relatives of Omieri had traveled more exhaustedly and, evidently, experienced capitalism at a much deeper level than the Nyakach python. It should be remarked that Norton, Virginia, was long noted for church congregations that actively incorporated snakes in church ritual—that is, up to the time prohibitive ordinances pushed such practices out of existence, or underground.

9. *Kenya Times*, 26 August 1989, 1.

10. *Weekly Review*, 3 February 1989, 18.

11. *The Standard*, 1 February 1989, 28.

12. For extended discussion on this point, see Cohen and Odhiambo, *Siaya*, chapters 2 and 3.

13. B. A. Ogot, "The Rev. Alfayo Odongo Mango," in Kenneth King and Ahmed Salim,

eds., *Kenya Historical Biographies* (Nairobi: East African Publishing House for the Department of History, University of Nairobi, 1971), 99–111. See also H. O. Nundu, *Nyuolruok Dhoud Ugenya* [Ugenya Genealogies] (Nairobi: Kenya Literature Bureau, 1987).

14. Siaya has been described as "the citadel of elitism" by one historian-journalist, Kwendo Opanga. *Daily Nation*, 17 April 1989, 12–13.

15. Such a breach, between the formal legal discourses on rights in property and inheritance, and the everyday world of improvisation, invention, and reinterpretation, is revealed at many points in the valuable collection of papers developing from a special conference on the S. M. Otieno case held at the University of Nairobi, 18 July 1987. See the collection of J. B. Ojwang and J. N. K. Mugambi, eds., *The S. M. Otieno Case: Death and Burial in Kenya* (Nairobi: Nairobi University Press, 1989).

16. From a perspective today, one sees that at a relatively young age SM entered into what was essentially a debt-and-dependency relationship with Tiras Waiyaki. Over four decades, SM's personal world shifted dramatically and SM was exercising patronage and generosity toward Tira's grandson, SM's stepson, also Tiras Waiyaki, who resided on SM's land at Upper Matasia.

17. Among those going to India were Josephat Njuguna Karanja, E. N. Gakuo, Omolo Agar, Joseph Gatuguta, Joseph Odero-Jowi, Adam Ogola, Isaac Omolo Okero, Polycarp Akoko Mboya (*Mudho*), and Zachariah Ogutu Nyamodi. See C. Ojwando Abuor, *White Highlands No More: A Modern Political History of Kenya*, vol. 1 (Nairobi: Pan African Researchers, n.d. [c. 1973]), 306–7.

18. As a seeming confirmation that colonial hegemonies may be virtually perpetual and may work their survival through many tortuous channels, one notes the argument at Justice Bosire's bench between the two lawyers, in which, the record notes, "Mr. Khaminwa complained to the judge that Mr. Kwach was asking him whether he studied law in India." Bosire then replied, "I wish you two were in my position. Why are you talking amongst yourselves? You are not saying things that can be understood so that I can give directions. When I started these proceedings, I said all of us are officers of the court and everyone is watching us" (Sean Egan, ed., *S. M. Otieno: Kenya's Unique Burial Saga* (Nairobi: Nation Newspapers, c. 1987), 34). On hegemony, see T. Jackson Lears, "The Concept of Cultural Hegemony: Problems and Possibilities," *American Historical Review*, 90, 3 (1985), 567–93.

19. In responding to Kwach's cross-examination, Wambui stated: "I had just come from detention. I was then running a hotel in Nairobi—the Princess Hotel, where I was one of the partners." Kwach then asked, "You were working at Princess Hotel." Wambui: "Yes, I was a partner and manager." (Egan, 28). The audience to Kwach's cross-examination recognized, with this portion of testimony, the innuendos about women working in bars and other demeaning employment.

20. In a report of an interview, published in the *Weekly Review*, 22 May 1987, Wambui was said to have met SM in the 1950s when visiting her father at the law courts, "but that it was only after his return from India in 1961, when they struck up a relationship. She had gone to seek her lawyer, the late Akoko Mboya, at the then Princess Hotel, and found him with a gentleman whom she had noticed at a bus stop on a number of occasions because he used to smile at her. She did not immediately recognise him as the young man who had worked with her father. . . ." In 1959, Wambui was arrested and fined eighty shillings in a Nairobi Magistrate's Court on Saturday, 28 March on charges of being a "rogue and vagabond" in collecting money for the Nairobi People's Convention Party at a pay parade at Nairobi City Council's administration center at Eastlands. She was observed collecting money from Council employees who had just been paid. See the *East African Standard*, 30 March 1959. The incident was cited by A. C. Onginpo-Ongutu, "The Role of the Nairobi People's Convention Party (NPCP) in the Nationalist Struggle for Uhuru in Kenya (1956–1960)," (University of Dar es Salaam,

University Examinations, 1971, Political Science, Paper 7 (a) Dissertation, March 1971), 21. This may have been the reason why she sought Akoko Mboya's legal assistance.

21. Details of the law careers of Kwach and Khaminwa are drawn from profiles published in the *Weekly Review*, 22 May 1987.

22. The *Weekly Review* 22 May 1987, reported that Kwach was a member of Nyamuot Union, "the association that unites the members of the Kanyamuot clan in the countryside" (13). In his own argument before the High Court, Kwach was, like all of his witnesses, careful to distinguish the notion of "home" from that of "house." In his closing argument, Kwach argued, "My lord, as we have been sitting in this court, I have been looking at the coat of arms. It features a cock and an axe. These are very necessary when someone wants to build a house and that is why they are carried by the first son. It is symbolic to us Luos. And that is why Lavington [Kwach's Nairobi residence] is my house and not my home" (Egan, 96).

23. From an oral communication, Peter Omondi Haggai.

24. Egan, 29.

25. See chapter 7, which follows.

26. That High Court battle, which lasted for some three months, was closed with a decision by the court, Justice Gachuhi ruling, to give Mburu's corpse to neither widow, but rather to his clan for burial at a "neutral site." The case is recorded as Camelina Ngami Mburu v. Mary Nduta and Two Others (H.C.C.C. No. 3209 of 1981).

27. See J. B. Ojwang. *Constitutional Development in Kenya: Institutional Adaptation and Social Change* (Nairobi: ACTS Press, African Centre for Technological Studies, 1990), 90–93. Not only was John Khaminwa one of the first individuals placed under detention orders by the Moi government, he found himself in detention once again in 1990, in the wave of "fresh" detentions that closed down upon lawyers and activitists speaking up for reform and change in the political party system in Kenya. See the *Weekly Review*, 13 July 1990.

28. See E. S. Atieno Odhiambo, "Democracy and the Ideology of Order in Kenya, 1888–1987," in Michael G. Schatzberg, ed., *The Political Economy of Kenya* (New York: Praeger, 1987); also, David Throup, "The Construction and Destruction of the Kenyatta State," in the same volume, 33–74; and P. Anyang' Nyong'o, "State and Society in Kenya: The Disintegration of the Nationalist Coalitions and the Rise of Presidential Authoritarianism, 1963–78," *African Affairs*, 88, 351 (April 1989), 299–51, and Joel D. Barkan and Michael Chege, "Decentralizing the State: District Focus and the Politics of Reallocation in Kenya," *Journal of Modern African Studies*, 27, 3 (1989), 431–53.

29. This is the point that Blaine Harden makes in *Africa: Dispatches from a Fragile Continent* (New York: W. W. Norton, 1990) "The verdict was almost certainly fixed by Kenya's president" (124)—but with the flimsiest of evidence and logic on Harden's part.

30. One is even further apprised of this as one notes that Justice Gachuhi of the Court of Appeal panel that heard the Otieno case was earlier, as a High Court judge, hearing the Mburu burial case in which John Khaminwa represented Mary Nduta; and then, in 1989, Richard Kwach, as Mr. Justice Kwach of the Court of Appeal, ruled—with Justices Nyarangi and Justice Platt (who heard Kwach represent the clan in the Otieno case)— that, in respect to another burial case. "There is individual, family, and clan interest and concern in the burial of a Kenya African. Departure from the customary procedures is not only incomprehensible but unacceptable." In this case, P. D. K. Maingi v. R. K. Maingi (Civil Appeal No. 66 of 1984), the Court of Appeal discounted the significance of a written will against what was recognized as the standing of "African customary law applying to an African." Curiously, the court remarked in Maingi v. Maingi that "the widow of a deceased African man has real interest in the burial place of her deceased husband . . .," but the judges did not view the issue in the way Wambui did, for they went on to explain what the basis of her interest was: "when she dies, her grave would

be located next to her deceased husband's." For a report of Maingi v. Maingi, see the *Daily Nation*, 6 August 1990, 14.

31. The vulgar, or déclassé, confronted with *culture*, high culture, are parodied in other lands as well. "Not having the right perceptions left one in the category of the Texas millionaire in the British Museum who complained to one of the guards, 'You know, I've looked at all of these pictures, and I sure don't see anything so great about them.' 'But sir,' replies the guard icily, 'the *pictures* are not on trial.'" From Frank D. McConnell, "The Lit-Crit Wars," *The Wilson Quarterly*, 14, 1 (Winter 1990), 104.

32. Personal communications, James A. Freedman and Gabrielle Spiegel. See also James A. Freedman, "Orality versus Textuality in the Reformation: The Origin and Influence of Textuality on Theological Perspectives in the Reformation" (Ph.D. Diss., Department of Religious Studies, Rice University, 1990). Additionally, Carlo Ginzburg, *The Cheese and the Worms: The Cosmos of a Sixteenth-Century Miller* (Baltimore: Johns Hopkins University Press, 1980), situates his subject, the miller Menocchio, as a reader of texts in the largely oral world of northern Italy in the sixteenth century.

33. See the important critical work of Brian V. Street, for example his "Literary Practices and Literacy Myths," in Roger Saljo, ed., *The Written World: Studies in Literate Thought and Action* (Berlin: Springer, 1988), 59—71).

34. There is an immense literature produced in Indian universities on Shakespeare. See, for example, S. Nagarajan and S. Viswanathan, eds., *Shakespeare in India* (Delhi: Oxford University Press, 1987).

35. There are certainly other entries into the study of such transnational cultural and intellectual experience in the period between the end of World War II and the "era of the new nations" of the 1960s. See, for one, David McCutchion, *Indian Writing in English* (Calcutta: Writers Workshop, 1969) and his brief portrait of Sudhin Ghose, the controversial Indian man of letters, whom McCutchion found in a London flat in 1957, in something of an exile. Or we can examine the lives of Salman Rushdie and V. S. Naipaul. In a new work, Michael M. J. Fischer and Mehdi Abedi, *Debating Muslims: Cultural Dialogues in Postmodernity and Tradition* (Madison, Wis.: University of Wisconsin Press, 1990), xxiii, and pp. 1—201 focus on the "resonances and dialogue across cultural traditions ..." that underlay the contemporary situation of "multilinguistic and multicultural interreference." The authors note that Jacques Derrida and other analysts of such a "postmodern" situation are themselves products of transnational, transcultural, conditions. Did SM and Okero and others from Kenya move within this world—in both its Indian and Kenyan settings of the 1950s and 1960s?

36. Of course, Shakespeare was also considered a requisite in the formation of the new elite of postwar colonial Africa. The recollected transcripts of Julius Nyerere and Milton Obote place them together within the performance of a student production of *Julius Caesar* at Makerere College in Uganda in 1949.

37. Jyotsna Singh, "Different Shakespeares: The Bard in Colonial/Postcolonial India," *Theatre Journal* 41, 4 (December 1989), 445—58. We are grateful to Kamran Ali for bringing this article to our attention.

38. The education of women in Kenya was long delayed. When Alliance Girls' High School was launched in the 1950s the emphasis was upon study of the Romantics rather than Shakespeare. "Beauty" was highly valued, and Okoth-Ogendo now Professor of Law, University of Nairobi, became—in the mid-1960s—the "Black Beauty" across the valley at the Alliance High School.

39. In his study of the 1977 United States Federal District Court case Mashpee Tribe v. New Seabury *et al.*, James Clifford could have been commenting somewhat presciently, on the Otieno case. "But doesn't the adversary system for producing recordable facts and durable judgements assume a mediating culture surrounding its theatrical confrontations? After all, the abstractly opposed viewpoints are resolved by the common sense

of a jury of 'peers.' And what if this shared culture and its common sense assumptions are precisely what is at issue in the proceedings?" "Identity in Mashpee," in Clifford, *The Predicament of Culture: Twentieth-Century Ethnography, Literature, and Art* (Cambridge, Mass.: Harvard University Press, 1988), 329. In still another setting, Justice Michael S. Stegman, rendering judgment on Winnie Mandela in a Johannesburg court—she was convicted of kidnapping and of being an accessory after the fact to assault with intent to commit grievous bodily harm—reflected on Mrs. Mandela's "remarkable absence of candor," and noted: "To imagine that all of this took place without Mrs. Mandela as one of the moving spirits is like trying to imagine 'Hamlet' without the Prince." As reported in the *New York Times*, 14 May 1991, A1, A7.

40. We are grateful to Professor Linda Gerstein, Haverford College, and especially to Mr. Hogie Hansen, Secretary of the College, for assistance on this point.

41. From a personal communication from one of the lecturers present at the Kabarak meeting with the president.

42. In July 1990, Imanyara was arrested, kept in solitary confinement for several weeks, and charged with the publication of a seditious magazine. He was released, pending trial on the charges, and the *Monthly* was banned at the end of September 1990 (see "Kenyan [sic] Bans a Journal That Upholds the Law," *New York Times*, 1 October 1990, A9). Once again on 2 March 1991, Imanyara was arrested and his offices searched (Reported by Jane Perlez in the *New York Times*, 3 March 1991, 8. Perhaps coincidentally, an adjoining article (in the Chicago edition) on evidence of the growing numbers of Kenyan women postponing or avoiding marriage, also by Perlez, cites both Imanyara and his wife Florence: "There is an inferiority complex among these men (citified Africans) that an educated women who can do what he can do is a threat,' said Mr. Imanyara, whose wife, Florence, said he was liberated because among other things he will enter the kitchen").

43. The *Weekly Review*, 3 August 1990, and his reiteration of his views, 24 August 1990.


## Chapter 7
## Owino Misiani's Lamentation, 1987

1. Popular song, "Otieno Waiko Nyalgunga" ("We must bury Otieno at Nyalgunga"), composed and sung by Owino Misiani, Orchestra Shirati Jazz (Nairobi: Wamenyo Bwana Otieko Weche label, Wamenyo Recording Company, P. O. Box 68118, Nairobi, Kenya, early 1987), 45 rpm, mono, in Luo; translated by E. S. Atieno Odhiambo.


## Conclusion

1. One might have found within the High Court building the simple proclamation: "The making of men is more important than the making of empires." It is, however, not found there but rather on a plaque in Harris Hall which contains the History Department, Northwestern University.

2. Caroline Walker Bynum, "Fast, Feast and Flesh: The Religious Significance of Food to Medieval Women," *Representations* 11 (1985), 1—25; Valie Export, "The Real and Its Double: The Body," *Discourse* 11, 1 (Fall-Winter 1988—89), 3—27; Emily Martin, *The Woman in the Body: A Cultural Analysis of Reproduction* (Boston: Beacon, 1987); and Mary Poovey, *Uneven Developments: The Ideological Work of Gender in Mid—Victorian England* (Chicago: University of Chicago, 1988). Also, Peter Stallybrass and Allon White, *The Politics and Poetics of Transgression* (Ithaca, N.Y.: Cornell University Press, 1986), 23—26. Perhaps still more importantly, see the writings of Charlotte Perkins Gilman (*Women and Economics* and *The Yellow Wallpaper*) and Tillie Olsen (*Silences*).

3. *The Cheese and the Worms: The Cosmos of a Sixteenth-Century Miller* (Baltimore, Johns Hopkins, 1980).
4. The authors are particularly grateful to Hans Medick who, over a number of years, has drawn attention to the importance of understanding the often complex interconnections between civil society and private spaces both removed from and connected to the workings of state and market. See Hans Medick and David Sabean, eds., *Interest and Emotion: Essays in the Study of Family and Kinship* (Cambridge: Cambridge University Press, 1984).
5. From an opening commentary presented to the PARSS Seminar, University of Pennsylvania, 27 April 1989.
6. This is not to exclude the possibility that such "tribal conflicts" have in fact been constructed by parties interested in the power that seems to reside around "defenses of civilization." See Marianna Torgovnick, *Gone Primitive: Savage Intellects, Modern Lives* (Chicago: University of Chicago Press, 1990) and Sally Price, *Primitive Art in Civilized Places* (Chicago: University of Chicago Press, 1989). No less an authority on Kenya than President Moi has declared that a multiparty political system in Kenya would mean a collapse into "tribalism."
7. Sally Falk Moore, *Social Facts and Fabrications* (Cambridge: Cambridge University Press, 1980), 11.

## Afterpiece

1. Thanks to Johannes Fabian and Ivan Karp for comments on my comment in first draft form.
2. Duncan Okoth-Okombo, "Semantic Issues," in J. B. Ojwang and J. N. K. Mugambi, eds., *The S. M. Otieno Case*, (Nairobi: Nairobi University Press, 1989), 89–97.
3. Joan Wallach Scott, *Gender and the Politics of History* (New York: Columbia University Press, 1988), 60.
4. bell hooks, *Yearning: Race, Gender and Politics* (Boston: South End Press, 1990), 76.
5. See p. 3.
6. In this light, it is interesting to note Siranga's progressive promotion in the course of this book. First identified as a "member of the clan", he then becomes chair of the burial committee and begins to interact with Wambui and to chair meetings. Siranga is next called "head of the clan", later simply identified as "an official of the Umira Kager Association and Ger Union."
7. See J. W. van Doren, "African Tradition and Western Common Law: A Study in Contradiction," J. B. Ojwang and J. N. K. Mugambi, eds., *The S. M. Otieno Case: Death and Burial in Modern Kenya* (Nairobi: Nairobi University Press, 1989), 129.
8. James Clifford, "Identity In Mashpee," in James Clifford, *The Predicament of Culture: Twentieth-Century Ethnography, Literature, and Art* (Cambridge, Mass.: Harvard University Press, 1988), 310.
9. See *Weekly Review*, 19 October 1990, 26–28, and *Weekly Review*, 26 October 1990, 17–18. Ironically, Mr. Justice Richard Otieno Kwach was one of the commissioners and questioned the Ominde clan's representation.
10. See p. 95.
11. Ernest Renan, "Qu'est-ce qu'une nation?," in H. Psichari, ed., *Oeuvres complètes de Ernest Renan, I* (Paris: Calman-Lévy, 1947), 904.
12. Benedict Anderson, *Imagined Communities: Reflections on the Origin and Spread of Nationalism* (London: Verso and New Left Books, 1983).
13. Michael G. Whisson, "The Journeys of the Joramogi," East African Institute of Social Research conference paper, Makerere University, 1962, mimeo.
14. These Kikuyu debates are discussed in chapter 7 of Bruce Berman and John Lonsdale,

*Unhappy Valley: Clan, Class and State in Kenya* (London: James Currey, 1991); for the lives of some female Kenyans of the time see, Luise White, *The Comforts of Home: Prostitution in Colonial Nairobi* (Chicago and London: University of Chicago Press, 1990).

15. H. K. Wachanga, with Robert Whittier, *The Swords of Kirinyaga: The Fight for Land and Freedom* (Nairobi: East African Literature Bureau, 1975), 43.

16. *Kenya Land Commission Evidence, I* (Nairobi: Government Printer, 1933), 638–39.

17. David M. Gitari, *Let the Bishop Speak* (Nairobi: Uzima Press, 1988), 40.

18. For examples, see Agnes Chepkwony, *The Role of Non-Governmental Organizations in Development: A Study of the National Christian Council of Kenya, 1963–1978* (Uppsala: Studia Missionalia Uppsaliensia, xliii, 1987), 156, 274–75.

19. David William Cohen and E. S. Atieno Odhiambo, *Siaya: The Historical Anthropology of an African Landscape* (London: James Currey, 1989), 34, 39.

20. Appeals Court judgment, Casebook, Case No. 88, p. 344, cited in E. Cotran, "The Future of Customary Law in Kenya," in J. B. Ojwang and J. N. K. Mugambi, eds., *The S. M. Otieno Case: Death and Burial in Modern Kenya* (Nairobi: Nairobi University Press, 1989), 161.

21. P. W. Kariuki, citing the *Viva* magazine article "Wambui's Defeat is a Defeat for Women." In "Loss and Bereavement," in J. B. Ojwang and J. N. K. Mugambi, *The S. M. Otieno Case: Death and Burial in Modern Kenya* (Nairobi: Nairobi University Press, 1989), 58.

22. David William Cohen and E. S. Atieno Odhiambo, "The Surveillance of Men: Notes Towards an Essay on Gender in Kenya," paper presented to "The Male Gender in Africa" workshop at the University of Minnesota, May 1990, 18.

23. Present volume, pp. 45–6.

# TEXTS CITED IN COURT

(The texts are cited here as presented in court transcripts.)
Achebe, Chinua, *Things Fall Apart*
Allen, *Law in the Making*
Allott, *Judicial and Legal System in Africa*
Allott, *Essays on African Law*
Arnold, *New Essence in African Law*
*Black's Law Dictionary*
Blackstone, *Commentaries on Law*
Chanock, Martin, *Law, Custom and Social Order*
Chesire, G. C., *The Private International Law*
Cotran, Eugene, *Restatement of African Law*
Denning, Lord, *The Family Story*
Denning, Lord, *Landmarks of Law*
Dyers, *Jurisprudence*
Eliot, George, —————
*Farmers Magazine*
Ford, Lena Guilbert, "...," [a limerick]
"former chairman of the Ger clan," —————
Gardner, Earl Stanley, *Perry Mason* ...
Gertzel, C., et. al., *Government and Politics in Kenya*
Goldsworthy, D., *Tom Mboya: The Man Kenya Wanted to Forget*
Halsbury, *Laws of England*
Hollis, A. C., *The Nandi*
Hobley, C. W., *Bantu Beliefs and Magic*
Kuloba, Richard, *Judicial Hints and Civil Procedures*
Leakey, L. S. B., *The Southern Kikuyu Before 1903*, vol. 2
Malusu, Joseph, *The Luhya Way of Death*
Manchester, H. A., *Machinery of Justice*
Massam, G. A., *The Cliff-Dwellers of Kenya*
Mbiti, J. S., *Love and Marriage in Africa*
Mbiti, J. S., *Introduction to African Religion*
Mbuya, P., *Luo kitgi gi Timbegi*
Middleton, John, *The Kikuyu and the Kamba*

Moi, Daniel Arap, *Kenya Africa Nationalism*
*The New Testament*
Ocholla-Ayayo, A. B. C., *Traditional Ideology and Ethics*
Odera Oruka, Henry, *Punishment in Traditional Africa*
Odera Oruka, Henry, *Thoughts of Traditional Kenyan Sages*
*The Old Testament*
Ominde, S. H., *The Luo Girl*
Otunga, Maurice Cardinal, *The Catholic Church in Western Kenya Oxford English Dictionary*
Paden, John, *The African Experience*
Pala Okeyo, Achola, "The Participation of Women in Kenya Society"
p'Bitek, Okot, *Song of Lawino*
p'Bitek, Okot, *Song of Ocol*
Peristiany, J. G., *The Social Institutions of the Kipsigis*
Philips, Arthur, and Henry E. Morris, *Marriage Laws in Africa*
Routledge, *With a Prehistoric People*
Shakespeare, William, *Julius Caesar*
Shaw, Bernard, ———
Snell, G. S., *Nandi Customary Law*
United Nations, *Legal Status of Rural Women*
*Viva* [magazine]
Wako, D. M., *The Western Abaluhyas and their Proverbs*
Wanjala, C., ed., *Standpoints in African Literature*
Welbourn, F. B., and B. E. Kipkorir, *The Marakwet of Kenya*
Whisson, Michael, *Change and Challenge*
Wilde, Oscar, *Book of Catholic Quotations*
Woodward, Llewellyn., *The Age of Reform*
?———, *The African Christian Marriage*
?———, *Aid to Bible Understanding*
?———, *The Business Encyclopaedia*
?———, *Changing Law and Law Reform in Ghana*
?———, ——— [a dictionary]
?———, *Dictionary of Quotations*
?———, *The Encyclopaedia of Forms and Precedences*
?———, *A History of Thomas Jefferson*
?———, *An Introduction to the Legal Systems of East Africa*
?———, *Legal Adviser*

# BIBLIOGRAPHY

Abe, Toshisharu. "The Concept of 'Chira' and 'Dhoch' among the Luo: Transition, Deviation and Misfortune." In *Themes in Sociocultural Ideas among Six Ethnic Groups in Kenya: The Gusii, The Isukha, the Logooli, the Kipsigis, the Luo, and the Kamba*, edited by Nobuhiro Nagashima, 127–40. Tokyo: Hitoshubashi University, 1979.

———. "Preliminary Report on Jachien among the Luo of South Nyanza," Unpublished report, n.d.

Abuor, C. Ojwando. *White Highlands No More: A Modern Political History of Kenya.* Vol. 1. Nairobi: Pan African Researchers, n.d. [c. 1973].

Achebe, Chinua. *Things Fall Apart.* London: Heinemann Educational Books, 1958, c. 1957.

Amis, Philip. "Commercialized Rental Housing in Nairobi, Kenya." In *Spontaneous Shelter, International Perspectives and Prospects*, edited by Carl V. Patton, 235–57. Philadelphia: Temple University Press, 1988.

Amuka, Peter S. O. "Ngero As A Social Object." Master's Thesis, University of Nairobi, 1980.

———. "A Preliminary Discussion of the Literary Value of Two *Dodo* Songs by Obudo of Homa Bay." UNESCO Seminar on Oral Traditions, Past Growth and Future Development in East Africa. Kisumu, Kenya, 1979.

———. "Towards a Synthesis of the Oral and Written Text: A Reading of Two *Dodo* Songs." *Passages* 1 (1991), 1.

Anderson, Benedict. *Imagined Communities: Reflections on the Origin and spread of Nationalism.* London: Verso and New Left Books, 1983.

Anyumba, H. Owuor. "The Historical Dimensions of Life-Crisis Rituals. Some Factors in the Dissemination of *Juogi* Beliefs among the Luo of Kenya up to 1962." Paper presented at the Limuru Conference on the Historical Study of East African Religions, 26 June 1974.

———. "The Making of a Lyre Musician." *MILA* 1, 2 (1970), 28–33.

———. "Spirit Possession among the Luo of Central Nyanza, Kenya (1953 entry for Arts Research Council Prize Essay)." *Occasional Papers in African Traditional Religion*, Makerere University, Department of Religious Studies and Philosophy, 3 (November 1971), 1–46.

Ayany, Samuel. *Kar Chakrouk Mar Luo.* Kisumu Kenya: Equatorial Publishers, 1952.

Ayot, Henry O. *Historical Texts of the Lake Region of East Africa.* Nairobi: Kenya Literature Bureau, 1977.

———. *A History of the Luo-Abasuba of Western Kenya from A.D. 1760–1940.* Nairobi: Kenya Literature Bureau, 1979.

Barkan, Joel D., and Michael Chege. "Decentralizing the State: District Focus and the Politics of Reallocation in Kenya." *Journal of Modern African Studies* 27, 3 (1989), 431–53.

Bass, Thomas A. *Camping with the Prince and Other Tales of Science in Africa.* Boston:

Houghton Mifflin, 1990.

Berg-Schlosser, Dirk. *Tradition and Change in Kenya.* Paderborn, Germany: Ferdinand Schoningh, 1984.

Berman, Bruce J. *Control and Crisis in Colonial Kenya: The Dialectic of Domination.* London: James Currey, 1990.

Berman, Bruce J., and John Lonsdale, *Unhappy Valley: Clan, Class and State in Kenya.* London: James Currey, 1991.

Bettelheim, Bruno. "Freud's Vienna." *The Wilson Quarterly* 14, 2 (Spring 1990), 68–77.

Blount, Ben G. "Agreeing to Agree on Genealogy: A Luo Sociology of Knowledge." In *Sociocultural Dimensions of Language Use,* edited by Mary Sanches and Ben G. Blount, 117–35. New York: Academic Press, 1975.

———. "Acquisition of Language by Luo Children." Ph.D. Diss., University of California, Berkeley, 1969.

———. "Aspects of Luo Socialization." *Language and Society* 1 (1979).

Blount, Ben G., and Richard T. Curley. "The Southern Luo Languages: A Glottochronological Reconstruction." *Journal of African Languages* 9, 1 (1970), 1–18.

Boltanski, Luc. *The Making of a Class: Cadres in French Society,* translated by Arthur Goldhammer. Cambridge: Cambridge University Press, 1987.

Braaten, Jane. "Towards a Feminist Reassessment of Intellectual Virtue," *Hypatia* 5, 3 (Fall 1990), 1–14.

Brodzki, Bella, and Celeste Schenk, eds. *Life/Lines: Theorizing Women's Autobiography.* Ithaca: Cornell University Press, 1988.

Bujra, Janet M. "Women 'entrepreneurs' of early Nairobi." *Canadian Journal of African Studies* 9 (1975), 213–34.

Burke, Edmund. *Reflections on the Revolution in France.* In *Burke: Selected Works,* edited by E. J. Payne. London: Clarendon Press, 1898.

Butterman, Judith M. "Luo Social Formation in Change: Karachuonyo and Kanyamkago, c. 1800–1945." Ph.D. Diss., Syracuse University, 1979.

Bynum, Caroline Walker. "Fast, Feast and Flesh: The Religious Significance of Food to Medieval Women." *Representations* 11 (1985), 1–25.

Chanock, Martin. *Law, Custom, and Social Order: The Colonial Experience in Malawi and Zambia.* New York: Cambridge University Press, 1985.

Clifford, James. *The Predicament of Culture: Twentieth-Century Ethnography, Literature, and Art.* Cambridge, Mass.: Harvard University Press, 1988.

Clifford, James, and George E. Marcus, eds. *Writing Culture: The Poetics and Politics of Ethnography.* Berkeley: University of California Press, 1986.

Cohen, David William. "Doing Social History from Pim's Doorway." In *Reliving the Past: The Worlds of Social History,* edited by Olivier Zunz, 191–235. Chapel Hill: University of North Carolina Press, 1985.

———. "The Face of Contact: A model of a Cultural and Linguistic Frontier in Early Eastern Uganda." In *Nilotic Studies: Proceedings of the International Symposium on Languages and History of the Nilotic Peoples, Cologne, January 4–6, 1982,* edited by Marianne Bechhaus-Gerst and Rainer Vossen Rainer, 341–55. Berlin: Dietrich Reimer Verlag, 1983.

———. "Food Production and food Exchange in the Precolonial Lakes Plateau Region." In *Imperialism, Colonialism, and Hunger: East and Central Africa,* edited by Robert I. Rotberg, 1–18. Lexington, Mass. Lexington Books, 1983.

———. "La Fontaine and Wamimbi: The Anthropology of 'Time-Present' as the Substructure of Historical Oration." In *Chronotypes: The Construction of Time,* edited by John Bender and David Wellbery. Stanford, Calif.: Stanford University Press, 1991, 205–25, 249–53.

———. "Luo Camps in Seventeenth Century Eastern Uganda: The Use of Migration Tradition in the Reconstruction of Culture." *Sprache und Geschichte in Afrika (SUGIA)* 5 (1983), 145–75 [a paper originally prepared for and presented to the International Congress of

Africanists, Addis Ababa, December 1973].

———. "Natur und Kampf—Uberfluss und Armut in der Viktoriasse-Region in Afrika von 1880 bis zur Gegenwart." *SOWI* 14, 1 (1985), 10−23.

———. "Pim's Work: Some Thoughts on the Construction of Relations and Groups—the Luo of Western Kenya." Paper presented to a conference on "The History of the Family in Africa," School of Oriental and African Studies, London, September 1981.

———. "The Political Transformation of Northern Busoga." *Cahiers d'Etudes Africaines* 22, 3−4 (1982), 465−88.

———. "The River-Lake Nilotes from the Fifteenth to the Nineteenth Century." In *Zamani: A Survey of East African History, New Edition*, edited by B. A. Ogot, 136−49. Nairobi: East African Publishing House and Longman, 1974.

———. *Womunafu's Bunafu: A study of Authority in a Nineteenth Century African Community.* Princeton: Princeton University Press, 1977.

Cohen, David William, and E. S. Atieno Odhiambo. "Ayany, Malo and Ogot: Historians in Search of a Luo Nation." *Cahiers d'Etudes Africaines* 27, 3−4, 107−8 (1987), 269−86.

———. *Siaya: The Historical Anthropology of an African Landscape.* London: James Currey; Nairobi: Heinemann Kenya; Athens, Ohio: Ohio University Press, 1989.

———. "The Surveillance of Men: Notes Towards an Essay on Gender in Kenya." Paper presented to "The Male Gender in Africa" workshop at the University of Minnesota, May, 1990.

Comaroff, Jean. *Body of Power, Spirit of Resistance.* Chicago: University of Chicago Press, 1985.

Cooper, Frederick, ed. *Struggle for the City: Migrant Labor, Capital, and the State in Urban Africa.* Beverly Hills, Calif.: Sage, 1983.

Cotran, E. "The Future of Customary Law in Kenya." In *The S. M. Otieno Case: Death and Burial in Modern Kenya*, edited by J. B. Ojwang and J. N. K. Mugambi, 148−63. Nairobi: Nairobi University Press, 1989.

Crazzolara, J. P. *The Lwoo.* 3 vols. 1950 and 1951. Verona: Editrize Nigrizia, 1954.

Dinesen, Isak (Karen Blixen). *Out of Africa.* New York: Random House, 1937.

DuPre, Carole E. *The Luo of Kenya: An Annotated Bibliography.* Washington, D.C.: Institute for Cross-cultural Research, 1968.

Egan, Sean, ed. *S. M. Otieno: Kenya's Unique Burial Saga.* Nairobi: Nation Newspapers, 1987.

Evans-Pritchard, E. E. "Ghostly Vengeance among the Luo of Kenya." *Man* 50, 133 (1950), 86−7.

———. "Luo Tribes and Clans." *Rhodes-Livingstone Journal* 7 (1949), 24−40.

———. *The Position of Women in Primitive Societies and Other Essays in Social Anthropology.* New York: The Free Press, 1965.

Export, Valie. "The Real and its Double: The Body." *Discourse* 11, 1 (fall-winter, 1988−89), 3−27.

Fearn, Hugh, *An African Economy: A Study of the Economic Development of Nyanza Province of Kenya, 1903−1953.* London: Oxford University Press, 1956.

Feierman, Steven. *Peasant Intellectuals: Anthropology and History in Tanzania.* Madison, Wis.: University of Wisconsin Press, 1990.

Fischer, Michael M. J., and Mehdi Abedi. *Debating Muslims: Cultural Dialogues in Postmodernity and Tradition.* Madison, Wis.: University of Wisconsin, 1990.

Forrest, Leon. "Spiritual Flight of Female Fire." *Passages* 1 (1991), 5.

Freedman, James A. "Orality versus Textuality in the Reformation: The origin and Influence of Textuality on Theological Perspectives in the Reformation." Ph.D. Diss., Rice University, Houston, 1990.

Furedi, Frank. "The African Crowd in Nairobi: Popular Movements and Elite Politics." *Journal of African History* 14, 2 (1973), 275−90.

Gilbert, Michelle. "The Sudden Death of a Millionaire: Conversion and Consensus in a

Ghanaian Kingdom." *Africa* 58, 3 (1988), 291–314.

Ginzburg, Carlo. *The Cheese and the Worms: The Cosmos of a Sixteenth-Century Miller.* Baltimore: Johns Hopkins University Press, 1980.

Gitari, David M. *Let the Bishop Speak.* Nairobi: Uzima Press, 1988.

Goldfarb, Alan. "A Kenyan Wife's Right to Bury Her Husband: Applying the Convention on the Elimination of All Forms of Discrimination Against Women." *ILSA Journal of International Law* 14, 1 (1990), 1–21.

Great Britain. *Kenya Land Commission: Evidence and Memoranda.* Vol 2. Col. 191. Native Evidence, Nyanza Province, 1933.

Hamilton, Carolyn. "A Positional Gambit: Shaka Zulu and the Conflict in South Africa." *Radical History Review* 41 (Spring 1989), 5–31.

Hanley, Gerald. *Warriors and Strangers.* London: Hamish Hamilton, 1971.

Harden, Blaine. *Africa: Dispatches from a Fragile Continent.* New York and London: W. W. Norton, 1990.

Hartmann, H. "Some Customs of the Luwo (or Nilotic Kavirondo)." *Anthropos* 23, 1 and 2 (1923), 263–75.

Hartwig, Gerald. "The Victoria Nyanza as a Trade Route in the Nineteenth Century." *Journal of African History* 9, 4 (1970), 535–52.

Hauge, Hans-Egil. *Luo Religion And Folklore.* Oslo: Scandinavian University Books, 1974.

Hay, Margaret Jean. "Economic Change in Luoland: Kowe 1890–1945." Ph.D. Diss., Unversity of Wisconsin, Madison, 1972.

———. "Local Trade and Ethnicity in Western Kenya." *African Economic History Review* 2 (1975), 7–12.

———. "Luo Women and Economic Change During the Colonial Period." In *Women in Africa: Studies in Social and Economic Change,* edited by Edna G. Bay and Nancy J. Hafkin, 87–109. Stanford: Stanford University Press, 1976.

Henige, David. *Oral Historiography.* New York: Longman, 1982.

Herring, Ralph. "The Influence of Climate on the Migrations of the Central and Southern Luo." *Kenya Historical Review* 4, 1 (1976), 35–62.

———. "The JoLuo Before 1900." Paper presented to the Nairobi History Seminar, 1978.

———. "Political Development in Eastern Africa: The Luo Case Re-examined." *Kenya Historical Review* 6, 1–2 (1978), 126–45.

Herring, Ralph, David William Cohen, and B. A. Ogot. "The Construction of Dominance: The Strategies of Selected Luo Groups in Uganda and Kenya." In *State Formation in Eastern Africa,* edited by Ahmed I. Salim, 126–61. Nairobi: Heinemann, 1984.

Hill, Christopher. *The World Turned Upside Down: Radical Ideas During the English Revolution.* London: Temple Smith, 1972.

Hobley, Charles W. "Kavirondo." *The Geographical Journal* 12 (1896), 361–72.

———. *Kenya: From Chartered Company to Crown Colony.* London: Witherby, 1929.

———. "Nilotic Tribes of Kavirondo." In *Eastern Uganda: An Ethnological Survey.* Occasional Papers 1, 26–32. London: Royal Anthropological Institute, 1902.

Hobsbawm, Eric J., and Terence Ranger, eds. *The Invention of Tradition.* Cambridge: Cambridge University Press, 1983.

Holquist, Michael. "From Body-Talk to Biography: The Chronological Bases of Narrative." *The Yale Journal of Criticism* 3, 1 (1989), 1–33.

hooks, bell. *Yearning: Race, Gender and Politics.* Boston: South End Press, 1990.

Huxley, Elspeth. *A New Earth.* 1960. Westport, Conn.: Greenwood Press, 1973.

James, C. L. R. *At the Rendezvous with Victory: Selected Writings.* London: Allen and Busby, 1984.

Johnson, Steven L. "Changing Patterns of Maize Utilization in Western Kenya." *Studies in Third World Societies* 8 (1979), 37–56.

———. "Production, Exchange, and Economic Development among the Luo-Abasuba of Southwestern Kenya." Ph.D. Diss., Indiana University, Bloomington, Indiana, 1980.

Kanogo, Tabitha M. J. "Rift Valley Squatters and Mau Mau." In *Some Perspectives on the Mau Mau Movement*, edited by William R. Ochieng' and Karim K. Janmohamed. Special issue of the *Kenya Historical Review* 5, 2 (1987), 243—52.

———. *Squatters and the Roots of Mau Mau, 1905—1963*. London: James Currey, 1987.

Karani, Florida. "The History of Maseno School, 1906—1962, the Alumni and the Local Society." M. A. Thesis, University of Nairobi, Nairobi, 1974.

Karimi, Joseph, and Philip Ochieng. *The Kenyatta Succession*. Nairobi: Transafrica, 1980.

Kariuki, P. W. "Loss and Bereavement." In *The S. M. Otieno Case: Death and Burial in Modern Kenya*, edited by J. B. Ojwang and J. N. K. Mugambi, 55—64. Nairobi: Nairobi University Press, 1989.

Karp, Ivan, and Patricia Karp. "Living with the Spirits of the Dead." In *African Therapeutic Systems*, edited by Z. A. Ademuwagun, John A. A. Ayoyade, Ira Harrison, and Dennis Warren, 22—25. Boston: Crossroads Press, 1979.

Kenny, Michael G. "Pre-Colonial Trade in Eastern Lake Victoria." *Azania* 14 (1979), 97—107.

———. "The Relation of Oral History to Social Structure in South Nyanza, Kenya." *Africa* 47, 3 (1977), 276—88.

———. "Salt Trading in Eastern Lake Victoria." *Azania* 9 (1975), 225—28.

Kenyatta, Jomo. *Facing Mount Kenya*. London: Secker and Warburg, 1953.

King, Kenneth, and Ahmed I. Salim, eds. *Kenya Historical Biographies*. Nairobi: East African Publishing House for the Department of History, University of Nairobi, 1971.

Kipkorir, B. E., ed. *Biographical Essays on Imperialism and Collaboration in Colonial Kenya*. Nairobi: East African Literature Bureau, 1980.

Kitching, Gavin. *Class and Economic Change in Kenya: The Making of an African Petite-Bourgeoisie, 1905—1970* New Haven: Yale University Press, 1980.

Kokwaro, J. O. "Traditional Medicine as One of the Oldest African Sciences." UNESCO Seminar on Oral Tradition, Past Growth and Future Development in East Africa, Kisumu, Kenya, 1979.

LaCapra, Dominick. "Rethinking Intellectual History and Reading Texts." In *Modern European Intellectual History: Reappraisals and New Perspectives*, edited by Dominick LaCapra and Steven L. Kaplan, 47—85. Ithaca, N.Y.: Cornell University Press, 1982.

Lears, T. Jackson. "The Concept of Cultural Hegemony: Problems and Possibilities." *American Historical Review* 90, 3 (1985), 567—93.

Lionnet, Françoise. "Dissymmetry Embodied: Feminism, Universalism and the Practice of Excision." *Passages* 1 (1991), 2—4.

Lipsitz, George. *Time Passages: Collective Memory and American Popular Culture*. Minneapolis: University of Minnesota Press, 1990.

Little, Peter D. "Woman as Ol Pa'yian [Elder]: The Status of Widows among the Il Chamus (Njemps) of Kenya." *Ethnos* 52, i—ii (1987), 81—102.

Lonsdale, John, "A Political History of Nyanza: 1883—1945." Ph.D. Diss., Cambridge University, Cambridge, 1964.

———. "When Did the Gusii or Any Other Group Become a Tribe?" *Kenya Historical Review* 5, 1 (1977), 355—68.

Lonsdale, John, Stanley Booth-Clibborn, and Andrew Hake. "The Emerging Pattern of Church and State Cooperation in Kenya." In *Christianity in Independent Africa*, edited by E. Fashole-Luke *et al.*, 267—84. Bloomington and London: Indiana University Press, 1978.

Lonsdale, John, and Michael Whisson. "The Case of Jason Gor and Fourteen Others: A Succession Dispute in Historical Perspective." *Africa* 45, 1 (1976), 50—65.

Lubogo, Y. K. *A History of Busoga*. 1960. Jinja, Uganda: East African Literature Bureau, 1962.

Macgoye, Marjorie Oludhe. *Coming to Birth*. Nairobi and London: Heinemann, 1986.

———. *Present Moment*. London: Heinemann, 1986.

———. *Street Life*. Nairobi: Heinemann, 1987.

Malo, Shadrack. *Dhoudi Mag Central Nyanza*. Nairobi: Eagle Press, 1953.

Martin, Emily. *The Woman in the Body: A Cultural Analysis of Reproduction*. Boston: Beacon, 1987.

Matsetela, Ted. "The Life Story of Nkgono Mma–Pooe: Aspects of Sharecropping and Proletarianization in the Northern Orange Free State, 1890–1930." In *Industrialization and Social Change in South Africa*, edited by Shula Marks and Richard Rathbone, 212–37. Harlow, Essex: Longman Group, 1982.

Mboya, Paul. *Luo Kitgi gi Timbegi*. 1938. Nairobi: Equatorial Publishers, 1967.

McConnell, Frank D. "The Lit–Crit Wars." *The Wilson Quarterly* 14, 1 (Winter 1990) 199–209.

McCutchion, David. *Indian Writing in English*. Calcutta: Writers Workshop, 1969.

Medick, Hans, and David Sabean, eds. *Interest and Emotion: Essays in the Study of Family and Kinship*. Cambridge: Cambridge University Press, 1984.

Miguda, Edith. "The Luo of Nairobi and Mau Mau." M.A. Thesis, University of Nairobi, 1988.

Molnos, Angela. *Cultural Source Materials for Population Planning in East Africa*. 2 vols. Nairobi: East African Publishing House, 1972–73.

Moore, Sally Falk. "Explaining the Present: Theoretical Dilemmas in Processual Ethnography." *American Ethnologist* 14, 1 (1987), 727–36.

———. *Social Facts and Fabrications: "Customary" Law on Kilimanjaro, 1880–1980*. Cambridge: Cambridge University Press, 1986.

Mugambi, J. N. K. "The African Heritage—Change and Continuity." In *The S. M. Otieno Case: Death and Burial in Modern Kenya*, edited by J. B. Ojwang and J. N. K. Mugambi, 165–79. Nairobi: Nairobi University Press, 1989.

Munro, J. Forbes. *Colonial Rule and the Kamba: Social Change in the Kenya Highlands, 1889–1939*. Oxford: Oxford University Press, 1975.

Mutai, Chelagat. "Still Committed to the Struggle" [an interview of Wambui Otieno]. *Viva* (April 1979), 10–12

Mwangi, Meja. *Going Down River Road*. London: Heinemann, 1976.

Nagarajan, S., and S. Viswanathan, eds. *Shakespeare in India*. Delhi: Oxford University Press, 1987.

Ndisi, John W. *A Study in the Economic and Social Life of the Luo of Kenya*. Lund, Sweden: Berlingska Boktryckeriet, 1974.

Nelson, Nikki. "'Women Must Help Each Other': The Operation of Personal Networks among Busaa Brewers in Mathare Valley, Kenya." In *Women United, Women Divided*, edited by Patricia Caplan and Janet Bujra, 77–98. Bloomington, Indiana and London: Indiana University Press, 1979.

New, Charles. *Life, Wanderings and Labours in Eastern Africa*. London: Hodder, 1873.

Ng'anga, James Mwangi. *Kenya: A Subject Index. A Select Bibliography of Articles, 1967–1976*. Nairobi: African Book Services, 1983.

Njoya, Timothy M. *Human Dignity and National Identity*. Nairobi: Jemisik Cultural Books, 1987.

Nundu, H. O. *Nyuolruok Dhoud Ugenya* [Ugenya Genealogies]. Nairobi: Kenya Literature Bureau, 1987.

Nyong'o, P. Anyang'. "State and Society in Kenya: The Disintegration of the Nationalist Coalitions and the Rise of Presidential Authoritarianism, 1963–78." *African Affairs* 88, 351 (April 1989), 229–51.

Nzomo, Maria. "The Impact of the Women's Decade on Policies, Programs, and Empowerment of Women in Kenya." *Issue* 17, 2 (Summer 1989), 9–17.

Ochieng, Philip. "What does the S.M. Case Teach Kenyans? *Daily Nation* 17 May 1987.

Ochieng', William R. "Clan Settlement and Clan Conflict in the Yimbo Location of Nyanza, 1500–1915." In *Ngano: Nairobi Historical Studies*, edited by B. G. McIntosh, 48–71. Nairobi: East African Publishing House, 1969.

———. "Colonial African Chiefs: Were They Primarily Self-Seeking Scoundrels?" *In Politics and Nationalism in Colonial Kenya*, edited by B. A. Ogot, 46–70. Nairobi: East African Publishing House, 1972.

——. *A History of the Kadimo Chiefdom of Yimbo in Western Kenya*. Nairobi: East African Literature Bureau, 1975.

——. *An Outline History of Nyanza up to 1914*. Nairobi: East African Literature Bureau, 1974.

——. "Political and Structural, Continuity in Yimbo, c. 1700–1972." In William R. Ochieng', *The First Word: Essays on Kenya History*. Nairobi: East African Literature Bureau, 1975.

——. "The Transformation of a Bantu Settlement into a Luo Ruothdom: A Case Study of the Evolution of the Yimbo Community in Nyanza up to A.D. 1900." In *Hadith 6: History and Social Change in East Africa*, edited by B. A. Ogot, 44–64. Nairobi: East African Literature Bureau, 1976.

Ochieng', William R., and Karim K. Janmohamed, eds. *Some Perspectives on the Mau Mau Movement*. Special issue of the *Kenya Historical Review* 5, 2 (1987).

Ocholla-Ayayo, A. B. C. *The Luo Culture: A Reconstruction of the Material Culture Patterns of a Traditional African Society*. Weisbaden: Franz Steiner Verlag, 1980.

——. "Marriage and Cattle Exchange among the Nilotic Luo." *Paideuma* 25 (1979), 173–93.

——. *Traditional Ideology and Ethics among the Southern Luo*. Uppsala, Sweden: Scandanavian Institute of African Studies, 1976.

Odaga, Asenath B. "Some Aspects of the Luo Traditional Education Transmitted through the Oral Narratives: *Sigendini*." UNESCO Seminar on Oral Traditions, Past Growth and Future Development in East Africa, Kisumu, Kenya, 1979.

Odera Oruka, Henry. "Traditionalism and Modernisation in Kenya—Customs, Spirits and Christianity." In *The S. M. Otieno Case: Death and Burial in Modern Kenya*, edited by J. B. Ojwang and J. N. K. Mugambi, 79–88. Nairobi: Nairobi University Press, 1989.

Odhiambo, E. S. Atieno. "Democracy and the Ideology of Order in Kenya, 1888–1987." In *The Political Economy of Kenya*, edited by Michael Schatzberg, 177–201. New York: Praeger, 1987.

——. "Economic Mobilization and Political Leadership: Oginga Odinga and the Luo Thrift and Trading Corporation to 1956." In *Politics and Leadership in Africa*, edited by William Ochieng' and Aloo Ojuka. Nairobi: East African Literature Bureau, 1975.

——. "From Warriors to *Jonanga*: The Struggle Over Nakedness in Western Kenya." Paper presented at the African Studies Center, Boston University, Seminar on Popular Culture and the Performing Arts, 11–12 May 1989; in *Matatu* 3 (Institut fur Ethnologie und Afrikastudien, University of Mainz), forthcoming.

——. "Gor Mahia Deconstructed." Paper presented at the Conference on Prophesy and Leadership in East Africa, Birkbeck College, London, 10–12 December 1989.

——. "The Movement of Ideas: A Case Study of Intellectual Responses to Colonialism among the Liganua Peasants." In *History and Social Change in East Africa*, edited by B. A. Ogot, 165–85. Nairobi: East African Literature Bureau, 1976.

——. "A Note on the Chronology of African Traditional Religion in Western Kenya." *Journal of Eastern African Research and Development* 5, 2 (1975), 119–22.

——. "A Portrait of Protestant Missionaries in Kenya Before 1939." In E. S. Atieno Odhiambo, *The Paradox of Collaboration and Other Essays*. Nairobi: East African Literature Bureau, 1974.

——. "The Rise and Fall of the Kenya Peasant. 1888–1922." In *African Social Studies: A Radical Reader*, edited by Peter C. W. Gutkind and Peter Waterman. London: Heinemann, 1977. (Originally published in *East African Journal* 9, 5 (1972), 5–11.)

——. "'Seek ye first the Economic Kingdom': A History of the Luo Thrift and Trading Corporation (LUTATCO), 1945–56." In *Hadith 5: Economic and Social History of East Africa*, 218–56. Nairobi: East African Literature Bureau, 1975.

——. "Siasa: African Politics and Nationalism in East Africa, 1919–1935." In E. S. Atieno Odhiambo, *Siasa: Politics and Nationalism in East Africa, 1905–1939*, 91–148. Nairobi:

Kenya Literature Bureau, 1981.

———. "Some Aspects of Religious Activity among the Uyoma Fisherman: The Rites Connected with the Launching of a Fishing Vessel." *MILA* 1, 2 (1970): 2–14.

———. "Towards a History of African Traditional Religion: A West Kenya Case." Unpublished paper, 1974.

Odhiambo, O. J. H. "Dholuo Phonology: A study of the Major Vowel Processes. M.A. Diss., University of Nairobi, Nairobi, 1981.

Odinga, Oginga. *Not Yet Uhuru: An Autobiography*. 1967. New York: Hill and Wang, 1969.

Odongo, Onyango Ku, and J. B. Webster, eds. *The Central Lwo during the Aconya*. Nairobi: East African Literature Bureau, 1976.

Ogot, B. A. "British Administration in the Central Nyanza District of Kenya." *Journal of African History* 4, 2 (1963), 249–73.

———. *History of the Southern Luo: Migration and Settlement*. Nairobi: East African Publishing House, 1967.

———. "Kingship and Statelessness among the Nilotes." In *The Historian in Tropical Africa*, edited by Jan Vansina, R. Mauny, and L. V. Thomas, 284–302. London: Oxford University Press, 1964.

———. "The Rev. Alfayo Odongo Mango." In *Kenya Historical Biographies*, edited by Kenneth King and Ahmed Salim, 90–111. Nairobi: East African Publishing House for the Department of History, University of Nairobi, 1971.

Ogot, B. A., and William R. Ochieng'. "Mumboism: An Anti–Colonial Movement." In *War and Society in Africa*, edited by B. A. Ogot, 149–77. London: Frank Cass, 1972.

Ogot, Grace. *The Promised Land*. Nairobi: East African Publishing House, 1966.

Ogutu–Obunga, Gilbert Edwin Mesheck. "A Case for Oral Traditions in the Study of Belief Systems and Ritual." UNESCO Seminar on "Oral Traditions, Past Growth and Future Development in East Africa," Kisumu, Kenya, 1979.

———. "An Unholy Trinity: Customs, Superstition and Witchcraft Among the Kamageta." *Kenya Historical Review* 2, 2 (1974), 235–41.

———. "The Ideas of Time and History with Special Reference to the Kenyan Luo." *Kenya Historical Review* 2, 1 (1974), 13–21.

Ojwang, J. B. *Constitutional Development in Kenya: Institutional Adaptation and Social Change.* Nairobi: ACTS Press, African Centre for Technological Studies, 1990.

———. "The S. M. Otieno Case and the Problems It Raises: An Introductory Note." Nairobi Faculty of Law Seminar, Death, Burial and Society: Social, Cultural and Legal Perspectives, Nairobi, 18 July 1987.

Ojwang, J. B., and J. N. K. Mugambi, eds. *The S. M. Otieno Case: Death and Burial in Modern Kenya*. Nairobi: Nairobi University Press, 1989.

Okaro-Kojwang, K. M. "Origins and Establishment of the Kavirondo Taxpayers' Welfare Association." In *Ngano: Nairobi Historical Studies I*, edited by B. G. McIntosh, 111–28. Nairobi: East African Publishing House, 1969.

Okoth-Okombo, Duncan. *Dholuo Morphophonemics in a Generative Framework*. Berlin: Dietrich Reimer Verlag, 1982.

———. "Semantic Issues," In *The S. M. Otieno Case: Death and Burial in Modern Kenya*, edited by J. B. Ojwang and J. N. K. Mugambi, 89–97. Nairobi: Nairobi University Press, 1989.

Okullu, H. *Church and State in Nation-Building and Development*. Nairobi: Uzima Press, 1984.

Oliver, Roland. "The Nilotic Contribution to Bantu Africa." In *Nilotic Studies: Proceedings of the International Symposium on Languages and History of the Nilotic Peoples, Cologne, January 4–6, 1982*, edited by Marianne Bechhaus-Gerst and Rainer Vossen, 357–74. Berlin: Dietrich Reimer Verlag, 1983.

Oloo (Aringo), Peter C. "History of Settlement: The Example of Luo Clans of Alego (1500–1918)." B.A. Thesis, University of Nairobi, 1969.

Ominde, Simeon H. *The Luo Girl from Infancy to Marriage*. Nairobi: East African Literature

Bureau, 1952.

Omondi, Lucia Ndong'a. *The Major Syntactic Structures of Dholuo*. Berlin: Dietrich Reimer Verlag, 1982.

Ongong'a, Jude. *Life and Death — A Christian/Luo Dialogue*. Eldoret: AMECEA Pastoral Institute, Gaba Publications, 1983.

Onstad, Eric. "The History of the Nairobi Street Hawkers." M.A. Thesis, University of Nairobi, Nairobi, 1990.

Onyango-Abuje, John. *Fire and Vengeance*. Nairobi: East African Publishing House, 1971.

Onyango-Ogutu, B., and A. A. Roscoe. *Keep My Words: Luo Oral Literature*. Nairobi: East African Publishing House, 1974.

Othieno-Ochieng', N. A. *Luo Social System with a Special Analysis of Marriage Rituals*. Nairobi: Equatorial Publishers, 1968.

Otieno, Margaret. "The Biography of Ex-Chief Muganda Okwako (1903–1952)." B.A. Thesis, University of Nairobi, Nairobi, 1972.

p'Bitek, Okot. *Religion of the Central Luo*. Nairobi: Kenya Literature Bureau, 1971.

Pala Okeyo, Achola. "Daughters of the Lake and Rivers: Colonization and Land Rights of Luo Women in Kenya." In *Women and Colonization: Anthropological Perspectives*, edited by Mona Etienne and Eleanor Leacock, 186–213. New York: Praeger, 1980.

———. "The Joluo Equation: Land Reform = Lower Status for Women." *Ceres* (May/June 1980), 36–42.

———. "Women in the Household Economy: Managing Multiple Roles." *Studies in Family Planning* 10, 11/12 (1979), 337–43.

———. "Women's Access to Land and Their Role in Agriculture and Decision-making on the Farm: Experiences of the Joluo of Kenya." *Journal of Eastern African Research and Development* 13 (1983), 69–85.

Parkin, David. *The Cultural Definition of Political Response. Lineal Destiny Among the Luo*. London: Academic Press, 1978.

———. "Emergent and Stabilized Multilingualism: Polyethnic Peer Groups in Urban Kenya." In *Language and Ethnicity and Intergroup Relations*, edited by Howard Giles, 185–209. London and New York: Academic Press, 1977.

———. "Kind Bridewealth and Hard Cash: Eventing a Structure." In *The Meaning of Marriage Payments*, edited by John Comaroff, 197–220. London and New York: Academic Press, 1980.

———. "Language Choice in Two Kampala Housing Estates." In *Language Use and Social Change: Problems of Multilingualism with Special Reference to Eastern Africa*, edited by W. H. Whiteley, 345–63. London: Oxford University Press for the International African Institute, 1971.

———. "Tribe as Fact and Fiction in an East African City." In *Tradition and Transition in East Africa: Studies of the Tribal Element in the Modern Era*, edited by Philip H. Gulliver, 273–96. Berkeley: University of California Press, 1969.

Parkin, David, and David Nyamwaya, eds. *Transformations of African Marriage*. Manchester: Manchester University Press for the International African Institute, c. 1987.

Poovey, Mary. *Uneven Developments: The Ideological Work of Gender in Mid-Victorian England*. Chicago: University of Chicago, 1988.

Potash, Betty. "Marriage Stability in a Rural Luo Community." *Africa* 48, 4 (1978), 381–97.

———. "Wives of the Grave: Widows in a Rural Luo Community." In *Widows in African Societies: Choices and Constraints*, edited by Betty Potash, 45–65. Stanford: Stanford University Press, 1986.

Price, Sally. *Primitive Art in Civilized Places*. Chicago: University of Chicago Press, 1989.

Republic of Kenya. *Report of the Judicial Commission Appointed to Inquire into Allegations Involving Charles Mugane Njonjo (former Minister for Constitutional Affairs and Member of Parliament for Kikuyu Constituency)*. Nairobi: Government Printer, 1984.

Roberts, Richard, and Kristin Mann, eds. *Law in Colonial Africa*. New York: Heinemann,

1991.

Schatzberg, Michael, ed. *The Political Economy of Kenya*. New York: Praeger, 1987.

Scheppele, Kim Lane. *Legal Secrets: Equality and Efficiency in the Common Law*. Chicago: University of Chicago Press, 1988.

Schiller, Laurence D. "Gem and Kano: A Comparative Study of Stress in Two Traditional African Political Systems in Nyanza Province, Western Kenya, c. 1850–1914." Paper presented to the History Seminar, University of Nairobi, Nairobi, 1977.

Scott, Joan Wallach. *Gender and the Politics of History*. New York: Columbia University Press, 1988.

Shepard, Richard F. "About Men." *New York Times Magazine*. 30 September 1990, 26, 46.

Shipton, Parker M. *Bitter Money: Cultural Economy and Some African Meanings of Forbidden Commodities*. Washington, D.C.: American Anthropological Association, 1989.

———. "Lineage and Locality as Antithetical Principles in East African Systems of Land Tenure." *Ethnology* 23, 2 (1984), 117–32.

———. "Strips and Patches: A Demographic Dimension in some African Land-Holding and Political Systems." *Man* 19 (1984), 613–34.

Simmonds-Duke, E. M. "Was the Peasant Uprising a Revolution? The Meanings of a Struggle over the Past." *Eastern European Politics and Societies* 1, 2 (1987), 187–224.

Singh, Jyotsna. "Different Shakespeares: The Bard in Colonial/Postcolonial India." *Theatre Journal* 41, 4 (December 1989), 445–58.

Southall, Aidan. "From Segmentary Lineage to Ethnic Association: Luo, Luyia, Ibo, and Others." In *Colonialism and Change: Essays Presented to Lucy Mair*, edited by M. Owusu. The Hague: Mouton, 1975.

———. *Lineage Formation among the Luo*. London: Oxford University Press, 1952.

Southall, Aidan, ed. *Urban Anthropology: Cross-Cultural Studies of Urbanization*. New York: Oxford University Press, 1973.

Spittler, Gerd. "Administration in a Peasant State." *Sociologia Ruralis* 23 (1980), 130–44.

Stafford, R. L. *An Elementary Luo Grammar, with Vocabularies*. Nairobi: Oxford University Press, 1967.

Stallybrass, Peter, and Allon White. *The Politics and Poetics of Transgression*. Ithaca, N.Y.: Cornell University Press, 1986.

Stam, The Rev. N. "The Religious Conceptions of the Kavirondo." *Anthropos* 5 (1910), 359–62.

Stamp, Patricia. "Burying Otieno: The Politics of Gender and Ethnicity in Kenya." *Signs* 16, 4 (1991), 808–45.

Street, Brian V. "Literary Practices and Literacy Myths." In *The Written World: Studies in Literate Thought and Action*, edited by Roger Saljo, 59–71. Berlin: Springer, 1988.

Swainson, Nicola. *The Development of Corporate Capitalism in Kenya*. London: Heinemann, 1980.

Tamarkin, M. "Social and Political Change in a Twentieth Century African Urban Community in Kenya." Ph.D. Diss., University of London, London, 1973.

Thomas, Lynn M. "Contestation, Construction, and Reconstitution: Public Debates Over Marriage Law and Women's Status in Kenya, 1964–1979." M.A. Thesis, Johns Hopkins University, Baltimore, Md., 1989.

Throup, David. "The Construction and Destruction of the Kenyatta State." In *The Political Economy of Kenya*, edited by Michael Schatzberg, 33–74. New York: Praeger, 1987.

Torgovnick, Marianna. *Gone Primitive: Savage Intellects, Modern Lives*. Chicago: University of Chicago Press, 1990.

Tosh, John. "Lango Agriculture During the Early Colonial Period: Land and Labour in a Cash-Crop Economy." *Journal of African History* 19 (1978), 415–39.

Tucker, A. N., and M. A. Bryan. *Linguistic Analyses: The Non-Bantu Languages of North-Eastern Africa*. London: Oxford University Press, 1953.

van Doren, J. W. "African Tradition and Western Common Law: A Study in Contradiction." In *The S. M. Otieno Case: Death and Burial in Modern Kenya*, edited by J. B. Ojwang and J. N. K. Mugambi, 127–32. Nairobi: Nairobi University Press, 1989.

Van Onselen, Charles. "Race and Class in the South African Countryside: Cultural Osmosis and Social Relations in the Sharecropping Economy of the South-Western Transvaal, 1900–1950." *American Historical Review* 95, 1 (1990), 99–123.

Vansina, Jan. *Oral Tradition*. London: Routledge and Kegan Paul, 1965.

Vansina, Jan. *Oral Tradition as History*. Madison, Wis.: University of Wisconsin Press, 1985.

Van Zwanenberg, R. M. "The Missionary Conscience and Colonial Injustices: The Life and Times of W. E. Owen of Nyanza." In *Politics and Leadership in Africa*, edited by William R. Ochieng' and Aloo Ojuka, 63–84. Nairobi: East African Literature, 1975.

Verdery, Katherine. *National Ideology Under Socialism: Identity and Cultural Politics in Ceauşescu's Romania*. Berkeley, Ca.: University of California Press, 1991.

Wachanga, H. K., with Robert Whittier. *The Swords of Kirinyaga: The Fight for Land and Freedom*. Nairobi: East African Literature Bureau, 1975.

Waligorski, Andrzej. "Kinship Terminology of the Luo." *African Bulletin* 8 (1968), 57–63.

Weinberger, Eliot. *The Collected Poems of Octavio Paz, 1957–1987*. New York: New Directions, 1987.

Were, Priscilla O. "The Origin and Growth of the Iron Industry and Trade in Samia (Kenya). B.A. Thesis, University of Nairobi, Nairobi, 1972.

Whisson, Michael G. *Change and Challenge: A Study of the Social and Economic Changes among the Kenya Luo*. Nairobi: Christian Council of Kenya, 1964.

———. "The Journeys of the JoRamogi." Paper presented to the East African Institute for Social Research, Kampala, Uganda, 1962.

———. "Some Aspects of Functional Disorders among the Kenya Luo." In *Magic, Faith, and Healing: Studies in Primitive Psychiatry Today*, edited by Ari Kiev, 283–304. New York: Free Press, 1964.

———. "The Will of God." Paper presented to the Makerere Institute for Social Research, Kampala, Uganda, 1962.

White, Luise. "A Colonial State and an African Petty Bourgeoisie: Prostitution, Property, and Class Struggle in Nairobi, 1936–40." In *Struggle for the City: Migrant Labor, Capital, and the State in Urban Africa*, edited by Frederick Cooper, 167–94. Beverly Hills, Calif.: Sage, 1983.

———. *The Comforts of Home: Prostitution in Colonial Nairobi*. Chicago: University of Chicago Press, 1990.

Wilson, Gordon, *Luo Customary Law and Marriage Customs*. Nairobi: Government Printer, 1968.

# INDEX

Abonyo, Jane Obuong', 4
Ackoro, Mary, 34
Ackoro, Pius Gumo, 34
Adagala, Seth, 28
Adema, Alfred, 12
Adema, Juta Johanna, 12
African Christian Marriage Act, 9, 22
African culture
  Bomas of Kenya Centre and, 28–29
  interpretation of, 105–107
  Luo customs and, 92
  SM case and, 97–98
AIDS, levirate and, 113
Akinyi, Felgona, 28
Alego Ragar Association, 7
Alego Ulafu clan, 34
Allende, Salvador, 16
Amuka, Peter, 103–105
Anderson, Ben, 109
Anthropology, Luo culture and, 64
Anyango, Pamela (Monday), 36–37
Argwings Kodhek, C. M. G., 16
Argwings-Kodhek, Joanna, 69
Arina, Richard, 27
Atieno, Stefano, 70
Ayah, Ndolo, 76–77
Ayany, Samuel Chweya, 43

Benjamin, Walter, 118
Bible, 110
Blixen, Karen (Isak Dinesen), 2, 36
Boltanski, Luc, 39
Bomas of Kenya Centre
  Kenyan culture and, 28–29
  SM's Corner at bar, 1–2, 16–17, 22–23, 29
Born-again Christians, 30–31
Bosire, Justice S. E. O., 21, 30, 36, 60, 61, 66, 71, 94, 102
  judgment of, 48, 49, 51
British American Tobacco Company (BAT), 63
Bujra, Janet, 46
Buliro, Elizabeth, 3–4
Buliro, Joshua, 4

Burial customs. See also Luo burial customs
  Luo vs. Kikuyu, 113
Burials
  of Francis Otieno Pala, 37–38
  of Mary Ackoro, 34
  of Pamela Anyango, 37
  of Zachariah Ogutu Nyamodi, 34–36
Bynum, Caroline Walker, 93

"Change-in-the-making," 98
Chanock, Martin, 105–107
Chieno (outer skirt), 69
Christian church, 63, 110
  Bible, 110
  conflict of Luo burial customs with, 68–69
  opposition to state policies by, 31–32
  reborn Christians, 30–31
Cigarettes. See also Tobacco
  Luo meaning of, 63
Clans. See also Umira Kager clan
  Alego Ulafu, 34
  Kager Kogolla, 59
  Kaugagi, 37
  legal standing of, 101–103
  Luo vs. Kikuyu, 113
  Ominde, 102–103
  Otieno, 19
Clifford, James, 102
Clothing
  of deceased, in Luo culture, 69–70
  of widows, in Luo culture, 69
Cohen, David William, 101, 106, 107–108, 110, 114, 117–19
Common law, 13–14
Cotran, E., 113
Court of Appeals, 8–10, 93
Cultural Definition of Political Response: Lineal Destiny among the Luo (Parkin), 20
Currey, James, 20
Customary law, 13–14. See also Luo customary law

Daily Nation (Nairobi), 6, 17, 71

*Dala* (home), 42, 81–82
Death. *See also* Luo burial customs
  causes of, Luo culture and, 115
  Luo culture and, 59, 104–105, 109
  SM discussions of, 22, 23
Dholuo, meanings of house and home in, 42
Dinesen, Isak. *See* Karen Blixen

Economy of the law, 78
Evans-Pritchard, E. E., 42
Expert witnesses, perception of, 49–51, 53
Export, Valie, 93

Feminism, 111–12. *See also* Women
  critical studies of, 93–94
  rights of women, 30, 32, 39
  Wambui's position and, 36
Fischer, Michael M. J., 111–13
Funeral rites. *See also* Luo burial customs
  Luo custom and, 54–55, 64–65, 114–15

Gachuhi, J. Mugo, 8
Gender. *See also* Feminism; Men; Women
  issues raised about, 93–94, 109
Ger Union, 28, 101–102
Ginzburg, Carlo, 94
Gluckman, Max, 116
*Goyo ligala* (home building), 59–60

High Court of Kenya, 30–31. *See also*
    Bosire, Justice S. E. O.; Shields, Justice
    Frank S.
  gender and, 93
  judgment of, 48, 83
  testimony before, 21–28
  Wambui's reaction to ruling by, 30–31
History, production of, 20
Home, Luo meaning of, 24, 40–42, 59–60
House, Luo meaning of, 40–42
House Number One, Ojijo Road. *See* One
    Ojijo Road
Huxley, Elspeth, 36

*Janeko* (lunatic), 66–69
Judicial codes, 13
Jumbe, Mfahaya, 46

Kager Kogolla clan, 59
Kakaire, 18–19
Karanja, Dr. Josephat, 5, 26
Karen-Langata, 2
Kariuki, J. M., 16
Karp, Ivan, 112
Kaugagi clan, 37
Kenya African Union (KAU) party, 28
Kenyan culture
  Bomas of Kenya Centre and, 28–29
  interpretation of, 105–107
  Luo customs and, 92, 97–99, 119

SM case and, 97–99
Kenyan government. *See also* Bosire, Justice
    S. E. O.; Shields, Justice Frank S.
  church opposition to, 31–32
  Court of Appeal, 8–10, 93
  High Court, 21–28, 30–31, 48, 83, 93
  law, 13–14
  role in SM case, 83–84
Kenyan press, coverage by, 15
Kenya Railways Corporation, 5
*Kenya Times*, 77
Kenyatta, Jomo, 27, 32
*Ker*, 75
Khaminwa, John, 59
  admonished for lack of understanding of
      Luo culture, 64, 86
  cross-examination of Albert Ong'ang'o
      by, 39–40
  *dala* of, 81–82
  detention of, 87
  discussion of house and home by, 40–42
  education of, 82–83
  honorary degree awarded to, 86
  information provided by, 4, 9, 24, 94
  injunction filed by, 10
  Luo burial customs and, 38, 54–55, 57, 62,
      79
  perception of in rural countryside, 52–53
  pleas filed by, 6–7
  positions presented by, 21
  presentation of Patrick Otieno by, 72
  *raia* and, 95
  testimony of Mama Koko and, 47, 95
  testimony of Odera Oruka and, 49–50
Kiano, Dr. Julius Gikonyo, 4, 5, 13
"Kick the coffin open" declaration, 22, 24
Kikuyu, 109–10, 112
  customs, vs. Luo customs, 113, 114
Kikuyu lady, 6
Kimani, Mrs., 4
Kinuthia, Samwel, 6–7
Kiserian (Ngong)
  SM choice for burial, 5, 11, 22
  SM purchase of land in, 1
Koko, Mama. *See* Murikira, Mariamu
Kokwaro, Joseph Ong'ayo, 79
Kratz, Corinne A., 100–103
Kwach, Richard
  appointment of to Court of Appeal, 86
  *dala* of, 81–82
  education of, 80–82
  house and home discussed by, 41, 42
  literacy issues discussed by, 13
  Luo burial customs and, 24–26, 54–55,
      61–62, 66–69, 79
  Mariamu Murikira (Mama Koko) and,
      45–47
  Johannes Mayamba discussed by, 59–61,
      62

Odera Oruka testimony and, 49–51
Otieno sons and, 66–67, 72
perception of in rural countryside, 52–53
pleas filed by, 6–9
*raia* and, 95
treatment of women's role in burial
    arrangements by, 36, 38
Wambui and, 57, 94

Langata, Nairobi
    Kikuyu burials in, 114
    as matrimonial residence of SM, 14
    as SM burial place, 4, 6
Law, economy of, 78
Law Society of Kenya, 17
Law of Succession Act, 35
Lenin, N., 16
Levirate, 63, 68–69, 113–14
Literacy, orality and, 12–13
Lonsdale, John, 108–111
Luo burial customs, 35, 37–39, 54–55,
    59–62
    anthropology and, 64
    Pamela Anyango burial and, 37
    Christian belief and, 68–69
    court argument in favor of, 24–26
    importance of funerals in, 54–55, 76
    *janeko*, 66–69
    John Khaminwa and, 38, 54–55, 57, 62, 79
    vs. Kikuyu burial customs, 113, 114–15
    Richard Kwach and, 24–26, 54–55,
        61–62, 66–69, 79
    levirate, 63, 68–69, 113–14
    misunderstanding of, 63–65
    rites involving widows, 65–71
    rituals, 24–26, 37–39, 64–71
    *tero buru*, 60, 63, 104, 105, 114
Luo customary law, 14
    applicability of, 21
    court decision and, 9
    Umira Kager clan arguments and, 39
    Wambui's defense and, 30
Luo customs
    African development and, 97–99
    anthropology and, 64
    corpses and, 18–19
    death and, 104–105, 109
    ethnicity, 77
    exclusion of experts on, 79
    interpretation of, 95–99
    Kenyan culture and, 92, 97–98, 119
    vs. Kikuyu customs, 113, 114–15
    marriage and, 22, 30, 38
    meaning of house and home in, 24,
        40–42, 59–60
    political and social leadership and, 75–76
    public debate about, 12
    role of, 20
    SM burial and, 7, 9

    social class and, 76
    testimony of Henry Odera Oruka and,
        50–51
    understanding of, 62–65
    Wambui and, 55–57
    widows in, 24, 65–71
    women writers and scholars on, 36
Luo Union, 75

Maathai, Wangari, 35
Mama Koko. *See* Murikira, Mariamu
Marcos, Imelda, 16
Marriage
    African Christian Marriage Act, 9, 22
    between SM and Wambui, 26–28, 32–33,
        55, 105, 115
    death and, 105
    Luo custom and, 38
    rights of women in, 38
Marriage Act, 9, 22
Martin, Emily, 93
Mashpee Wampanoag Tribal Council, Inc.,
    102
Masolo, Dr. D. A., 37
Mayamba, Johannes, 59, 62
*Mbira* (traditional oath), 53
Mboya, Pamela, 69
Mboya, Tom, 16, 47, 118, 119
Media. *See* Press
Men, issues raised about, 93
Miller, Chief Justice C. H. E., 17, 43
Miller Commission of Inquiry, 22
Modernism, vs. traditionalism (tribalism),
    15, 51, 92
Modi, Odhiambo, 2, 3
Moi, Daniel Arap, 11, 78, 83, 84, 86, 107
*Le Monde*, 39
Moore, Sally Falk, 20, 99, 107–108
Mourning dress, 69–70
Muchina, Jane Njeri, 13
Mugambi, J. N. K., 112
Muge, Reverend Alexander Kipsang
    Arap, 16
Mugo, Harry, 12, 22–23, 27
Muhuni, Rahab Wambui, 12–13, 24
Muna, Musa, 12
Murder, of SM, rumors of, 115
Murikira, Mariamu (Mama Koko), 12, 13,
    45–47, 93, 95
Mutai, Chelagat, 32
Muthoga, Lee, 12
Mwangi, Peter Kenneth, 24
*Mzee* (elder), 2

*Nairobi Law Monthly*, 87
Nassir, Shariff, 84
National Council of Women of Kenya
    (NCWK), 32, 35
Nationality, 109–110

*Nation* (Nairobi), 6, 17, 71
*New York Times*, 15
Ngari, Charles Machina, 54
Ngong (Kiserian)
  SM choice for burial, 5, 11, 22
  SM purchase of land in, 1
Ng'weno, Hilary, 77
Njonjo, Charles, 22, 44–45
Njugi, Timan, 12, 22
Nyalgunga, 2, 14, 71, 72, 77–79
  burial, 4–9, 17–18, 28, 31, 40, 65–67, 71, 77, 78, 103–105
*NyaLuoly*, 92
Nyamayoga, Athieno, 34
Nyamila village, Nyalgunga
  Luo customs argument in favor of, 24–26
  Nyalgunga as word for "home," 14
  SM attitudes toward, 13, 65–66
  SM birthplace, burial place, 4, 5
  SM burial in, 11, 17–18, 104
Nyamodi, Veronica, 35
Nyamodi, Zachariah, 35–36, 75
Nyarangi, Justice J. O., 8, 55

Obonyo, John, 4
Ochieng' Oganga, Christopher, 52–53
Ochieng' Ougo, Joash, 55, 101–102
  *Daily Nation* coverage of, 6, 17
  judgment in favor of, 9, 11
  news of SM death received by, 4–5
  ownership of One Ojijo Road, 5
  represented by R. Kwach, 24, 25–26
  sponsorship of funeral meetings at One Ojijo Road by, 4
  suits filed by and against, 6–10
  understanding of Luo customs by, 42, 62–63
Ochieng' Ougo, Rispa, 4
Ochola, Hilary, 23, 29
Ocholla-Ayayo, A. B. C., 114, 115, 116
Odera Oruka, Henry, 48–51, 68, 94
Odera, Zachariah, 76, 77
Odhiambo, E. S. Atieno, 101, 106, 107–108, 110, 114, 117–119
Odhiambo, Simeon (Simon), burial of, 27, 45, 46, 49
Odhiambo, Tom, 122
Odhiambo, Umira, 2, 3
Odinga, Oginga, 35, 53–54, 75, 78, 80, 83–84, 96
Odongo, Idalia Awino, 4, 29, 59, 93
Ogot, B. A., 79, 111, 125, 134
Ogot, Grace, 34–36
Ojuka, Aloo, 80
Ojwang, J. B., 38–39, 112
Okero, Issac Omolo, 84, 85
*Okola* (skirt), 69
Okoth-Okombo, Duncan, 41–42, 101
Okullu, Henry, 32

Okumu, Victoria, 17–18
Okungu, Omondi, 37
Ole Tameno, James Ligia, 12, 13
Oloitiptip, Stanley, 84
Olunga Obillo, Robert, 29
Omieri (snake), 76–77
Ominde clan, 102–103
Omollo, Oluoch, 77
Ondieki, Mary Orie-Rogo, 37
One Ojijo Road
  burial discussion at, 4–6
  as place of public assemblies, 5–6
Ong'ang'o, Albert, 22, 26, 39–40, 45, 94, 95
  testimony of, 47–51
Ongwama, Albert, 52–53
Onyango-Abuje, Dr. John, 6
Onyango, Barrack Angoya, 7
Otieno, Frederick, 2
Otieno, Jairus Michael Ougo, 27, 66–67
Otieno, Patrick Oyugi, 2, 66, 67, 71–73
Otieno, Silvano Melea (SM)
  Bomas of Kenya Centre and, 1–2, 16–17, 22–23, 29
  burial of, 11, 17–18, 71, 104
  burial of father by, 27
  burial wishes of, 1, 12, 12–13, 21, 65–66
  career of, 26–28
  children of, 27
  death of, 2–3
  education of, 79–80
  genealogy of, xi
  hospitalization of (1985), 23
  interpretation of case, 19–20, 107–108, 111–112
  interpretation of life of, 24, 92–93, 103
  languages spoken by, 27
  lifestyle of, 21, 22–24, 27, 92
  Luo customs and, 55–56
  marriage to and relationship with Wambui, 26–28, 32–33, 71, 80, 115
  matrimonial residence of, 14
  property owned by, 27
  public discussion of case, 11–12, 18, 45, 52–53, 72–74, 94–95, 103–104, 106, 116–17
  purchase of land by, 1
  *raia* and, 45
  reverence for Shakespeare by, 84–85
  rumors of murder of, 115
Otieno, Virginia Wambui, 2, 16, 25, 96
  absence from SM's funeral, 71
  African customs and, 115–116
  arrogance of, 116
  authority of, 93, 101
  as born-again Christian, 30–31
  burial wishes for SM, 4, 5, 65–69
  career of, 32–33
  *Daily Nation* coverage of, 6
  genealogy of, 19

grave of, 71
Justice Shield's decision in favor of, 7–9, 116
Kikuyu custom and, 115
lack of information about, 112
Luo customs and, 55–57
Mariamu Murikia (Mama Koko) and, 45–47
marriage to and relationship with SM, 26–28, 32–33, 55, 80, 105, 115
opposition to government by, 32
as *pim*, 55–57
property owned by, 27
reaction to High Court ruling, 30–31
rumors about, 115
suits filed by and against, 6–10
support for, 34–36, 54, 119
testimony before High Court, 21–28
as widow, 65–71
women's rights and, 30, 32–33, 36, 39, 93, 109
Ougo, Joash Ochieng'. *See* Ochieng' Ougo, Joash
Ougo Oyugi, Jairo, 27, 55, 56, 63, 66, 67
Ouko, Dr. Robert, 102–103
Ouko, Robert, 16
Ouma, Fred, 4
Overseas press, coverage by, 15
*Owino Misiani's Lamentation*, 88–91
Owira, Amoth, 52–53
Owiti, Horace Ongili, 37
Oyugi, George Michael, 27

*Pacho*, 42
Pala, Francis Otieno, 37–38
Pant, Apa, 80
Parkin, David, 20
Paz, Octavio, 99
P'Bitek, Okot, 55
Perón, Juan, 16
Phombeah, Gray, 77
*Pim*, Wambui as, 55–57
Pinto, Pio, 16
Platt, H. G., 8
Poovey, Mary, 93
Power
  public debate regarding SM burial and, 12
  sociology of, 96
Press. *See also* specific periodicals
  Kenyan, coverage by, 15, 103
  overseas, coverage by, 15
Production of history, 20
Property ownership, of SM and Wambui, 27

*Raia* (ordinary people), 43–45, 47, 95
Ramogi, George, 40
Rang'enga, Philip, 5, 7
Renan, Ernest, 108

School children, discussion by, 72–74, 103–105
Scott, Joan, 101
Scriptures, 110
Sewe, Anyango, 34
Shakespeare, William, 84–85
*Shamba* (farm), 2
Shields, Justice Frank J., 7–9, 28, 29, 102, 116
Siaya, 20, 95
Singh, Jyotsna, 85
Siranga, Omolo, 24, 25, 101–102
  announcement of SM burial location by, 6
  *Daily Nation* coverage of, 6
  house and home discussed by, 40–42
  initial discussion of SM burial place by, 4, 5
  judgment in favor of, 9, 11
  suits filed for and against, 7–8
Skoch, Okola, 34
SM. *See* Otieno, Silvano Melea
Social class
  expertise and authority and, 49–51
  Luo culture and, 76
  *raia*, 43–45, 47, 95
  rural countryside, 52–53
*Social Facts and Fabrications: "Customary" Law on Kilimanjaro, 1880–1980*, 99
Sociology of power, 96
*Song of Lawino* (p'Bitek), 55
Spiegel, Gabrielle, 96
*Standard*, 77
Stevens, Robert, 86
"Sunstone" (Paz), 99

Tameno, James Ligia, 47
*Tero buru* (burial rite), 60, 63, 104, 105, 114
*Tero Buru* (song), 73–74
Tipton, Billy, 16
Tobacco, Luo meaning of, 63, 68
Traditionalism
  vs. modernism, 15, 92
  testimony of Henry Odera Oruka and, 51
  tribalism, 15
Turner, Victor, 116

Ugenya Association, 7
Ugenya moiety, 28
Umira Kager clan, 4, 5
  African development and, 97
  arguments against burial customs of, 62
  *Daily Nation* coverage of, 6
  decision to take over burial arrangements by, 6
  effort to silence opinion by, 53–55
  injunction against, 10
  legal standing of, 101–103
  Luo customary law and, 39
  Luo ethnicity and, 78

SM friends in, 28
testimony before High Court for, 25–26
Wambui's knowledge of, 55–57
Umira Kager Welfare Association, 102
Upper Matasia
SM's improvement to farm at, 23–24
Umira Kager clan opposition to burial in, 25–26

Voice of Kenya (VOA), 5, 52

Wachira, Godwin, 12, 13
Waiyaki, Tiras, 2, 3, 4, 23, 25, 80
Waiyaki, Virginia Wambui, 27. *See also* *Otieno*, Virginia Wambui
Waiyaki wa Hinga, 109–110
Wambui tribe, 15
Wananchi, Bomas of Kenya Centre and, 28–29

Wasow, Barbara, 28
*Washington Post*, 15
*Weekly Review*, 34–35, 77
White, Luise, 46
Widows
authority to arrange spouses' funerals, 36
clothing of, 69
inheritance (levirate), 63, 68–69, 113–14
in Luo culture, 65–71
respect for wishes of, 34–35
Wambui as, 65–71
Women. *See also* Feminism
issues raised about, 93–94
rights of, 30, 32
suppression of voice of, 106
Wambui as leader of, 32–33

Yahuma, Japheth, 41
Youth, SM case and, 72–74, 103–105